Profit From Unlimited Thinking
Learn To Use The Creative Powers Of
Your Mind To Transform Your Life
by
Euphrosene Labon

Floreo Publishing

©Euphrosene Labon 1989, 2003, 2004, 2007

First published in Great Britain in 2004 by
floreo Publishing
Brambletyne Close
Angmering
West Sussex
BN16 4DD

Second Edition

All rights reserved.

No part of this book may be reproduced or transmitted in any form without permission in writing from the publisher except for the purpose of review.

ISBN 10 1-905402-10-4
ISBN 13 978-1-905402-10-6

Self-Discovery/ Personal Development/ Spiritual

Design and word-processing *floreo* Publishing

Distribution: http://www.floreo.org
Email: euphrosene@floreo.org

Acknowledgement and Special Thanks

To all the writers and metaphysical gurus I have quoted for my readers to pursue further. Although I have given the full title and name of the author in every possible instance, I have been unable to clarify current publisher status for all and will happily remedy this in the next edition.

To Kamala Germaine, my mother, whose mental illness prevented me from writing about metaphysics for years - for obvious reasons

To Dad RIP

To family, friends and the many strangers who encouraged me over the years and still do and to all floreo NEWS subscribers

FIRST WORDS 7

PART 1 — WHO ARE YOU? 14

You and Your Life 15
Goals: Techniques and Timelines 22
Key Desires 26
Making a Difference 40

PART 2 - KEEPING ON TRACK 46

Techniques & Tips 46
Self-Discovery In Words 56
Stimulating Your Imagination 63

PART 3 - UNLIMITING YOUR MIND 83

Keeping an Open Mind 83
Tools To Expand Consciousness 93
Mind & Spirit Basics 117
Intelligence: IQ Emotion Spirit 146
T+E+V=M 157

PART 4 - MANAGING CHANGE 165

Things Happen 165
Keeping Tabs on Your Thoughts 186
Understanding Metaphysical Principles 191
Problem Solving 214
Managing Your Expectations 215

PART 5 - GURUS AND YOU 225

Self-Help Gurus 227
Creating Your Perfect Guru 230
How Will You Know? 248
Coaching Yourself 253
Benefiting from Self-Hypnosis 257
Sample Hypnosis Script 261

SOME LAST WORDS 272

ABOUT THE AUTHOR 274

TASK NOTES 275

TASK NOTES 276

TASK NOTES 277

TASK NOTES 278

TASK NOTES 279

TASK NOTES 280

TASK NOTES 281

FIRST WORDS

> *Profit: benefit; gain; good; of help; of use; good; make money -Roget's Thesaurus; Unlimited: infinite; godlike; omnipotent; unrestricted Roget's Thesaurus*
>
> *
>
> *"The smell of profit is clean, And sweet, whatever the source." Juvenal*
>
> *
>
> *"He who lives in the realisation of his oneness with this Infinite Power becomes a magnet to attract to himself a continual supply of whatsoever things he desires." Ralph Waldo Trine*[1]

Unlike Thoreau, I do not think "the mass ... lead lives of quiet desperation". Artists, philosophers, writers, poets and scientists may seek meaning to life, and sometimes despair, but the mass generally gets on with each day's tasks expecting nothing, possibly hoping for a little more. When they do want more, they want it to be rather more subjective: pay off debts, find a job, or a partner, buy the house or the car of one's dreams, get a promotion, lose weight and so forth.

Successfully manifesting any of those fine goals is an aspect of unlimited thinking, and will be achieved, not only through reading Profit From Unlimited Thinking, but also proactively creating your own Tasks from each of the sections. However, I am also aiming for a little bit more for my readers.

> *"Men learn while they teach" Seneca*

It is said that one should write with a firm image of a reader in mind. Try as I might, mine remains the open-minded cynic! So perhaps I have given myself a parallel challenge.

God definitely has a sense of humour in giving tasks to people. It's a divine paradox that those who can best mentor and teach are those whose successes are constantly being rebalanced by further challenges in their lives. It keeps the energy at maximum flow if nothing else!

---

[1] In Tune with the Infinite: Ralph Waldo Trine

I have long been fascinated by the mystical and the power of the mind. Indeed my bookshelves are groaning with similar-themed topics. But it takes a lot of chutzpah to believe that my flavouring of words and truths can make a difference for other people - even if they have created minor miracles for me.

Successful sales coaching comes from my consistent and regular personal triumphs in frontline selling. I have "been-there-done-that" to recognition and respect. With unlimited thinking, contrarily, this divine dissatisfaction means the mentor never stops learning or chasing knowledge. Success can then become a continuously-moving target, frequently with no tangible evidence. All we can do is aim to share our passion.

> *"[The bourgeois] prefers comfort to pleasure, convenience to liberty, and a pleasant temperature to that deathly inner consuming fire." Hermann Hesse*

We all have the choice to draw a line around our newly-created comfort zones at any time. A writer of unlimited thinking however, does not! I am chasing more knowledge that you can choose to use or ignore, and I accept the challenges that go with it, so who is to say when success has been reached?

> *"A teacher affects eternity; he can never tell where his influence stops."*
> *Henry Brooks Adams*

It is mindboggling how many gurus there are, all promising happiness, deep and meaningful relationships, radiant health, wealth, control of our destiny, developing charisma, strength, confidence and much more. But as I said earlier, despite the evident growth market in self-help books, most people live in relative ignorance of their potential benefits.

Yet when life suddenly slaps down challenges, we all want answers – and we want them instantaneously. We all want to progress from the situation cleanly and speedily. Mortgage difficulties, severe illness, redundancy, business problems, divorce, death, climbing the corporate ladder, increasing your income, losing weight, giving up bad habits, getting out of the 9-5 work rut and doing your dream job, and so forth. Present a workable solution and you will be flavour of the month.

So books continue to be churned out because one day you too will need to find the right doors to push open to find a 'workable solution' to your particular challenge.... to say nothing of the writer's challenge, bearing in mind George Bernard Shaw's truism "He who can, does. He who cannot, teaches."

> *"It is almost impossible to bear the torch of truth through a crowd without singeing someone's beard." Aphorism*

Universal truths are not new as Ecclesiastes is often quoted, and sharing them is not the preserve of a select few. Every author has his or her own perspective based on subjective values and interests. There are no firm guarantees but what I do promise is to enthusiastically open a few doors to an enhanced world. Who knows? It may be just what you are about to need! And if something sounds familiar, that's excellent too. Recognition is a primary step in learning – and it also serves as a prompt to action.

By providing enough tools including quotations and further reading[2], you can control how much or how little you want to expand and unlimit yourself. You can take a giant step out of your comfort zones, or assess and absorb little by little. The choice is up to you.

> *"Leadership is lifting a person's vision to higher sights, the raising of a person's performance to a higher standard, the building of a personality beyond its normal limitations." Peter Drucker*

Profit From Unlimited Thinking is based on a creative thinking workshop I first ran in the late 80s. (It also explains the familiarity of my writing style).

---

[2] suggested reading or authors to further explore unlimited ideas

While I continue to be absorbed by all aspects of spirituality and mysticism, I also like to achieve my goals with some financial comfort. It may not be very evolved, but the workshops sprang from what I call pragmatic spirituality. However, these workshops were of necessity limited by time. This meant that I could only provide soundbyte metaphysics. Although written in a similar vein, I have included a lot more that would not have been practical in a one-day workshop.

Along with a few specific Tasks, I have purposely included further reading as well as references to other writers, specific books and some websites. Curiosity springs from enhanced thinking, and their inclusion is to make the search easier for you – rather than as a firm recommendation.

> *"It is for life... that we learn."* Seneca

A very successful salesman once told me that you can never read too many books on sales methods. Not only would you refresh the parts that had become stale through habit, but you might also find a killer tip that could help close a big deal. That goes for self-help books too.

Many of you may already be familiar with much that is covered within these pages. Many will be seeking fresh ways to manifest secret dreams and desires. I want to refresh and confirm as well as to provide a solid foundation for profiting and achieving more in your life through an unlimited mindset.

Unlike many other books, I highly recommend that you jump in wherever you feel the urge. I very rarely, if ever, read a non-fiction book from cover to cover. I end up hearing the writer's voice in my ear, and not my own, guiding and advising me. I want you to hear your own voice and your own truth. As Benjamin Disraeli said "The greatest good you can do for another is not just to share your riches but to reveal to him his own ".

> *"Keep away from those who try to belittle your ambitions. Small people always do that, but the really great make you believe that you, too, can become great."*
> Mark Twain
>
> *
>
> *"Like a good lens, a typology system will help us to focus more clearly on the important issues."* Robert Frager[3]

As well as concrete guidance through specific techniques, Tasks and tools, I have also used ancient wisdoms, philosophies and contemporary spiritual sources. Through these, you will begin to have a greater understanding of yourself. Through greater self-understanding comes greater choice. You may discover your life purpose and make startling changes in your life.

If you follow through with even one small exercise you will begin a voyage of discovery. But the most fascinating journey of all will be in unlimiting your mind.

By harnessing, stimulating and expanding the powers of your imagination you will achieve your personal goals more easily, and success will make you want to set your limits higher and higher. And by learning to think unlimitedly, you will understand the role of the individual within the whole and use this knowledge to develop balanced and effective relationships with others.

By recognising patterns of behaviour and limitations in both yourself and others, you will be able to more readily provide creative solutions to overcome problems and achieve even your most secret dreams.

> *"I am part of all that I have;*
> *Yet all experience is an arch wherethrough*
> *Gleams that untravelled world, whose margin fades*
> *For ever and for ever when I move."* Tennyson

It is said that a mediocre teacher tells and that a good teacher explains, while the superior teacher demonstrates. However, a great teacher inspires.[4] I believe that you may well find further reading to tell or tease or even irritate but equally there will be something

---

[3] Who Am I? Ed Robert Frager
[4] William Ward

that will inspire as well. As a "teacher", I am still learning but I have enjoyed enlightenment or success with each of the methods written about. They do work, and I want them to work for you as well.

> *"What is it that every man seeks? To be secure, to be happy, to do what he pleases without restraint and without compulsion." Ralph Waldo Emerson*

One of the most important elements of unlimiting your mind is to think freely. While you will be prompted to try different types of Tasks, how you do them is up to you. You can use the given tools to train your mind and stretch your imagination in any way you please. My only intention is to lead you to profit from your true, unlimited, self and enjoy whatever you wish your life to be.

Euphrosene Labon
Angmering 2004

PART 1 – WHO ARE YOU?

> *"It is good to know what a man is, and also what the world takes him for. But you do not understand him until you have learnt how he understands himself."*

Everyone wants a sense of identity. It is a reason why so many adopted children try to seek out their biological parents.

Genealogical sites are one of the most popular on the Internet. Curiosity about where we come from is healthy. But it is as easy to discover much about yourself without tracing lost ancestors. The Enneagram, for example, an ancient metaphysical system, popularised by Gurdjieff, is one popular method based on nine basic personality types. HR departments and recruitment companies have a whole range of not dissimilar profiling systems. They all serve a purpose, albeit a limited one.

While understanding our parents does provide invaluable information about our motivations and genetic make-up, it is not wholly necessary for unlimited thinking. With unlimited thinking, you can create an image of the person you would like to be, develop the mental attitude and posture of that person, acting as if you are already who you want to be, in essence, and you will (eventually) become that person.

The fake-it-till-you-make-it philosophy works because it works firstly in the invisible layers of the mind. In other words, you have to know who and what you are now, and then change those core frequencies to those of who you wish to be. You do have to have self-knowledge. But even those with unknown starts in life can retrain their minds to accept knowledge gaps, and to convert perceived negative experiences into positive ones.

YOU AND YOUR LIFE

> *"Our life is what our thoughts make it."* Marcus Aurelius[1]
>
> *
>
> *"Man is obviously made to think. It is his whole dignity and his whole merit."* Pascal, Pensees
>
> *
>
> *"To find out what one is fitted to do and to secure an opportunity to do it is the key to happiness."* John Dewey

Take a look at your life right now. Are you happy with it? Well done! Now, take another look. Better still, see yourself from another person's viewpoint? Still Mr or Mrs Perfection? Not even a teensy bit that could be improved in some way?

For the more honest amongst us, we can all do with a tweak here and there even when our comfort zones are fairly satisfied. The mortgage repaid? More customers but less aggro? Bills paid on time? Neighbours' appalling parking habits? The daily commute?

Unlimited thinking does not mean suddenly discovering an ability to levitate or to read minds. It could do, though transcendent spiritual gifts are usually given to those who tend to live far from the material world. But unlimited thinking does not have to drag you kicking and screaming from your comfort zones either.

Anyone can profit from unlimited thinking and small profits will lead to the bigger ones in more manageable ways. You can stretch that comfort zone to suit. Yet even those who enjoy a rare level of satisfaction and contentment share smaller problems and challenges. Not enough hours in the day, how to prioritise... Stress at work. Communication issues with the boss or colleagues. There might even be bigger issues which get buried under the minutiae of daily living. Changing attitudes towards their marriage or their faith are big issues that most people prefer to forget about rather than confront. From the outside, you may enjoy a life of plenty, but there is a dissatisfaction.

---

[1] Meditations: Marcus Aurelius

PART 1: WHO ARE YOU?

In mysticism, this is usually referred to as divine dissatisfaction. However you may view your Creator - and even atheists were "created" - you get the odd feeling that the job could be improved upon in some way. Yes? So which area of your life needs to benefit from a touch of the unlimited? Increasing sense of achievement at work? Getting more help and support from your family and friends? Making stress work for you? Becoming respected within your community? Improving your health? Getting promoted? Starting your own business?

Okay, let's not labour that point any more. You have got this far because you are curious. You do want to see if there might be some magic in you. Or you simply want to stretch that comfort zone a tad.

Developing a greater self-awareness will open you up to your potential. You may choose then to do nothing about it but you will have stretched your mind beyond its current horizons and you might even discover true freedom.

TASKS
!How would you describe your reactions so far?
!Outline your life as it currently is

> "The value, or worth of a man, is as of all other things, his price; that is to say, so much as would be given for the use of his power." Thomas Hobbes

According to self-help gurus, success comes to those who have a burning desire who pursue that desire with utter, blinkered, determination. Experience or talent take a back seat to fixed purpose and driving persistence. The other main criterion is a complete belief in a power within themselves – although this is not necessarily seen as the Almighty of traditional faiths.

Most of us unfortunately have limited self-esteem, flickering drive and a long-distance relationship with our personal Almighty. We limit our potentiality probably because it is less uncomfortable.

Our potential is also limited by the values we set for ourselves, or have had set on us through education, culture, families, religion and work. When pursuing or even investigating the idea of unlimited thinking, we have to identify and be aware of any potholes and hurdles within ourselves as they will have an impact on the realisation of our goals.

TASKS
!What value do you place upon yourself?
!How valuable do others think you are?
!How important are others to your sense of self-esteem?

> *"Thought: this alone is inseparable from me. I am, I exist – that is certain. But for how long? For as long as I am thinking. For it could be that were I totally to cease from thinking I should totally cease to exist."*
> Rene Descartes

You are the sum of your thoughts. Philosophical clichés are very rarely allowed to intrude into our mundane daily existence. Stuck in a traffic jam, bored in a meeting, arguing with the in-laws or cleaning blocked loos for a living, our thoughts tend to reinforce the everyday realities of our work and home life.

We generally neither know nor care that we are responsible for these simple moments. Unfortunately, they have a tendency to self-replicate as we give mental power to them and our potentiality is waylaid along with the last bus home. If only to avoid missing our transport, or to make sure our transport is a limousine and not the rush hour tube, we do need to pay attention to what thoughts crowd our minds.

If we want more positive things to happen in our lives we need to be aware of any negative thoughts that stray or weed our energy flow. Positive thinking can also make our world a brighter place. One positive statement will cancel one thousand negative ones. By filling your mind with happy thoughts, you will increase your confidence and positivity which in turn will magnetise more of the same. You will still have your arm down the blocked loo, but your attitude will be much lighter and

PART 1: WHO ARE YOU?

brighter. There again, you may find yourself motivated to change your career or hire subcontractors.

Awareness of your thoughts will identify whether you are truly happy despite the odd glitches or whether it is time to make changes.

TASKS

!What are you thinking right now?
!Where would you place your positivity ratio?
!Write down a list of ten positive statements
!Write down any thoughts that came into your head as you did so

> *"Dreams provide access to [this] inner world, and when explored and understood, create a connecting bridge."*
> *Montague Ullman & Claire Limmer*[2]

Daydreaming is another form of thinking. Some of the greatest minds in history have made major discoveries through daydreaming. Daydreaming can be either totally original or unlimited thought, or it can be free-form thoughts around a particular issue. I call the latter perspective thinking.

Perspective thinking will allow you to see things differently. It means you can expand your inner vision where expanding the structure may not be possible – for example in employment or marriage. You can enjoy perspective thinking by imagining job opportunities or promotion and checking out the pros and cons till you are ready to make tangible your desire.

TASKS

!Allow your mind to take a flight of fancy
!Jot down any key points

---

[2] The Variety of Dream Experience: Montague Ullman & Claire Limmer

> *"You've got to create a dream. You've got to uphold the dream. If you can't, then bugger it. Go back to the factory or go back to the desk."*
> Eric Burdon

Unlimited thinking on the other hand comes from discovering yourself who you are, what you want from life what dreams and fantasies you may have, extending and expanding those desires and then taking the steps to make them happen. Unlimited thinking means allowing your daydreams to take flight till you hit your inner reality buffers. For example, you may daydream about being rich and famous, seeing yourself accepting awards for your latest film plus all the glitz and glamour that comes with such a lifestyle - till the reality buffer snaps you out of it and back into the call centre. Unless of course it pushes you to join a theatre group or take acting lessons.

Daydreaming is excellent thought therapy if it provides positive escapism or fosters an action plan. If it is simply lusting after the colleague who works beside you, to get you through the working day, then it is a waste of mindpower. How do you use your daydreams? Why are you daydreaming? We daydream for good reasons and we need to find out what they are trying to tell us – even the farfetched fantasies.

TASKS

!Do your daydreams involve celebrities?
!Do you dream of escape or fantasy?
!Do you follow up any signs from your daydreams?

> *"Men can starve from a lack of self-realisation as much as they can from a lack of bread."* Richard Wright
>
> *
>
> *"One of the strongest motives... is the urge to flee from everyday life, with its drab and deadly dullness and thus to unshackle the chains of one's own transient desires, which supplant one another in an interminable succession so long as the mind is fixed on the horizon of daily environment."* Einstein

Do you know what your motivators are? What really drives you?

PART 1: WHO ARE YOU?

Try some of these for size. Do you thrive on praise? Do you feel like a victim? Perhaps you want someone to take care of you? How do you feel if someone criticises you? Do you hate yourself if you make a mistake? Are you afraid of being alone? Are you in a destructive relationship? Are you afraid to show anger? Are you miserable if someone dislikes you? Do you want to be the best at whatever you do? Are you critical of others? Do you make decisions off the top of your head or do you feel panic when presented with changes? Are you frightened of failure? Do you have concerns about success?

Hidden in these questions are your particular motivators. Sex may have been Freud's driving force, the rest of us have moved on a shade.

Ohio State University identified fifteen basic desires that colour our attitudes and needs (not in any order): food, honour, prestige, independence, learning, avoidance of pain, avoidance of rejection, time with family, order, social contact, sex, power, vengeance, citizenship, physical exercise.

Our motivators are keys to a sense of self-realisation. Our fears and concerns keep us from achieving it.

TASKS
!List your key motivators
!Do you feel anything is holding you back?
!List potential solutions

> *"There is no failure except in no longer trying."* Elbert Hubbard[3]

Failure happens to everyone at some time. Fear of failure stops most of us from setting out to achieve our dreams. Failures though should be seen as either temporary setbacks or as a way of learning. Most of the greatest achievers faced quite a few periods of failure – but in whose eyes? Failure was and is usually how you

---
[3] Elbert Hubbard's Selected Writings

PROFIT FROM UNLIMITED THINKING

perceive yourself through other people's eyes. But don't concern yourself with what other people may think. You will not get very far if you do. You motivate yourself by your passion and your ability to be good at what you enjoy doing.

TASKS

!Have you ever felt a sense of failure?
!Did it make you progress or regress?
!What did you feel about the reactions of others?

> *"What your destiny is depends upon what you will do with yourself in relationship to your ideal. " Edgar Cayce[4]*

What Color Is Your Parachute[5] is a classic in career guidance. It is also a wonderful book to set the bones for your life purpose as it forces you to define your motivators in terms of your career.

Perhaps you have a hero or role model whose life you admire and wish to emulate? Whatever comparisons you make in order to define your life purpose should boost your confidence. Observe your life with gentle criticism. What could you dedicate yourself to achieving? Why would you do it? Can you be single-minded about it? How and who would support you?

So far you have created a skeleton for your goals and desires. You have a vague idea how you value yourself and how you would like to be valued. You may even have got a better view of your conscious and unconscious motivations. Now you have to be more specific. Now you have to flesh out those bones.

TASKS

!Do you have any role models or heroes/heroines?
!If existing circumstances were no objection what would you do?

---

[4] The Edgar Cayce Companion: compiled by B Ernest Frejer
[5] What Color Is Your Parachute: Richard Nelson Bolles

PART 1: WHO ARE YOU?

GOALS: TECHNIQUES AND TIMELINES

> *"Not every end is the goal. The end of a melody is not its goal, and yet if a melody has not reached its end, it has not reached its goal. A parable."*
> Nietzsche

No guru worth their salt will gloss over goal setting. Anthony Robbins, a renowned speaker in the arena of personal development, writes at great length[6] of the importance of goals. His fire and drive are tangible in all his books, if somewhat wearing to lesser mortals.

Stephen Covey posits:[7] "In the field of personal development, one of the few things than can be empirically validated is that individuals and organisations that set goals accomplish more. The reality is that people who know how to set and achieve goals generally accomplish what they set out to do". Deepak Chopra calls it the Law of Intention and Desire.[8] An intention is a goal. "Intention triggers transformation of energy ... Intention organises its own fulfilment."

So there you have it. Goal setting is important. But then you knew that anyway. You want to know how to achieve your goals in the easiest most enjoyable ways though, don't you? Don't we all? Well it can be fun, if you tell yourself it will be. There you have goal number one: *I intend to enjoy the process of manifesting each and every one of my goals.*

Everyone has goals. Even a seemingly aimless Sunday driver has an overall goal – a relaxing spin on a fine day, lunch in a country pub and then back home. To annoy as many people as possible by driving well below the speed limit in the middle lane is presumably an additional benefit.

Brian Tracy[9] advises those setting goals to ask themselves "What would you dare to dream if you knew you couldn't fail?" Apparently many people struggle to

---

[6] Awaken The Giant Within: Anthony Robbins
[7] First Things First: Stephen Covey
[8] The Seven Spiritual Laws of Success: Deepak Chopra
[9] The Psychology of Achievement: Brian Tracey

PROFIT FROM UNLIMITED THINKING

write much down. Their consciousness has become limited or indeed was never expanded to start with. In metaphysical terms this is called poverty consciousness. Although limited thinkers may have money in the bank or a comfortable lifestyle, they have begun to limit themselves to just what they can see and enjoy, and have sown the seeds of poverty consciousness.

But goals do not necessarily have to be world-shattering or life changing. They can be as simple as making time to regularly ring friends or to go for a walk every Sunday morning instead of lying in and fretting about the weekend being practically over.

You can have goals to learn a different word every day or take the stairs instead of the lift. You can make it a goal to shave your legs even if your social life consists of vegging out with your favourite TV personality. Goals could and should be fun – even the serious ones concerning money, health and love.

The key to goal-setting is to define your comfort zones and satisfaction limits and then take them a step further. Rather than using that old chestnut of having six months left to live, think in terms of what your life would mean to others. How would you like to be remembered? Having hair-free smooth limbs probably does not count when considering one's immortal soul.... However, it does not mean that our goals and desires should ignore the mundane: pay gas bill, get a job, learn a new language, spring clean the house or whatever. Start with your immediate needs, and then shift them up a key till you reach the realms of the fantastic. Stranger things have happened.

There are several goal-setting programmes you can try, and each is valuable in its own way as a tool to focus the mind, and to get on the first rung of self-awareness. SMART[10] goals are specific, measurable, achievable, realistic and have a set time limit. You should be constantly aware of your goals without obsessing daily about the detail.

---

[10] Coach Training Alliance

PART 1: WHO ARE YOU?

Treasure maps are a fun way to help you paint mental images and organise a plan of action. Mind maps[11] are similar in concept: write down your goal and list all the actions that will lead you to achieving it. List alternative methods.

Another fun exercise is to use a snakes and ladders board[12]. Label it to suit your own personal circumstances, and run through what will help or hinder you in getting to your goal. Mind maps can be constructed organically over time to encompass different events and circumstances.

Take a large sheet of plain paper and write your goal at the top of the page. At the bottom, draw a stick person. That is you. Now write down everything you have to do or think you have to do to achieve this goal. Write down all the challenges, real and imaginary. Use a different colour to link up each action-route and put squares around the obstacles and diamonds around the key milestones. I find this easier on the eye than some other forms of mind mapping which can end up looking like spaghetti junction on a bad day. But to each their own. The choices are many and varied to help you unclog and prepare your mind. Seeing everything laid out also provides at-a-glance perspective.

Once you have an outline of all your goals, you need to make sure your subconscious is in agreement. You can do this by stating your goals in the affirmative as an intention. This is what you want to happen. You fully intend that these goals will be realised.

If your subconscious has any doubts or fears, they will begin to surface with small criticisms or delaying tactics, or even tension in your gut. Should this happen, make sure they appear on your map. You will then need to create a separate intention or goal to either negate the fear or transmute it. For example, if you want to be a singer but have only entertained your family or your bathroom mirror, you may have to take an interim course of action through singing lessons prior to recording that demo tape.

---

[11] Tony Buzan: Use Your Head; cf also Vernon Howard
[12] Inner Resources ©1989 Euphrosene Labon

Most schools of thought say you should review your goals every day. If there are a lot of underlying issues to address first then I would not recommend this course of action. To frequently check-up on your various goals can result in frustration which will negate any progress you have made.

Regular reviews can be made about once a month or even quarterly. Much more important is to feed your imagination and desire with the fruits of the realised goal. Hear the applause. See the cash piling up. Feel the engine purring. By merging with the sensation of the desire, you will keep your energy fresh and progressive. By contrast, if you keep thinking of all the words you still have to write, then your bestseller will remain a few rough drafts on your laptop.

In metaphysics, there is a saying: "Let go and let God". Meaning that once you have taken the time and effort to tell your Self what you want and when, then let It get on with the business of prompting your next actions as well as creating the right timing, circumstances and momentum to make it happen.

Goals of course change. Or other interim goals seem to intrude. You may need other people as part of your goals but your goals themselves should never be dependent on anyone else. Your goals should reflect your life and yearnings.

Goals should be prioritised: short-term goals, intermediate goals, long-term goals. You should have goals to identify further education or training. Goals should identify any dependencies: if you want to be married, does your partner feel the same way? if you are single, what are you doing about increasing your social circle?

Goals should have at least five to ten enhancing statements to energise its potential. For example, if you want a house, describe it. Describe its location. Is it spacious? What are the neighbours like? Are the shops nearby? Is it quiet?

TASKS

!Before reading on, list some key goals

PART 1: WHO ARE YOU?

KEY DESIRES

> *"Desire keeps me alive..."* Little Steven

Years ago, despite being top salesperson, my boss pointed out that I always just exceeded my sales targets and then happily tailed off. In those days there were no accumulators to tantalise and anyway I seemed to have reached a limit that satisfied. But then I moved to a more expensive house and, unnoticed, the satisfaction limit crept up and kept creeping up.

However, there came a time when money alone failed to satisfy. Signs from my subconscious came in the form of fault-finding. I had to set some fresh goals or they would be forced on me. In fact, lacking courage, fresh goals were forced on me, many times. Although the circumstances differed, frequently the script remained the same.

One way of discovering what's important to you is by defining your ideal day[13] or daydreaming to see where you are lead by your inner voice. With most people, there are key areas to address when setting goals. These are shown below and encompass universal desires:

- Love and Marriage
- Home and Stability
- Creative Self-Expression
- Daily Work
- Material Desires
- Social Family Friends
- Mind and Body
- Success Money Wealth
- Value and Purpose

Tasks

!Do you agree with these categories?
!What other categories would you choose?

---

[13] Carole Gaskell www.lifecoaching-company.co.uk

PROFIT FROM UNLIMITED THINKING

> "Great energy comes only from a correspondingly great tension between opposites." Carl Gustave Jung
>
> *
>
> "Wealth cannot make a life, but Love." Robert Herrick

Everyone needs love in their lives. Unless you have chosen to be a hermit, you probably desire a loving partnership, to nurture or be nurtured. Whether you seek marriage or are celibate by choice, love can find a number of ways to express itself individually in your life.

Finding a perfect partner or transforming your existing relationship is, according to scientists, all in the mind. Those with a positive outlook on life, are usually careful in their choices and are more likely to make longer-lasting partnerships.

Paradoxically, some of the most successful partnerships have been those of opposites. One half of the couple will probably have the emotional or spiritual characteristics that the other lacks, or has repressed. Through the partner, the other person, has the ability to experience a different world or find balance and wholeness within himself or herself.

Finding a soulmate is not as hard as it may seem. The problem is much more likely to be a conflict between your inner and outer realities. You may have an image of your ideal but attract those who only carry a fleeting essence of that. Until the inner and outer merge in perfect harmony, then you will doubtless still be chasing the unattainable. The exception is in choosing to be with an interim soulmate. While it is possible for interim soulmates to evolve into THE soulmate, usually, they have come into your life to help you progress into the next stage of your spiritual and emotional development.

Most soulmate meetings are highly-charged. Some can prove very traumatic indeed since they represent powerful lessons needing to be learned. Getting some of your needs met by another person could bring out elements of yourself that you may be unaware of and unable to handle. You will have to learn what personal

PART 1: WHO ARE YOU?

essences you are prepared to hand over to another, and that requires a high level of trust

Compatibility is less important than mutual trust, but first you will need to be comfortable with yourself. By thinking of yourself and your future, you will start to attract to yourself those who share similar essences.

Perfect mates are not born. According to Edgar Cayce, a soulmate or perfect mate is someone "with whom you can work through life's challenges and difficulties, even when that individual may appear to be the source of them."[14] These perfect partnerships are made through months of effort. Too often, relationship patterns mirror those we had or have with one or both parents. We will keep repeating our mistakes, attracting the same type, until we not only recognise the pattern but break free of it. However keen you may be to rush up the aisle, goal-planning should take into account previous relationship patterns and what you may or may not have learned from them. You should be aware of your contribution to that pattern before expecting Miss or Mr Perfect to wander into your orbit.

Tasks

!How can your love life be improved?
!Do you have fantasies of a perfect partner?
!Write down your first reactions to the above section

> *"A home is not a mere transient shelter: its essence lies in its permanence, in its capacity for accretion and solidification, in its quality of representing, in all its details, the personalities of the people who live in it."* H L Mencken

William Congreve might have thought security an "insipid thing" and "uncertainty and expectation .. the joys of life". Most of us, however, would prefer to know where our income was coming from, and that we could be sure of always having a roof over our heads. A nomadic way of life is pleasurable to most in youth yet increasingly

---

[14] Edgar Cayce on Soulmates: Kevin J Todeschi

less so with the challenges of age. Even unlimited latter-agers who spend their retirements flitting round the globe, tend to have a home somewhere as an anchor.

There are many people who quite contentedly live without a permanent home or money in the bank. Quite a few of these people literally have nothing and no human support and still have a sense of joy in living. For the greater mass though, home and stability are vital. No matter what your current situation, you can, not only aspire to, but actually achieve far more with some focused goal-intentioning.

Some years ago, in a catastrophic financial downturn, I had to sell my house losing a lot of money and having a pile of business debts on top. Although I had to move to rented property while I sorted out the financial problems, I found the right place for me, at that time, at the right price, in a village setting. I had written down the ten most important things I required from my next home – and I got them all. Perhaps if I had moved my satisfaction limit I could have manifested something even better. Ultimately, your subconscious can only bring to you what you are capable of receiving. And even if you can receive it, the time may not be right. Location, price, peace, parking, shops, travel ... add some essence – light, airy, spacious and test it out.

TASKS

!**What does money mean to you?**
!**Describe your current financial status?**
!**How can it be improved?**
!**Write down any other money goals to aspire to**

> *"It's tough, but I came to realise that some of the most interesting things you can do in life are the least lucrative."*
> Laura Cantrell
> *
> *"A musician must make his music, an artist must paint, a poet must write, if he is to ultimately be at peace with himself."*
> Abraham Maslow

PART 1: WHO ARE YOU?

What gives us our creative urge? Are we all creative or is it just the gifted few and those with a high capacity for self-deception?

I believe a lot of people crush their creative urges because that creativity reflects their much deeper selves. Creativity frequently requires a leap into the dark. The creative thought is the opposite to rational logical thought. Creative self-expression requires more than a degree of openness. But very few people are prepared to lay themselves too far open. It is almost a divine Catch-22 to have the seeds of talent and then remove the self-belief to fulfil it.

Self-belief is usually nurtured by our parents yet one study shows that many creative greats have either lost one or both parents in childhood. Prodigies and highly successful business people may come from happy and integrated families but the truly creative have had a lack of family support which may have caused them to create private inner worlds.

Creative self-expression does not just mean forsaking the corporate world to paint in a Parisian attic. Employment patterns have been changing for some time. With well-paid retirement not available to all, we have to tap our inner abilities to keep us "flowing". Whether you are a nascent creative great or just want your latter years to be financially secure, then now is the time to identify your creative potential in your goal-setting.

By the way, it is abundant output that marks out a creative great. They may have a lot of failures under their belts but the sheer volume of productivity effectively fuelled their success too. So, what would you happily spend a lot of time doing? What hobbies have you buried under daily pressures and responsibilities?

If you think you have no creative abilities at all, then now is the time to set a goal to attend evening classes and find out what you are capable of uncovering.

TASKS

!Describe your hobbies and interests
!Do you feel you have a buried talent?
!What would you feel if your talent became your career?

PROFIT FROM UNLIMITED THINKING

!How knowledgeable are you at your hobby?

> *"Work as though you would live forever, and live as though you would die today". Og Mandino*[15]
>
> *
>
> *"One of the saddest things is that the only thing a man can do for eight hours a day, day after day, is work. You can't eat eight hours a day, nor drink for eight hours a day nor make love for eight hours."*
> *William Faulkner*

I am sure some of you would argue with both Mandino and Faulkner. The reality, however, is that we do spend a terrific amount of time at our daily work. In fact, if you count travel time, it is far more than eight hours a day. It stands to reason that you should find some enjoyment then to get out of bed and put in those hours... yes?

Most of us only ask to be valued and to be of value in our daily work. We want to enjoy what we do, have a measure of freedom to be creative, and have a reasonable salary. If our daily work is our career, then we tend to apply more detail to our desire. We want the ability to learn freely with excellent career advancement. We need a friendly and harmonious working atmosphere. We desire the trust and respect of management and colleagues and indeed to be trusted and respected in return. We may want control and autonomy in our actions, contributing to the strategy and growth of the company we are working for.

In this current age of insecurity, we want a better quality of life, with flexibility and choice of multiple revenue streams. We most likely want to transform our lifestyle without necessarily cutting our incomes – although many high-fliers have done so. The interesting thing is that as their satisfaction limit had already been set high in say the area of wealth, the successful ones have achieved similar salaries eventually, along with greater purpose and fulfilment.

---

[15] The Greatest Secret in the World: Og Mandino

PART 1: WHO ARE YOU?

Did you know that high levels of job changes are supposed to produce very bright people? Their intelligence is manifested in their insecurity.

If you are a road sweeper or a call centre operative or whether you clean loos for a living, your work is valuable in the scheme of things – and, of course, it is not static. You can change to something else as soon as you set your mind to it.

Whether you choose to work for yourself or for others, whether your work is glamorous and exciting or backbreakingly dull, smile, do your work with pride and provide a good service. That will be your foundation for achieving bigger and better as your limits start to expand.

TASKS

!Do you enjoy your job?
!If you could do anything at all, what would it be?
!What are your reasons for doing this job?

"Acquisition means life to miserable mortals." Hesiod

*

"We are never further from our wishes than when we imagine that we possess what we have desired." Goethe

*

"How few are our real wants! and how easy to satisfy them!" Julius Charles Hare & Augustus William Hare

---

Gandhi once said that one must "not possess anything which one does not really need". Do we really need that beautiful painting or those pieces of porcelain? Another piece of jewellery or exquisite carving? Probably not. Simplistic needs boil down to having something to eat, a roof over one's head and something to wear. Yet where would that leave the carpenter or the artist?

Not all of us are made in the mould of the Mahatma or Mother Teresa. Indeed the Big E[16] would not have given us the great variety of the human race if homogeneity was the divine diktat. So there is nothing

---

[16] Wakan Tanka - the Prairie Plains Indian name for the Great Everything

PROFIT FROM UNLIMITED THINKING

undivine in desiring material goods, even if it is more of the same. Who of us does not want a flashier car, another pair of shoes, that state of the art computer? Treat it as your ability to create and enjoy unlimited abundance. As with all things, think and act accordingly. We might flex our credit cards for smaller goodies, but the max-items have to be goal-intentioned to avoid being in serious debt. Fashion comes and goes and it may not be worth the punitive interest charges to jump time. Anyway, time allows you to check how passionate your desire really is.

In my seriously impecunious days, I kept pictures of all the material desires I felt I needed: dinky but supercharged laptop, sporty car, Nile cruise, revamped wardrobe and much more. I've manifested and enjoyed them all... and created fresh ones of a more practical nature: decorate the house, redo the garden, buy new furniture. Time still plays its part whatever your material desire may be so just enjoy the process. However, even the healthiest bank balance cannot buy calibre gardeners and decorators or manifest plumbers just when you need them, or think you need them.

TASKS

!List your immediate material desires
!Do you find yourself daydreaming about something?

PART 1: WHO ARE YOU?

> *"We discover ourselves through others."* C G Jung
>
> *
>
> *"You can make more friends in two months by becoming interested in other people than you can in two years by trying to get other people interested in you."* Dale Carnegie[17]
>
> *
>
> *"The family is the association established by nature for the supply of man's everyday wants."* Aristotle
>
> *
>
> *"I believe that more unhappiness comes from this source (the family) than any other – I mean from the attempt to prolong family connections unduly and to make people hang together artificially who would never naturally do so."*
> Samuel Butler
>
> *
>
> *"How far you go in life depends on you being tender with the young, compassionate with the aged, sympathetic with the striving and tolerant of the weak and the strong. Because someday in life you will have been all of these."*
> George Washington Carver

I call this sector of goal-intentioning, social, family and friends. Other people. Other people seriously affect our goals and desires at all levels, for better or worse. Unfortunately, we cannot turn our nearest and dearest into paragons of faultlessness. We cannot set goals that make our bosses or neighbours become idealised perfection. Any change we would like to see in them has to come from a change in our own attitudes. If there are challenges at work or home with other people, then your primary goals should address your inner disquiet first.

Set goals to enjoy more harmony in your relations with family, colleagues and friends. You can set goals to change or improve your social lives. Or to put more – or less – effort into family life. If you have not been giving enough time and attention to your family or your partner, then target time for them. If your family has been draining you with demands and problems, target time for you and make sure you take it.

You can expand your horizons via Cyberspace, or go trekking with a group of complete strangers. Start with the mundane and necessary and move into fantasy and see what comes from it.

---

[17] How to Win Friends and Influence People: Dale Carnegie

If pressing goals involve your neighbours or the neighbourhood, such as parking and noise, then there are ways to achieve what you desire. They will be covered within this book. For now, log them down as immediate, medium or long-term goals.

To improve, expand or enhance your romantic prospects or current relationship, take a good look at what actions, if any, you are taking and set your goals accordingly.

Some metaphysical writers state that the people around us are aspects of ourselves. Since human reality is but an illusion, so it goes, those around us, are exaggerated forms of aspects we are either unaware of, or choose to ignore. The spiritual concept is that we evolve faster by accepting and overcoming these aspects in others, in order to see them changed in ourselves.

TASKS
!Do you have a wide social circle?
!How long have you known your closest friends?
!Do you try to make new friends?
!How would you describe your family relationships?

> *"The biochemistry of the body is a product of awareness. Beliefs, thoughts, and emotions create the chemical reactions that uphold life in every cell"*
> Deepak Chopra[18]

Mind and body - to which could be added thoughts, mind and body - is a major goal-setting area for most people. There is a very good reason why the ancients called the body the temple of the spirit. Our spirit is continuously reflected in our bodies through our thoughts and will. Even a seemingly frail baby can project its inner strength through its will to live. We may be seeing a tiny fragile body, but inside is a spirit every bit as powerful as our own, with a unique way of getting his or her needs met.

How many physically different bodies have made remarkable contributions to the betterment of our world?

---

[18] Ageless Body, Timeless Mind: Deepak Chopra

PART 1: WHO ARE YOU?

Stephen Hawking and Christie Brown are two that immediately spring to mind.

Unfortunately, it is only when we are physically underpar that we take any notice of our health and our bodies. The physical effect is the result of ignoring those inner chidings. As the temple of our souls, the body deserves a lot more respect. It needs to be listened to *before* it starts to suffer any physical effects. It needs a disciplined mind.

I still think longingly of Marmite spread lightly on a layer of butter on thick white bread. However, my overfondness for it eventually started to play havoc with my digestion. Now wheat and dairy play no part in my diet because I lacked the correct eating discipline.

We all know that everything should be taken in moderation. But when things taste so good, it is easy to make them an over-regular snack or meal. Deliciousness compensates for the discomfort of a bloated waistline. Eventually, self-preservation at the cellular level has its say with intolerances and allergies. Until I rediscovered my willpower, 'exclusion and replacement' topped the list of health goals.

Water is an excellent therapeutic aid. Not drinking enough can cause depression and mood swings. We also eat when in fact we are thirsty. Scientific studies have shown that increasing water intake sensibly can improve mental and emotional health. Increasing intake is a valid goal, and can show results relatively quickly. Alcohol and coffee have had mixed reviews. In some schools of spiritual thought, they are frowned on, if not expressly forbidden. Moderation should always be the key, and is quite an easy goal to achieve since it only involves reducing quantity. The added advantage is from increased pleasure from its infrequency.

Smoking continues to receive universal bad press, yet paradoxically is the most difficult to give up. Most people are aware that smoking is not only bad for the body, but it is also not very considerate, yet they still cannot stop. For these people, it has become an addiction, and is quite possibly a symptom of another, underlying, cause. Those underlying causes have to be treated first. I have included a self-hypnosis script[19] at the back for those who wish to add this to their list of goals. It can help to redirect thoughts and, if necessary, seek out professional help.

While I am a firm believer in self-healing[20], sometimes physical challenges may be part of our spiritual evolution. Unlimited thinking comes from making that illness or disability step out of physical limitation and into mental possibility. Think again of Christie Brown and Stephen Hawking. Or it may just be the need to accept. Often resolution and solution come from simple acceptance.

Anyone who has ever read my ezine, floreo NEWS, will know that I am passionately against pigeonholing. It is the very antithesis of unlimited thinking. Age is a pigeonholer, whether you are perceived as too young or past it. In almost the same breath, we are told we will be living for longer, more healthily, but with less money in the pot. Contrarily however, we will not be accepted in traditional employment. Why? Why are our bodies and personas defined by a chronological factor? Experience and enthusiasm are what count - and they can come in various age ranges. Enthusiasm makes us seek out further challenges - and that keeps the spirit, and body, revitalised. Enthusiasm seeks out experience. Both ends of the age spectrum benefit. At one end of the scale are those starting out with few pre-conceptions. At the other, are those who are in their latter working years, thinking of nothing but retirement.

The concept of retirement is a major factor is neurone degradation. However, only the vainly singleminded would waste energy on thinking away their wrinkles. Ignore the wrinkles and set yourself some intellectual challenges for your goals.

The University of California suggests that as we "get older" (ie spend more time in our physical shells), intellectual challenges can stimulate the growth of neurones in our brains, compensating of any biological deterioration. Goals to increase your mental activities

---

[19] Inner Resources ©Euphrosene Labon 1989
[20] You Can Heal Your Life: Louise Hay

PART 1: WHO ARE YOU?

could include doing crossword puzzles, learning chess or a foreign language, becoming a political activist or joining a philosophical discussion group.

TASKS

!Are you healthy?
!Do you look forward to retirement?
!How do you react when asked your age?
!How do you keep your mind active?

"Wealth is a product of man's capacity to think." Ayn Rand

*

"How he does it is no secret, and no miracle. Hours and hours of practice and an iron will to stop even the tiniest doubts from creeping in[21]."

*

"All you need in this life is ignorance and confidence, and then success is sure." Mark Twain

*

"In all things, success depends upon previous preparation, and without such preparation there is sure to be failure." Confucius

*

"Fortune favours the brave." Anon

Ayn Rand's philosophy of Objectivism celebrates the power of man's mind, urging people to live by the codes of self-reliance, integrity, rationality and productive effort. And they are excellent means to generate wealth and success although I believe her philosophy focused more on the rational. She quite rightly saw that those in business were as much creators and benefactors of mankind as artists and philosophers. However, unlimited thinking sometimes requires switching off reason if wealth is to be created.

Wealth itself has very subjective meanings, as does success. There is no right or wrong definition if it is true for you – not what others may think is right for you. Charity workers are generally held in high regard but their income is usually quite low. As an aside: according to The Giving Campaign[22], research shows that wealthy people

---

[21] Rob Andrew about rugby star Jonny Wilkinson
[22] 2003 research paper

PROFIT FROM UNLIMITED THINKING

actually give proportionally less to charity than those less well off. In the same way, the principle of tithing seems to benefit the recipients rather more than the givers. Give from the heart. Be dictated to by compassion and not by inflexible laws.

Money is spiritual energy. It is vibrating all around us. Yes, I know that's hard to believe when the mortgage needs to be paid or if you are between jobs or the bank manager is foreclosing.

Some have tapped into the right money frequency and have made fortunes quite quickly. But equally most of them have lost similar or greater fortunes. The equivalent mental infrastructure did not exist to retain and build on that earlier burst of good luck. There is rarely much success in get rich quick schemes. Even for those first off the starting block.

Sometimes wealth can have an unwelcome kickback. J K Rowling has found writing much more difficult now that she is a wealthy woman. Apparently she says she even thought of breaking her arm to avoid putting pen to paper. So it is vital to understand your motivations and check out your satisfaction limits regarding wealth and success. Nothing is holding you back from visions of plenty, except yourself. You do not need an excellent education. Many wealthy men have had no formal education at all. Indeed, the drive to succeed can often come from having an unhappy background. What is important is defining your wealth and success satisfaction limits.

TASKS

!Define your concept of wealth
!Define your concept of success
!Do you feel either wealthy or successful?
!What would make you feel wealthy and/or successful?

> *"The conviction that life has a purpose is rooted in every fibre of man, it is a property of the human substance"* Primo Levi

PART 1: WHO ARE YOU?

While some traditional forms of religious worship have taken a battering, belief in a higher power has paradoxically increased. The desire to believe in *some*thing has lead to personal faiths which are a hotchpotch of the ancient and the fashionable. Our choice of enlightenment is dictated as much by our sense of value and purpose as our desire to experiment and progress. Modern living also requires a Convenient God and the Internet has been quick to respond.[23]

We are living in a time of counselling. From a starting point of life coaching, we move to inner exploration from where our sense of value and purpose become more defined and individual. We may still choose to belong to traditional churches, but we have an awareness that comes from spiritual maturity.

In Part 5, you will find out how to discover your own guru. For atheists, there is also a section on the value of creating your own genie or guru. For now, if some higher wisdom is missing from your life, add it to your list of goals.

Tasks

!Have you ever felt strongly about something?
!What did you do about it?

MAKING A DIFFERENCE

> *"The place God calls you to is the place where your deep gladness and the world's deep hunger meet."* Frederick Buechner

Most people desire to make a difference in some way. Maybe there is a subconscious desire to justify one's existence? We cannot all be brain surgeons or lead peaceful revolutions. Not all are blessed with the desire to write or paint or sing. Or run a Times 1000 company. But making a difference can come from the most seemingly humble corner.

---

[23] www.beliefnet.com

I once knew a road sweeper, a weather-beaten old man, with a curiously young aura. He had a huge repertoire of particularly bad jokes, and would playfully insist on recounting at least three whenever we met. Although he smiled as he rabbited on, his bright eyes would watch you carefully. I sometimes got the impression, it was the Good Samaritan's angel testing the waters. That man certainly made a difference. If you are lucky enough to know how you can make a difference, be thankful. The rest of us learn by trial and error, by switching off the ego and letting the still small voice within take over. There again, some may even ignore the 'ssv' because invariably it requires change, and change shifts us away from our comfort zones.

TASKS

!What would you define as a mission?
!Do you think you have a mission?
!Do you think you have ever made a difference?

> *"If you have been put in your place long enough, you begin to act like the place."* Randall Jarrell
>
> *
>
> *"..if a man really knew himself he would utterly despise the ignorant notions others might form on a subject in which he had such matchless opportunities for observation."* Santayana

Sometimes shifting comfort zones can mean the breaking down of the structures that have supported and guided us to our present position. Unlimited means breaking out of or expanding borders. Boxed thinking is usually the result of relying on too many structures.

Structures generally form a necessary backbone. However, they can unintentionally or even intentionally impede creative or unlimited thinking. Anything that does not conform is pushed out or not taken seriously. Structures like comfort zones usually include education, religion, class, sex, family, marriage, nationality and country. Work is a structure.

When you list your structures, make sure you jot down the first thoughts that spring to mind beside each

PART 1: WHO ARE YOU?

item heading. Log subsequent thoughts as you monitor their influence. The aim of unlimited thinking is not to impose anarchy into your lifestyle upsetting your nearest and dearest. Equally though, the aim is to avoid stagnation with the ultimate goal of transcendence.

At a mundane level, transcendence is heartfelt joy or even bliss in all areas of your life. The ripple effect of the ultimate - bliss - virtually guarantees that the other areas of your life will be enhanced - or changed.

TASKS

!List all the structures in your life
!Jot down any spontaneous thoughts as you do
!Do you feel anything is holding you back?
!How could you achieve your desires without hurting anyone?

> *"When you are fifty years old, you should know your destiny."* Confucius

Humans work to timescales. The Universe does not. Or rather, divine timescales are unquantifiable to mere human minds. So, with apologies to Confucius, age is neither here nor there. As an aside, to pigeonhole by age is supremely limited thinking... but that is another subject! Whether our destiny is that of a wisecracking roadsweeper, a caring mother, a conscientious office worker or something truly magnificent, we must always be ready, and to paraphrase the parable of the ten maidens: the five girls who were ready went in (to the feast), and those who were ill-prepared, found the door closed.[24]

To be ready for the Universe, we must at least prepare, and that means discovering any hidden purpose. One of the finest texts on finding out your mission in life can be found in Richard Nelson Bolles' classic[25].

Many writers in this genre, including myself, firmly believe in a Supreme Intelligence. Wakan Tanka, Jehovah, Allah or the various aspects in Hinduism are just

---

[24] Matthew 25:1-13
[25] What Colour is your Parachute?: Richard Nelson Bolles

PROFIT FROM UNLIMITED THINKING

some of the known terms for God. My own is the Big E. However, there have been, and still are, many people who have struggled with the idea of God. Yet many atheists have discovered their missions and made positive and significant differences to humanity. Having faith in a higher power, or a formal religion, is therefore not a pre-requisite to having a mission, far less making a difference. We are all born with untapped skills and talents - our inner resources - and these are the foundation stones of how we can make that difference.

We are told by self-help writers that we will know when we are "following our bliss[26]" - that is our destiny - because everything becomes effortless. Tragically, and far too often, the flowing sensation of "effortlessness" is blocked by what I call GFUDA – guilt, fear, uncertainty, doubt and anger.

A sense of destiny unfortunately can, and does, have widely differing impacts on humanity. A politician's sense of destiny, for example, can change the landscape of not only his or her country but also the wider world - and not, perceivably, always for the better. A serial killer, might delusionally believe he or she is ridding the world of a menace. The departed soul obviously would not agree. A sense of destiny therefore, while still incorporating the determination to do good, should recognise its effect on the lives of others.

Tolkien believed one should be committed to some greater cause than mere comfort and materialism. Helping others is the beginning. Increase your visibility in small ways and above all try and enjoy the process. In a similar way to Tolkien, Viktor Frankl[27] stated that humans should not pursue happiness but a purpose for living – "the task waiting for them to fulfil". If this purpose was found, then happiness would follow. This man spent three years in concentration camps where this concept germinated - and kept him alive. Your mission is your passion, and your passion is your purpose - and that is what drives you. That is your destiny.

---

[26] The Power of Myth: Joseph Campbell
[27] Man's Search for Meaning: Viktor Frankl

PART 1: WHO ARE YOU?

What if there is no burning passion in you? How can you also make a difference? Do something unselfish for a stranger. Take an interest in your local community and become one its spokespeople.

Anyone can create something special. Once you clarify the minimum elements of your life purpose, you will begin to start having bold dreams. You will start to become alert to opportunities. Nothing may come of them but you will start to recognise possibilities, and that in turn will increase your magnetism to more.

You are unique. Your needs are unique. Your family, friends and colleagues make up the jigsaw puzzle that is the unique you. Your uniqueness is coloured by your fears and phobias and habits. So while you may not yet be blessed with a driving desire, as you seek to find out more about your hidden self, often just such a gift creeps up on you. It will be more than just fifteen minutes of "fame" - that is, recognition and rewards. It will become your life's work which you choose to do, which you enjoy doing. It is fully following your bliss.

Thankfully driving desires are not the same as burning desires. Fulfilled desire, or destiny, will be happy pootling along at one mile an hour, rather than overshooting the speed limit. It is partaking that counts. Drive keeps you going. Fire burns out unless it is turned down and controlled.

The "Six Months" technique is frequently used to uncover hidden desires and destiny. What would I do if I only had six months left to live? What do I really want? How do I want to be remembered? Apart from its negative connotations, it can encourage dubious behaviour, so think about this carefully.

Sometimes self-hypnosis can help to discover hidden urges and drives. Taking time out to sit and fantasise or daydream is also an accepted form of creative imagining. Jot down the images and ideas that spring into your mind. Set goals and action plans around them. If you tell yourself that you are unlimited, you will be. Expect results and you will get them.

TASKS
- What do you feel passionate about - if anything?
- What makes you unique?
- How would you like to be remembered after you have gone?
- If you had six months left to live, what would you do?

PART 1: WHO ARE YOU?

PART 2 - KEEPING ON TRACK

TECHNIQUES & TIPS

In order to profit from the unlimited you have to switch off your logic and rational thinking modes. You have to develop fresher, more effective habits. As your knowledge and competence increase, new patterns of behaviour must be learned. Unlimited thinkers take responsibility, and, take action. Structured affirming and visualising will help you enormously in this.

> *"You cannot have a negative vocabulary and expect to be anything but poor; poor in health, poor in looks, poor in pocket. To break this habit, which can never bring out the magic in your mind, first cultivate a liking for positive words." Al Koran[1]*

Affirmations serve many purposes: to lift the senses, to change awkward thought patterns or to focus a stream of consciousness. However one of the primary functions of affirmations is to create new habits. Observe your automatic thoughts.

Language is a part of our identity. Our personal use of language as well as collective associations are all reflected in our daily lives. Paying attention to the volatility of language is important when addressing the issue of affirmations. Affirmations will help you to recognise instinctive thought patterns. They will allow you to replace destructive thoughts, and they will prompt the use of keywords to shift

---

[1] Bring out the Magic of your Mind: Al Koran

mental flow. Constant practise will instil a new pattern of behaviour.

Stephen R Covey writes[2] that habits can be learned or unlearned. He also wrote that creativity begins with the mind. True, and what better way to focus the mind then with affirmations. You can quickly make some quite startling changes in your life through the power of affirmations. There are, however, vital techniques to remember.

Affirmations should always be in the present tense. They should be short and sharp. They should be something your conscious, or subconscious, mind will not argue with. Coue's law of reverse effect will create the opposite of what you desire if your affirmation starts an internal argument. You cannot, for example, affirm "I am wealthy and successful" if you are on the dole. You can however affirm the words "wealthy" and "successful". You can affirm "I am open to wealth and success." These will then have the positive returns you seek.

Examples:
I am now enjoying more success.
I am increasing my income
I am succeeding more and more.
Everything is beginning to go my way
Wonderful things are now happening to me
My luck is turning around

Even better, though they are slightly esoteric:
I am vibrating with wealth and success energies
I am full of light and love
I am drawing to me all that I am

---

[2] Seven Habits of Highly Effective People

PART 2: KEEPING ON TRACK

"I am" statements are deeply powerful. Make sure your affirmations start with "I am".

TASKS

!What areas of your life do you most want to improve?
!Which goal do you most want to realise?
!Write a preliminary list of corresponding affirmations

> *"We begin with a thought that is planted in the mind and if you think this thought long enough, it becomes a habit. If you habitually think this thought habitually enough, it becomes a belief, something you believe to be true about yourself." Jerry Fankhauser*[3]

Affirmations can be used for building self-esteem, for finding love and for improving relationships. You can affirm for a job or for increasing abundance in your life. For increasing your creativity and self expression, for being on the path of bliss or simply to improve your daily work. You can affirm for prosperity, health and even for spiritual development.

As well as being in the present tense affirmations should use positive terms. Avoid anything with negative associations. You should affirm for what you do want, rather than what you do not want. "I am beginning to gain a fit and healthy body" does not contradict if you are currently overweight, and yet to start a slimming programme.

It is planting the seeds of activity and you will find yourself putting aside that packet of crisps and drinking a glass of water instead. You may find yourself paying more attention to a magazine article on weight loss or you may decide to walk to get the paper instead of hopping in the car. The statement is very powerful because it is positive, it reinforces your

---

[3] The Power of Affirmations: Jerry Fankhauser

desired goal and it sets in motion a chain of events that will ultimately result in your beautiful fit and healthy body.

Affirmations that are short, specific and easy to chant have an invisible and potent impact at a deep and hidden level of your mind. Power and energy come from constant repetition. Repetition is important. In fact repetition is vital and must be given time and focus. Repetition will imprint the affirmation into your subconscious mind and allow your hidden powers to come up with effective solutions.

Enjoy your affirmations. Use passion and creativity. Personalise them rather than copying something you have read in a book. Remember the volatility of language and make sure that the words you use do not have ulterior or unfortunate connotations!

Affirmations should be chanted persistently, regularly, morning and evening to get the results you require. Provided you have followed the basic rules, affirmations will work whether you believe they will or not. Obviously it helps, but belief actually will grow as you start to see the buds of success start to appear.

To gain maximum benefit from your affirmations, your mind should be in a receptive state. First thing in the morning, and prior to sleep are excellent. Still and quieten the mind first. Switch off any sensory stimulation. Close your eyes and focus on your breathing. Listen to your breathing. It has the most extraordinary effect of releasing the mind from its physical borders. You will get a sense of being both inside and outside of your physical body.

Start your affirmations and gently, hypnotically, keep repeating them. Stick to one or two that work together – remember they are focusing your inner energies and you do not want one statement to cancel out another.

PART 2: KEEPING ON TRACK

There is definitely a process and sequence to working successfully with affirmations. Feeling particularly intense or mind-stressed is not a good time to affirm for a key desire. You must affirm to clear the current condition first of all. Affirmations charge and energise, and you want your desire to be untainted.

Keep a log of any feedback. If you think nothing is happening, then that is precisely what you have created - nothing. Expect something to happen - and it will. There is a metaphysical law which states that everything happens invisibly first. As above, so below. Christians will recognise this similarity to the Lord's Prayer: On Earth, as it is in Heaven...

TASKS

!List any key issues in your life
!Prepare a list of corresponding affirmations
!Fine tune your earlier affirmations

> *"Every moment of your life is infinitely creative and the universe is endlessly bountiful. Just put forth a clear enough request, and everything your heart desires must come to you." Shakti Gawain*[4]

Positive, focused, visualisation can turn your life around. In Unlimited Thinking all desires are first manifested in our unconscious minds. For some, it is not always possible to actually see anything in their mind's eye. Jack Black[5], a leading practitioner of mind-management courses, simply *believes* he can see, and that, to him, is sufficient.

The brain and nervous system cannot differentiate between real and "unreal" and will act

---

[4] Creative Visualization: Shakti Gawain
[5] Mindstore: Jack Black

upon these images anyway. Imaginations are immensely powerful, so why not have fun with some controlled imagery? Script for yourself some ten minutes scenarios. For examples, imagine yourself rolling in money. Feel the texture of the notes and coins. Are you inside or outside? Is the sun shining? Are there other people around? What do you feel? Or how about standing on top of the world, with your boss sitting in the palm of your hand? Or the same place but with people queueing up to give you money? Or buy your services? Or offer you jobs?

If you know any annoying people, see them in your inner cinema as very small indeed... and unable to harm you. Tempting though it sometimes is to mentally step on them, thereby consigning them to imaginary Elysium, do not. It is far better to work on focusing on their finer natures. However hidden they may be, they do exist.

If your finances are fine but you have other challenges, imagine a powerful laser zapping away all your problems. Take care not to use your laser to harm anyone else though. If you do feel inclined to laser a person, make sure it is a cleansing one, releasing them of the negativity that has bounced on to you.

If you need protection, see yourself cloaked in golden light. For opportunity, create a picture of a house with many doors, all marked with the appropriate words: New Job, Promotion, Love, Success, Good Health and so forth. Then push open the door your require and step into the light behind. It will take care of the rest. Just remember to follow up all gut feelings that will result.

TASKS
!Create images to go with your key affirmations
!Use symbols and associations to reinforce the message

PART 2: KEEPING ON TRACK

> *"All our dreams can come true if we have the courage to fulfil them"* Walt Disney

An important part of visualising is taking time out to daydream. This is a logical step from the controlled imagery exercises described before. With daydreaming, you sit quietly and let your mind take its own journey. Just remember to write it down later.

Daydreaming, like night dreaming, is a mystery of the mind. We enter into a world where parallel time rules, where there are no boundaries – in fact, it is a world of unlimited possibilities. Jung believed that dreams were "remnants of a peculiar psychic activity taking place during sleep." By dreaming during the day, you will be able to better control the messages from your inner self.

Professor Susan Greenfield said that when we dream we are all schizophrenics. However, while schizophrenics seem unable to control their multi-aspected, altered egos, with daydreaming, you will have your hands firmly on the steering wheel. In the sci-fi drama, Quantum Leap, Sam Beckett never lost sight of who he was, but he tried to do the best he could to enhance the life of the body he had leaped into. You can imagine the same for whatever body your mind chooses to "leap into" during these states.

Whatever your key goals, they are already vibrating on an invisible plane, or dimension, waiting to be manifested. You have to be in tune with them, prior to manifestation, vibrating at their frequency, and to do that, you must feel that you are indeed doing so. This is not as difficult or as esoteric as it sounds. And you certainly will not be hexing yourself or anyone else. Just make sure your motives are compassionate and generous and you will be fine.

PROFIT FROM UNLIMITED THINKING

Take abundance as an example. Abundance is vibrating all around us. Abundance manifests not only as success, money and wealth, it also manifests as love, wellbeing, harmony and good health. To enjoy good health, tune your thoughts to that vibratory dimension of radiant good health. This applies even to those in hospitals - your physical body may be battered, but the foundations of your mind are perfect and healthy. When you vibrate with those foundations, you will discover ways to either heal yourself or to cope better.

Those suffering from most forms of mental illness will probably need a helper in this. Generally-speaking, schizophrenics are notoriously indisciplined, suffering "disordered thought". They prefer their own mind-world, no matter how much it may torture them. You, however, have more control over your choices.

Tasks
!Do you recall your dreams?
!Make an effort to remember at least one dream this week
!When you daydream, does it seem very real?
!Do you try and control your daydreams?

> *"It is now realised that a state of schizophrenia and the artistic vision are not mutually exclusive."* Carl Jung[6]

Visualisation is balancing what is with what you are creating. Controlled visualisation will ensure that your mental film-making stays within your pre-set boundaries. Thus to manifest wealth, you must feel wealthy and you must feel rich inside. However, you must ensure that this feeling of wealth does not manifest in bending the plastic enthusiastically before your bank account can handle it!

---

[6] Man and his Symbols: Carl Jung

PART 2: KEEPING ON TRACK

Sometimes visualisation needs help when the "leap" is too big. Scrapbooks are a useful tool for creating sensory images. You can rebuild self image, following the credo of fake-it-till-you-make-it. The subconscious, uncontradicted, has no means of knowing what is real or not. Paste in your scrapbook pictures of the car you want, then see yourself test driving it. Or even parking in your drive.

Whenever I have done these exercises, the sheer power that resulted, has energised me into achieving everything, although the means were perhaps rather more prosaic. Just be measured and balanced when you take risks.

Someone I once knew who subscribed to the fake-it-till-you make-it ideal, bought his Rolls Royce, but had rather big debts and a sad body language. Far better to see pictures of yourself feeling good in other ways first - then the Roller will follow. To manifest the bigger effects will almost certainly require you to unlimit various other aspects of your life and persona.

It is said in Eastern mysticism that when you have achieved the spiritual means to manifest whatever you want, at will, then you will no longer want to do so. Divine Catch-22! The amount of effort you put into training your imagination will show in unlimited results. The results you achieve, and you will achieve results, can be stretched as your satisfaction limit gets pushed further and further away from its current state.

Satisfaction limits are not exclusively related to wealth. You might want to express your inner artist, become your own boss or to adopt children. You might want to get married or explore a single life. Life in a village in Africa....

In a recent survey of activities to do before they die, the top-rated desire was swimming with dolphins. Other wishes included walking the Inca trail at Machu Picchu, trekking through a rainforest, riding a

PROFIT FROM UNLIMITED THINKING

motorbike on the open road, going white-water rafting, seeing the Northern Lights and skydiving. Why wait? Set your goal, visualise and see it manifest. Open and unlimit your mind - anything might happen!

TASKS

!Do you feel satisfied with your life?
!Do you feel you could achieve or give more?
!What you make you feel satisfied?
!What would increase your levels of satisfaction?

> "We may give advice, but we cannot inspire conduct." La Rochefoucauld...
> *
> "I make a habit of never having any sort of routine. It's bad to have a pattern to your life, because the three easiest times to kill a man are when he's on the toilet, when he's in bed or when he's eating."
> Masaaki Hatsumi

Unless you are a Ninja grand master, like Hatsumi, then you will value these daily practical tips, which should be habit-forming:

!Tell yourself you are a winner
!Have confidence in your abilities
!Smile
!Be friendly to people
!Speak with at least four people each day
!Take a chance on something
!Use affirmations with your daily routines
!Enjoy tasking your inner guru
!Believe miracles are possible
!Remember every day has creative power
!Think lucky and you will be lucky
!Spend ten minutes in stillness and silence
!Write down your problems
!Write down possible solutions
!Date and file what you have done
!Focus on something else

PART 2: KEEPING ON TRACK

!Be enthusiastic no matter what
!Follow up all your promptings
!Show your mind you are in control
!Stop any internal dialogue immediately
!Refuse to give up
!Be open to all opportunities
!Analyse failure and make it work for you
!Don't give a damn what other people think
!Fake it till you make it in your mind
!Avoid people who hold you back
!Read some words of wisdom every day

SELF-DISCOVERY IN WORDS

> "Why do I keep this voluminous journal? Partly because life appears to me such a curious and wonderful thing that it almost seems a pity that even such a humble and uneventful life as mine should pass altogether away without some such record as this, and partly too because I think the record may amuse and interest some who come after me." Rev Francis Kilvert
>
> *
>
> "If you do not tell the truth about yourself, you cannot tell it about other people." Virginia Woolf

I confess to keeping a personal journal with a similar view to the good Reverend. It also pleases my mother to receive written monthly updates. However, the main purpose of keeping a journal within the context of Unlimited Thinking, is to understand yourself better. Self-understanding comes from self-awareness and one of the best forms comes from what you share with your journal.

Keeping a journal can help you to explore and experience your feelings fully. Check your feelings by writing "I feel....". Unless you choose to share your pages with your mother, it is your private space to say exactly what you want. Indeed, you may even want your nearest and dearest to know what you really think

PROFIT FROM UNLIMITED THINKING

and feel, so your journal can be an ideal place to start developing forthrightness..

Piers Paul Read wrote that writing novels helped him to control and purge his more negative and destructive urges. Your journal can also provide a similar service, although, as in the case of Princess Diana's videos and letters, it might be kinder to add caveats in case you leave this mortal coil unplanned. Write freely, but add balance by trying to see the other person's perspective as well.

Journal writing should be a daily task. Your time just for you. Ira Progoff[7] wrote that recording your desires can trigger miracles. If there are no restrictions on your time, or money, what could you create for yourself. Write your life script, become an observer of your life: what needs improving, what is missing? How can you create something better? What is achievement to you?

Journal writing can be like praying on paper. As you create your life you can add or change the dramatis personnae, increase your physical attributes, your success quotient, intelligence, intellect and much more.[8] As it is written, so shall it be. No sooner written, then you will find yourself actioning it in "real life".

Tasks
!Buy or acquire a blank book
!Start writing down your thoughts, experiences and emotions
!Write down anything that comes to mind
!Make this your secret journal

---

[7] At A Journal Workshop – Ira Progoff
[8] Write It Down, Make It Happen – Henriette Anne Klauser

PART 2: KEEPING ON TRACK

> *"The human animal differs from the lesser primates in his passion for lists..."* H Allen Smith

Self-discovery from words can take many forms. For those who get no pleasure from lengthy writing, keeping lists is a step in the right direction. Writing lists can help to itemise feelings, intuitions and thoughts and allow you to unburden faster. Not everyone is a gifted writer, but almost everyone can write, even if it is only a shopping list... In this case, a personal shopping list, and that, believe it or not, is a great tool for self-discovery.

According to Wallechinsky/Wallace[9], everyone keeps lists. In fact, they say, lists are as old as written history. Hammurabi had a list of 282 laws, Moses had the 10 commandments. And then there is you with your shopping list or your business tasks of the day.

In Unlimited Thinking, lists are for various purposes. Lists suit lazy or inexperienced writers. Lists are good for at-a-glance keeping on track. Keep a special book reserved for your lists. List what you DON'T want – because they will tell you what you DO want and what you *should* be focusing on.[10]

Lists are good for applying detail to your desires and the more we think seriously about something, the faster we are going to attract it into our experience. Lists are good for setting timelines and observing potential obstacles. They are good for checking what you need to learn, who can help you, logging specific courses of action for each goal, and for listing the benefits you will enjoy when you have reached your goal/s.

---

[9] The Book of Lists
[10] Excuse Me, Your Life is Waiting: Lynn Grabhorn

Lists are good for writing down everything that is good in your life, everything that is a challenge and everything that is horrible, and that you want to change. Lists provide the basis for accurate goal setting. Lists will enable you to discover any contradictions in your goal setting. For example, if you want to be an artist but you crave financial security, you have an underlying goal which must be addressed first. List what makes you happy. "Happiness is not an ideal of reason but of imagination". What exactly is happiness?

Yogananda said that to be happy is to be in tune with God. Once contact is genuinely made the feeling of harmony and oneness never really disappears although it may get buried from inattention. However, someone else said that happiness is episodical - with Bernard Shaw adding that a lifetime of happiness would be hell on earth.

In untenable situations, it would seem like a bad joke to find something to be happy about, but there usually is something. Dependent on the level of pain and trauma, it might take an enormous effort of will to step outside of that emotion and situation and to seek something to be happy about. Paradoxically though, the very act of thinking of something that has made you happy will change your electro-magnetic frequencies and will generate some sort of change. It may only be a tiny change but it will add up.

For many, our challenges can seem immense and it can be difficult to find much to be happy about. Yet there are others, physically abused, trapped, starving and worse who have broken free by finding odd moments of happiness. Best of all is to find that happiness within. Happiness and success, like pain and despair are relative. Only your inner self knows its limits.

PART 2: KEEPING ON TRACK

Rousseau believed the secrets of happiness were a good bank account, a good cook and a good digestion - not a bad place to start.

TASKS

!Make a list of the first ten things that spring into your mind
!Use lists if writing is not your forte

> *"The unexamined life is not worth living."*
> *Socrates – Apology [Plato]*

Another tool for word self-discovery is a diary log. Not so intense as a personal journal, nor as brief as a book of lists, your diary log will contain snapshots: of thoughts, images, ideas, dreams, insights, coincidences, as well as the mundane - the plumber not turning up, or being bawled out by the boss, taking your wife out for a romantic meal, something about your children, having a touch of road rage .... these are typical logs you may want to include.

> *"So in each action 'tis success*
> *That gives it all its comeliness." William Somerville*

A success diary is exactly that: a log of each and every little, medium and big success that contributes towards the fulfilment of your goals. Success thoughts, ideas, events and actions should all be included.

TASKS

!What would you class as a success?

PROFIT FROM UNLIMITED THINKING

!Keep a log of everything that you class as a success
!Write down past successes

> *"If it is indeed true that each human soul contains a Bible within itself, may it not be that each person contains the possibility of new spiritual events and awarenesses taking place in his or her own experience?" - Ira Progoff PhD*

Keeping a personal journal is like having a conversation with yourself, or Self. Through your observations and judgements, it details your personal strengths and weaknesses, your fears and thought patterns, actions and inactions. It is a secret place to tell yourself what you really want, how much you really want it and what it will give you. It will show how deep your desires are and what your commitment is to those desires. As you log events in the wider world, it will also show how they can, and do, affect your thought processes and how they could impinge on your goal fulfilment. It is a place to scribble screenplays for your fantastic new life - where you can describe in glorious detail all the things and people you want to enhance what you already have. Or maybe even to creative a whole new world for yourself.

As previously stated, thoughts exist on an invisible plane or dimension, prior to manifestation – and this is where you will capture them first. They may appear disguised but the essence will absolutely manifest in time.

Use your journal to log any alternatives that may satisfy as well – or to see if your desire is unshakeable. Are you willing to change yourself to achieve your desires? Are you prepared to commit to your dreams? If you do not, then nothing will happen. Use your journal to log tasks to be done. When they are completed, you can transfer them to your success

PART 2: KEEPING ON TRACK

diary. Do not leave tasks undone. Use your journal to do mental dumps. Dump anything unfulfilling. If it gets you down, it is not right for you, and the best place to find out is from your journal.

Try writing a self-portrait. Start from your perspective, then write it as if it is your partner's words and feelings about you. Or a sibling, or your boss, maybe your children.... This is a particularly good exercise if you have any issues with a specific person.

> "..we can never know for sure whether channeling is a fabrication of our own minds, or true communication with other beings. But... the human mind has an amazing capacity to access wisdom far beyond our conscious knowledge.[11]" Kathryn Ridall PhD
>
> *
>
> "The Lord gives His blessing when He finds the vessel empty." Thomas à Kempis

Automatic writing is another form of what I call streaming – short for streams of consciousness. It is also a form of channelling: as your unconscious mind taps directly into its subconscious, it can uncover blocks or hidden emotions, or knowledge beyond our current experience. Obviously solitude is a must. Write away for however long or short you feel necessary and see where you are lead.

It is generally thought that handwriting is better for streaming than using a laptop, because the pen or pencil effectively becomes an extension of your hand. However, typing into a laptop, in my experience, has been more effective for me, as I have not been distracted by messy handwriting. Either way is acceptable, if the end result is less ego and more "still small voice".

---

[11] Channeling: Kathryn Ridall PhD

It is worth noting that many successful writers, including JK Rowling, have been handwriters. Many again talk of the words simply pouring from them. Of course, if you are feeling particularly adventurous, you can always try the exercise with your other hand. As part of my own self-taught exercises to make my broken hand useful again, I regularly practised left-hand writing and drawing. It had the added benefit of injecting humour into a non-humorous passage of time.

Try writing a letter to yourself, or to another person, real or imagined. Make sure to destroy the letter if it is to an existing person – especially if it is contentious in any way. Emotions and attitudes change over time, and bilious letters have a habit of turning up at precisely the wrong time!

Take a written journey. What do you see? Hear? Smell? Describe it in as much detail as you can. What are you doing and what are you wearing? What do you feel like? Who else is there with you? Who do you want to be with you? What is the purpose of your trip?

Writing, whatever form it takes, is definitely good for the mind and soul. As a method of unlimiting your mind, it cannot be stressed highly enough.

STIMULATING YOUR IMAGINATION

> *"The imagination is the secret and marrow of civilisation. It is the very eye of faith."* Henry Ward Beecher
>
> *
>
> *"People can die of mere imagination."* Chaucer
>
> *
>
> *"Because imagination created the world, it governs it."* Baudelaire

PART 2: KEEPING ON TRACK

Now that you have your diary, list log and journal, what else can you put in it? Now that you know how to visualise, how can you make your mental screenplays more vivid and exciting?

Albert Einstein famously talked of imagination being more powerful than knowledge. This is no doubt proved by the fact that many people have difficulty in creating their own mental pictures. To imagine is to create mental images and to fire them with emotion. Freeform imagining, or daydreaming, is allowing the hidden tunes within to play their song. Imagining provides possibilities and solutions. "Imagination is the power of the mind to consider things which are not present to the senses, and to consider that which is not taken to be real.[12]"

The sections that follow are intended to help to build and stimulate the imagination ...

> *"...let us chase our imagination to the heavens, or to the utmost limits of the universe..." David Hume*

Imagination and creativity are inseparable for artists and poets and writers. The rest of us in our everyday lives have barely the time or the inclination to challenge our imaginations. Daydreaming is fine but focused imagination is the province of those arty types. But you can of course stimulate your imagination with the practical and the tangible. Why take a leap of faith with something airy-fairy, when trying out a new recipe will do the trick almost as well?

You may not want to paint a landscape or write a book, but, as well as food, you may want to experiment with your garden, or redecorating the spare room. You may want to learn a new language.

---

[12] The Oxford Companion to Philosophy ed Ted Honderich

Getting your vocal chords wrapped around Chinese, as well as learning their immensely beautiful characters, will immediately transport you mentally into a vibrant, exciting and *different* world.

Stimulating the imagination involves cultivating curiosity. Develop a sense of wonder. Don't just use the expression "smell the roses" – go out and discover what they do smell like. Find something to be surprised about. Try something new.

Before you go to sleep each night, think of at least three exciting things you would like to do the next day. Remember this is an exercise for stimulating your imaginative processes – not for taking the day off to go golfing!

Your lists and daily journal will eventually throw up a pattern of interest that might be worth exploring or even turning into a fully-fledged major goal.

TASKS

!Do you use the television to stimulate your imagination?
!How often do you read books?
!What are you going to do now to stimulate your imagination?
!Have you any ideas you can share?

> *"The majority of Englishmen and Americans have no life but in their work; that alone stands between them and ennui... they are too deficient in senses to enjoy mere existence in repose; and scarcely any pleasure or amusement is pleasure or amusement to them." John Stuart Mill*[13]

Idleness is generally frowned on, yet many ideas have been born in moments of seemingly mindless inactivity. Isaac Newton and Einstein, as well

---

[13] The Importance of Being Idle: Stephen Robins

PART 2: KEEPING ON TRACK

as many artists and writers, gained valuable insight and ideas in their periods of wakeful idleness.

Wakeful idleness is not sitting in front of the box with a six-pack and a burger. It is not having a lie-in. Nor is it surfing the Internet. It is sitting and gently observing. It is letting your thoughts drift, allowing them to follow their own course. Become an observer of your thoughts and, when you hit Planet Earth again, scribble them down in your journal. If you are properly in tune with your intuition, you may get a relatively quick return. Generally, results happen over a period of time, which is why keeping records is quite important. Nothing is unimportant in the scheme of things, however many light years it may be from your current experience.

> *"The mystery of language was revealed to me. I knew then that 'w-a-t-e-r' meant the wonderful cool something that was flowing over my hand. That living word awakened my soul, gave it light, joy, set it free!" Helen Keller*

At a rough estimate, there are 6,000 languages spoken in the world today. Language distinguishes us. Despite fashionable views, language is more than a question of style.

Language is perceived as a human system of communication. In fact, the faculty of language is regarded as a defining characteristic of being human[14]. Some peoples deploy an incredible variety of sounds and sibilants to describe individual characteristics and even defects. There are peoples who have special languages for hunting, or circumcised males[15]!

---

[14] The Oxford Companion to the English Language
[15] Spoken Here: Mark Abley

PROFIT FROM UNLIMITED THINKING

Language diversity is as splendidly rich as the human race.

While English may dominate as the language of world trade and commerce generally, other nations, notably the French, have passed legislation to try and protect the power and beauty of their own mother tongues. Language is wonderful. It is alive, and constantly changing. Language is cross-cultural, lending and borrowing words to add to its richness and freshness.

There are so many games one can play with words, and there is an almost endless supply to stimulate our imaginations. For some though, language becomes a forgotten territory, requiring another perspective on unlimitedness.

Alzheimer's sufferers, sadly, lose the ability to communicate with words. From mild difficulty in finding words to a complete loss of language, people with Alzheimer's focus more on non-verbal communications[16]. Gestures, tone, facial expressions and body movements become their primary mode of communicating. So there is still a lesson that multi-abled people can take from them when learning to stimulate their own imaginations.

Learn a new word each week, or even each day. Find out its synonyms and antonyms using Roget's Thesaurus.

According to Steven Pinker[17], the brain hears speech content in sounds with a remote resemblance to speech. He calls it "sine-wave speech". Speech is in fact an illusion. This is excellent for the purposes of unlimited thinking. Choose your new words with care,

---

[16] New Approach to Living Positively: Joanne Koenig-Coste
[17] The Language Instinct: Steven Pinker

PART 2: KEEPING ON TRACK

and you could be vibrating at a wavelength with great potential.

TASKS

!Choose a new word and make sure you use it several times
!Do this every week with a new word
!Change one of your language mannerisms

> *"A person gets from a symbol the meaning he puts into it, and what is one man's comfort and inspiration is another's jest and scorn." Justice Robert Jackson*

According to Tom Chetwynd[18], symbols are treasured as a "means of releasing sources of energy from the unconscious". When unconscious knowledge is brought into the conscious mind, it can affect the quality of our lives, "bringing value and meaning". When Pope Urban Vlll believed his life was threatened by adverse astrological events (a sun's eclipse), he used the supposed symbolic influences of the magic squares of Jupiter and Venus to countermand their influence. He lived on for a further sixteen years.

The square of Jupiter is thought to bring prosperity and happiness, while Venus brings love. Urban felt protected and prospered by the symbolic resonances within those squares, and his life reacted accordingly. Albrecht Durer's engraving "Melancholia" also includes the magic square of Jupiter. It is traditionally associated with happiness, prosperity, good fortune, good health and long life. Durer believed its mere presence would aid the sufferer, helping to lift his or her spirits[19].

Another symbolic magic square is that of Saturn. It is used as a leveller, bringing down to earth

---

[18] A Dictionary of Symbols: Tom Chetwynd
[19] The Complete Fortune Teller: Francis X King

PROFIT FROM UNLIMITED THINKING

those afflicted with delusions of grandeur. Its significant number is fifteen. Each row, whether across, down, up or diagonal, adds up to the number fifteen.

    4 - 9 - 2
    3 - 5 - 7
    8 - 1 - 6

Believed to be the origin of the I Ching - Book of Changes[20] - it was said to be the pattern of life. This particular magic square is also used in intuitive[21] feng shui, and has been more effective for me than the classical school of feng shui which focuses on the use of a geomancer's compass. In fact, I first found out about the magic square many years before I knew of feng shui.

Each of the numbers represents elements in the journey of life. I used these symbolic associations to create energy flow for what I wanted to attract. And it worked. As with all energy though, it is important to avoid stagnation, even with symbols.

While there are universal symbols, or archetypes, our unconscious tries to communicate with each individual according to our own personal dictionaries. By paying attention to our dreams and coincidences, we can begin to discover our own inner language with its private codes and symbols. We can then immediately start to live richer lives.

TASKS

!Do any symbols have meaning for you?
!Or numbers?

---

[20] I Ching - The Richard Wilhem Translation
[21] Feng Shui Made Easy: William Spear

PART 2: KEEPING ON TRACK

> *"Who is there that, in logical words, can express the effect music has on us? A kind of inarticulate unfathomable speech, which leads us to the edge of the Infinite, and lets us for moments gaze into that!"* Thomas Carlyle

I have mixed feelings about science. On the one hand, science has proved many long-known mystical truths. On the other, if science does not believe it, it cannot be so, consigning spiritual metaphysics to the fools' junkyard.. Thankfully, however, scientists are in agreement about music.

Music can affect us in numerous ways – mostly to advantage. Penn State University asked students to keep diaries recording their moods and responses to music. The students reported back of positive emotions, regardless of the choice of music. Babies listening to music were shown to have increased their intelligence and curiosity. Unless you take after W.C. Fields, one of the most beautiful sounds is that of a baby burbling and chuckling away to him or herself, music to most people's ears.

Music can boost performance or relax. It can increase energy flow, or it can substantially reduce it. Your choice of music should reflect your circumstances. Because hard rock music can make you speed, it is not suitable for traffic jams, as it can exacerbate road rage. In fact, research[22] has proved that some forms of up-tempo music have increased the rate of accidents. Equally though, tranquil classical music on motorways can induce torpor, when alertness is vital.

Music has been used to treat ill-health as well as stimulate soldiers into battle. Technogrunge with its heavy thudding beat is fine in a night club. Unfortunately it has also been responsible for some

---

[22] Ben-Gurion University 2002

suicides as has country music. Music affects our nervous system. Even a deaf person can "hear" music – through bone conduction. Evelyn Glennie taught herself to sense musical sounds through the soles of her feet as well as through her lower body and hands. To her, music "isn't just a question of sounds... the seed.. comes from the heart... You don't need ears"

Mozart is well-known for increasing intelligence and improving concentration, far more than any other composer. Apparently it is because of the precise mathematical patterns of his music reflected in our mental processes. We get a sense of balance which helps to regulate our bodies thus helping them to function better. Music has even been shown to break down cancerous cells. Mark you, the case in question involved intoning scales for three and a half hours each day for a month, so I am not surprised the faulty cells took off. The story does not record what effect all that intoning had on other parts of her mind![23]

Pythagoras believed that both preventative and curative treatment should begin with the senses, especially hearing.[24] Using appropriate harmonies, it became possible to change or reverse emotional attitudes. Equally, music was viewed as a bridge to heaven. From the Whirling Dervishes to the shamans to wandering minstrels, music has had a purifying power. However if you are planning to use music to stimulate your imagination, choose with care. Lyrics should be avoided. Film soundtracks are also not a good bet. One of my favourite pieces is Zimmer's Gladiator but it resonates, for me, with the "Final Battle" and I am not yet ready for Elysium!

---

[23] Healing With The Voice: James D'Angelo
[24] Iamblicus: Pythagorean Life

PART 2: KEEPING ON TRACK

Before selecting your music, write down what you want to achieve: to raise your energy? to relax? to get ideas? to feel in tune with the divine? In our highly-blessed age there is an abundance of music to suit all needs. You can be mentally stimulated, unlock your creativity, be inspired and much more. The language of music must be learned. Opera generally is an acquired taste unless you are Italian. So too are many forms of Asian music. However its marriage with western pop has seen Indian bhangra hit the charts and open up a new world of the Bollywood musical. This in turn can foster exotic flights of fancy.

Music is very powerful in controlling and manipulating our emotions as soundtracks have proved. Listen to the first bars of Jaws and you can almost smell the deceptively peaceful ocean, as well as feel your hackles rise!

A proven and powerful musical form is chanting. Aside from its eastern, mystical traditions, it induces in the chanter a semi-hypnotic trance and can be very healing because of its vibrational energy. "Aum" is called the universal vibration or sound of the universe. It is beyond time and space. Posture is important when listening to music[25]. Either stand or sit upright, back straight, head erect. According to Dr Alfred Tomatis this enhances our receptive antennae enabling us to vibrate with the sounds.

Chanting is a primary part of most religious traditions. From Gregorian chant to Islamic call to prayer and Judaic vocal counterpoint, and all forms of Eastern mysticism, music and chanting have been key to inducing an altered state of consciousness. In The Sound of the Soul[26], the author writes that vocal exploration starts in the womb. The foetus creates

---
[25] The Power of Music: Cynthia Blanche & Antonia Beattie
[26] The Sound of the Soul: Arthur Samuel Joseph

PROFIT FROM UNLIMITED THINKING

vocal vibrations and sound waves almost similar to dolphins. We make sounds to express our aliveness. The essence of who we are is in our voices.

Toning uses voice in pure sound rather than melody, concentrating usually on elongated sounds. It is the focus on one note that sets up a vibration through the whole body. Typically using vowels, you can affect different areas of the body, balancing, healing and refreshing both mind and body. Sounds and tones can calm or stimulate: the sounds of waves lapping, or the roaring of motorcars round the circuit. To lift yourself out of a depressive slump, try some Tubthumping, or conducting to William Tell at full blast. It makes me burst out laughing seeing how daft I look, arms swinging wildly in tempo. Just make sure not to annoy your neighbours or family with high decibel therapy.

Another word of caution: music has different associations for each person, so make sure you choose your own. While I might get light-hearted pleasure from it, I once read that one man's rages were triggered by the William Tell overture - the theme tune to A Clockwork Orange. He was subsequently given two life sentences. Use music to scope and enhance your daydreams and flights of imagination but remember to select those with harmonious associations.

TASKS

Make a list of your moods and emotions
Select some pieces of music to go with those moods
Describe in your journal how they make you feel

PART 2: KEEPING ON TRACK

> *"The purest and most thoughtful minds are those which love colour the most."* John Ruskin

I love to paint big colourful pictures. I find the process of painting extremely therapeutic. Seeing something emerge from the colour, is both hypnotic and revealing. It is an unspoken, sensory truth pertinent to myself, as your colour exercises should be to you too. It does not matter what anyone else thinks because what you are doing is having a illustrative conversation with yourself. In colourism, the colours themselves convey space and emotion. Yellow is quick-thinking, red takes risks, white is refined, silver elegant. Blue is careful, green methodical and black is success and ambition.

No matter what your artistic skills, it is highly recommended spending time with paints or coloured pencils as part of your journey into unlimited thinking. Drawing colourful shapes and patterns should not just be a child's activity. It is extraordinarily therapeutic, even if you have the artistic skills of a gnat. Your choices of colours, designs and shapes will not only be entertaining and relaxing, they will also be highly revealing. There are many splendid books and courses available, with colour exercises and theories[27] to add some intellectual weight and dimension. You can even hire a colour consultant or do a college course and become a colour therapist yourself.

Colour impacts the retina the longer you look at it. Colour requires intense focus to truly gain benefit which makes it a wonderful medium for visual meditation. Howard Hodgkin believes that "nothing can compare with (colours') infinite possibilities, its infinite seductions; the multiplicity of its possible

---

[27] Colour: Edgar Cayce; The Luscher Colour Test; The Complete Book of Colour: Suzy Chiazzari; Creative Visualization with Colour: Brenda Mallon; Colour Healing: Lilian Verner-Bonds; Know Yourself Through Colour: Marie Louise Lacy etc

PROFIT FROM UNLIMITED THINKING

meanings from the most profound to the exceedingly trivial."

Max Luscher's famous colour test is believed to reveal personality through colour, discovering the real person through your strengths and weaknesses – all from selecting from eight colour combinations. Luscher theorised that a person's preference for certain colours is directly related to the emotional value of those colours. Before reading the following generalised summary of colour associations, you should write down your own preferences and dislikes, as well as any non-committal choices. Is your preference for undilute? Or pastel, calmer colours? Do you prefer interim shades or secondary colours?

Mediaeval painters believed the more brilliant and primary a colour, the more divine it was. Colours can create their own highs, and indeed lows. Greys, browns, blacks, though much-loved by fashionistas, can be very lowering tints taken to excess. Indeed all colours and tones have their positive and negative associations. The associations shown below should only be used as a generalised thumbnail sketch.

Red: fiery, passion, fast, sensual, power, determination
Pink: unconditional love, unbiased, spiritual renewal
Purple: royalty, delusional (violet), depth
Blue: divine light, healing, cold, melancholy
Green: abundance, reality, jealousy
Yellow: mind, sunshine, cowardice, spirituality, intellect
White: transfiguration, ethereal
Orange: communication, humour, happiness, joy

Colours have wavelengths, frequencies and vibrations. Red, for example, has the longest wavelength and the lowest frequency. It also has the slowest vibration, even though it is predominantly used in fast food restaurants for quick turnaround.

PART 2: KEEPING ON TRACK

Judicious use of colour can assist in a variety of ways. Because colours are associated with our chakras or energy centres, we can use them to increase or realign any imbalances in ourselves and in our lives. Green, for example, is the colour of the heart chakra. Green is also abundance and wealth, as well as love. Colour work can include wearing an item of that colour, painting pictures with said colour, eating colour foods or a little revamped interior design. Yellow can be worn to increase inspiration and problem-solving when taking exams. Obviously, not top to toe yellow... or any colour for that matter, because colours have such a subliminal and profound affect on our psyches. Quite apart from the ribbing you would have to take.

Water is excellent therapy[28] for virtually all ills. By adding colour, through coloured glass or gels, the benefits can be substantially increased. Walls painted pink in prisons have helped to reduce aggression. Green can aid depression, by lifting our inner life force: suicide levels dropped when a bridge was painted green. However, too much of a shade can tip the scales negatively: purple can foster delusions, red increases emotions. However, while moderation in anything is always advised, June McLeod, President of the Colour Therapy Association, states that "you cannot overdose... once the body has absorbed what it requires, the colour energy will cease to flow[29]."

TASKS

!What are your favourite colours?
!What images and sensations do they conjure up for you - if any?

---

[28] Your Body's Many Cries for Water: Dr F Batmanghelidj
[29] Colours of the Soul: June McLeod

PROFIT FROM UNLIMITED THINKING

> *"The consciousness of the planet is leading humanity to the re-discovery of an ancient and forgotten healing art in which the utilisation of crystals is prominent"* Melody[30]
>
> *"You set the seal on perfection; full of wisdom you were and altogether beautiful. You were in an Eden, a garden of God, adorned with gems of every kind: sardin and chrysolite and jade, topaz, cornelian and green jasper, lapis lazuli, purple garnet and green felspar. Your jingling beads were of gold, and the spangles you wore were made for you on the day of your creation."* Ezekiel 28:12, 13

In a recent article, the interviewee dismissed crystals as "all that crap". Yet it is a scientific fact that quartz disks or rods, cut and ground appropriately, are used for their ability to resonate at a particular frequency. By charging and discharging currents of electricity, such crystals can and do perform a number of vital modern-day functions. Most of the crystals and gemstones found in rather more esoteric books can also be found in dictionaries of science and technology. Since science is only concerned with the tangible and the useful, we can take it that crystals do perform valuable functions. As the human body is made up a trillions of electro-magnetic particles, it is entirely acceptable to imagine a benign gem increasing or decreasing our energy flow appropriately through its conductive powers.

The origins of crystal and gem "personalities" and characteristics are lost in the mists of time. These affiliations are many, many thousands of years old and cross cultures as well as time. From the earliest recorded days, we know that gems were used as symbols of spiritual as well as worldly authority.

In the Bible, God refers to gemstones several times, directing their use for protection or inspiration. Ancient Egyptians valued their gemstones so highly, they were buried with them. But does historical and

---

[30] Love Is In The Earth: Melody

PART 2: KEEPING ON TRACK

scientific validity matter with unlimited thinking? Any tools that help to keep the mind focused whether that comes from feng shui, colour or crystal therapy should be used pragmatically. I have found when wearing a particular gem favourite again, after a reasonable gap, that I am welcoming an old friend back into my energy field. I genuinely feel a positive charge, which of course is what they are meant to do. By wearing or keeping crystals close to your aura, you are charging them with your frequencies. They in turn can enhance receiving frequencies associated with their particular personality.

Crystals and gems can be used for colour therapy. Allow yourself to be drawn to a particular colour or gem and work your exercises around it. Tiger's Eye can aid confidence, bloodstone attracts creativity, green tourmaline for abundance, ruby for wealth, jade for unlimited potential... citrine is the merchant's stone, peridot can lift spirits, aventurine helps with stress and insomnia.

Most of the books dedicated to crystal usage, recommend rituals for washing and charging them. They would be most disappointed with me. I stick them under a running tap for a couple of minutes then wear them more or less continuously till they have absorbed my frequencies. I do not much care for standing under the light of a waxing or waning moon, but do like to think of my lighter, higher nature so that as it prepares to conduct electrical flow on my behalf, it kicks off with a "programme" of healthy and positive vibrations. For this reason, I would advise care with using a piece of jewellery with a history. I was once given gold bangles that had belonged to my grandmother. Some years later, I had a mammogram and was told I had a lump that required attention. As my grandmother had died of breast cancer, I promptly performed my own cleansing ritual and the lump disappeared, so I kept on wearing the bangles. Unfortunately, those gold bangles did still manage to exert a negative influence further down the line. My hand took the brunt of a car crash, with the thin gold wedging deeply into my hand, breaking bones and subsequently affecting my grip. I had foolishly removed other protective and balancing gems, but left the bangles because they were too difficult to remove. A&E delivered the coup de grace... and the insurance company claimed them in lieu of cash. Coincidence? Who knows? Just take care.

Crystals and gems are conductively used in space exploration and missiles as well as medical equipment. Programme yours to conduct positive energies for you.

> *"Is there anyone among the great men who has not imitated? Nothing is made with nothing."* Jean Auguste Dominique Ingres
>
> *
>
> *"Everyone alters and is altered by everyone else. We are all the time taking in portions of one another or else reacting against them, and by these involuntary acquisitions and repulsions modifying our natures."* Gerald Brenan

Ecclesiastes was a miserable so-and-so. As far as he was concerned, there is nothing new under the sun. Whatever had been done before would be done again, life was useless ... on and on, he moaned. So, since very little is truly original, how can we be unlimited? Is emulating a pioneer mere imitation? If so, why bother? Firstly, there is no-one like you. Someone might have the same build and colouring as you. They may even share the same birth date or name. This doppelganger may also have followed a similar career path. But they are not you. Even in the unlikely event that they popped out of your mother's womb at the exact same second as you, they would still not have your feelings and your thoughts. They will have their

PART 2: KEEPING ON TRACK

own experiences, which will colour their emotions and sensations, as will you. Identical twins, even separated at birth, frequently share similar likes and dislikes. But, they are still unique at a fundamental level.

So you are original. What you may choose to do with your life and self-expression may not be original, but how you choose to tell it or do it or be it, assuredly will be. You and only you have your unique inner melody, and that is what you will project whether you choose to be a plumber, a lawyer or a road sweeper.

TASKS

!Buy a crystal - the first one that grabs your attention
!Log any thoughts or changes you might experience
!Describe your uniqueness

> *"You do something* first *and then somebody comes along and does it pretty." Pablo Picasso*

Role models are an excellent way to trigger off the imaginative process. They provide a skeleton scenario for your imagination to flesh out. But this time it is your mind, your face, your body enjoying the rewards and respect.

Take an achiever in your chosen field, see how he or she worked their magic, and use it as a blueprint. But do you really want to be them? Does their life in all its aspects appeal to you? Or is it the achievement that you would like to emulate in your life? This is more than a twenty minute exercise. Ask yourself: what is it about this person that I would like to have for myself? Are there aspects of this person or their life that may not be right for me?

You may want to run a hugely successful business. However, you may not be prepared to risk your home or your marriage. You may want to step into a position, rather than starting in the post-room, so your role model will have used time and circumstance to favour them. The subconscious is tuned into an energy frequency which just happens to know all the ins and outs of your chosen role model's life and personality - including many hidden weaknesses and vices. Be specific with your subconscious as to what you want it to bring to you.

It amused me to read recently that businessmen love villainous historical role models. Best sellers have included those warm personalities of Machiavelli, Sun-tzu and Napoleon[31]. The journalist gently mocks with "Close That Deal the Gandhi Way" – but didn't Gandhi achieve Indian independence peacefully? Prior to that, didn't he help to topple the pass laws? He persisted. He was determined. He accepted the very rough times. But he won! Winning of course brings other challenges. Winning is not a dead end but another beginning.

Role models these days frequently are those who glitter and sparkle on the screen or football pitch. "My hero" is frequently used to describe those who have achieved in a particular field while possibly having a less than heroic home life. The object of worship takes on a rarified status where he or she can do no wrong. The worshipper's life is enhanced or reduced by the actions of the hero.... In fact, recent research has shown that hero worship can adversely affect the personality.

Celebrity Worship Syndrome is not the same as copying a winning mindset. Anthropologists agree that we need celebrities to show us the road to success. However, your choice of idol will colour your attitudes and ambitions. They may even keep you in a loop of

---

[31] Power The 48 Laws: Robert Greene

PART 2: KEEPING ON TRACK

vicarious living. Those who have reached the tops of their trees with relatively untarnished lives have had to adopt a number of styles to get there – and stay there. There have usually been some casualties along the way, as well as undoubted personal sacrifices. Think carefully, therefore, about what you will be emulating. Entrepreneurs are very rarely good at the day to day management of a company. Top salespeople do not usually make good sales managers. Actors frequently have troubled relationships.

Edward de Bono[32] also advocates looking to successful people. Learn from them, but improve upon their performance. Problems arise in hanging on to the same role models. Save the hero for yourself and let the model be the script with which to develop your desires – solely a prop for an under-utilised imagination.

Anthony Robbins too is a fan of role models, rightly stating that they are templates to coerce the imagination to take an individual nearer to his or her goals. The main task is to focus on the essence rather than each detail of a particular role model. This is especially true where role models may be thin on the ground. Despite the success of "pop and fame" reality shows, creating unlimited scenarios in your life should not just be dependent on being able to point to another and saying "if they can do it so can I". Of course, if fifteen-minute fame is what you seek, go for it.

Have faith in your dreams and create your own inner role model if necessary. Either way works.

---

[32] Tactics The Art & Science of Success: Edward de Bono

PART 3 - UNLIMITING YOUR MIND

> *"Minds are like parachutes. They only function when they are open."*
> James Dewar

KEEPING AN OPEN MIND

> *"The human body is the best picture of the human soul".* Ludwig Wittgenstein
>
> *
>
> *"I rely a great deal on animal instincts. .. I used the onset of acute pain as a signal that there was something wrong in my portfolio. The backache didn't tell me what was wrong... but it did prompt me to look for something amiss when I might not have done so otherwise."* George Soros

Someone once wrote that the development of the mind can only be achieved when the body has been disciplined. I believe the writer has it the wrong way round. The state of our minds is frequently reflected in our bodies over time and space, therefore minds need exercising every bit as much as our physical bodies. In fact minds probably need exercising even before our physical bodies. Minds need to be managed by challenging them in different ways.

Aches and pains in our bodies are the mind's way of engaging our attention. Challengingly, the longer we spend on the planet, the less able we are to remember what may be the underlying causes, hence physical degradation.

Learning new activities is one of many ways to excite fresh air and energy into our brainwaves. As mystics have always known, but scientists have recently come to accept, the brain can continue to grow and develop for all our lives. But what is the mind and body connection? Do all our mental frailties and fears really show up in our bodies? If so, how can we free ourselves from those limitations?

Hratch Ogali, an Armenian former jeweller, has achieved incredible success in helping his clients to conquer paralysis. Working as a mind instructor, he talks to his patients and gets them to focus on inactive muscles, activating the nerve endings and allowing energy to flow freely through them again. Similarly, when James Hall, previously a Jungian psychiatrist suffered what seemed to be a stroke, his friend, Patton Howell[1], refused to give up on him. Through painstaking work with a panel of letters, he confirmed that Hall had in fact retained his cognitive functioning and linguistic capabilities. "I demand to live, asshole" was his first fighting statement to the therapists – and twelve years on he lives, and co-authors, communicating via his computer.

The mind-body connection is well accepted in medical circles yet to suggest that a problem may have been caused in the mind is insulting to many a sufferer. This is especially true of illnesses such as ME. But negative stress does create feelings of anxiety which in turn trigger physical responses such as sweating, faster breathing and even increased heart rate. Optimistic thought and unfaltering belief have been shown to create remarkable changes in our health. Even terminal cases have exceeded gloomy forecasts of their life expectancies. The inspirational Chris Moon who had his right hand and right leg amputated is an amazingly positive thinker. He says "attitude is everything and we control our attitude." He runs for charity, achieved a master's degree and has set up his own business – all while "adjusting slightly" to the physical changes of

---

[1] Locked in to Life: Patton Howell & James Hall

limb loss. A positive attitude is a primary mental exercise.

Visualisation has been used to improve blood cells, reactions to previous allergies, reversals of breast cancer and much more. Regular self-hypnotic exercise has been shown over and over again to improve the quality of our health and the length of lives.

TASKS
!What does your body say about you?
!What would you like your body to say about you?

> *"Stress is the state manifested by a specific syndrome which consists of all the nonspecifically inducted changes within biologic system."* Hans Selye
>
> *
>
> *"Stress: a measure of the internal forces in a body between particles of the material of which it consists as they resist separation, compression, or sliding in response to externally applied forces."* OUP

Stress energy is thwarted energy. It has potential But its very power, undirected, can be deeply unpleasant. It can cause rippled bad experiences, as well as impact negatively on the body. Stress counselling, which focuses on the negative, often exacerbates the problem, while mental images of healthy, vital, bodies can create startlingly good progress.

Self-hypnosis or mindful self-conversation is not meant to take the place of medical treatment. After all, it is extremely difficult to focus on positive, mind-changing thought patterns if your head is throbbing wildly. If you've broken bones, they need to be fixed. And, being human, time has to be built into the equation. Your body has endured a build up of unacknowledged pressure. This has created the "disease" which has manifested as some form of bodily

PART 3: UNLIMITING YOUR MIND

failing. However, while cellular intelligence does work beyond time and space, not all sick bodies are reflective of the state of the mind. Great souls have often chosen physical challenges to prove the unlimited capacity of their minds. Their aura speaks for itself. For we lesser souls, healing has to take place on two levels. Fix the pain. Mend the breaks. Hold off the cancer. In parallel, address the underlying issues by using imagery and self-conversation to reprogram your intelligent cells.

Science is belatedly confirming age-old eastern philosophy that our minds are reflected in our bodies. It is no doubt why we can be so judgmental about external appearance, although a beauteous outlook does not necessarily prove a good heart. Equally, a physically-challenged body does not make its owner mentally-limited. Their chosen spiritual adventures may not require them to have the same human parts as the majority.

Physical food is as important as mind food. We are what we eat. It fuels the body. A biochemist writing[2] of helping his daughter to beat cancer, has a strategy checklist which seems to predominate with what to put, or not put inside our bodies. If the body is indeed the temple of the spirit, then it shows respect to this inner eminence to treat it well. Pythagoras abstained from meat in his pursuit of spiritual perfection. He believed, as do many eastern mystics, that the purity of veganism aided self-awareness. By not eating meat, one could become more aware of past lives and thus understand the patterns within the current life[3]. The Greeks did not care much for non-meat eaters. However, they did make an exception for those seeking the divine. They accepted that avoiding meat made spiritual connection easier. But for

---

[2] Everything You Need To Know To Help You Beat Cancer:Chris Woollam
[3] The Heretic's Feast A History of Vegetarianism: Colin Spencer

Pythagoras, there was also the recognition of the spirit in all living creatures. My own view is that as we merge with the particles of what we eat, so too do we take on their characteristics. Vegetus means lively, sprightly - an excellent barometer of good health, with the added bonus of slightly easier spiritual connection.

> *"Acne may result from inaccurate self-reporting and can be cured by good semantics." W C Ellerbroek MD*[4]

A wonderful result of paying attention to your body is that it does try and "talk" back to you. Snippets of advice suddenly pop up into your head. Or you feel compelled to eat a particular food, or try a specific exercise. Sometimes you will find yourself net-surfing and discover something which will trigger a spate of activities which positively affect your health. I regularly dip into Louise Hay's bestseller, You Can Heal Your Life, to check out the minor twinges and sometimes major challenges that my mind wants me to pay clear attention to. Even broken hearts can benefit from physical attention – no, not that sort!

Dr Roger Callaghan[5] believes that by tapping points on the body, in a similar way to acupuncture, we can unblock repetitive thought patterns and thus our energy field. That in turn will encourage behavioural change, and so the heart heals. Although almost Pavlovian, face-tapping allied to mental imaging is another way of discovering the mind-body connection.

---

[4] Your Body Believes Every Word You Say: Barbara Hoberman Levine
[5] www.thoughtfieldtherapy.co.uk

PART 3: UNLIMITING YOUR MIND

> *"And when we realise that our true Self is one of pure potentiality, we align with the power that manifests everything in the universe."*
> Deepak Chopra

We are made of trillions and trillions of intelligent, physical particles, each vibrating in a mini-microcosm, each transmitting and receiving information according to its individual programme. This could be a scary thought if they all decided to do their own thing. But another rule of physics is that like attracts like, so they vibrate together in general harmony to make up the physical you. Phew!

In laboratory tests, scientists have grown human ears onto the backs of mice, and presumably a lot more Twilight Zone stuff that we are probably not yet ready to accept. So, can we test out our own particles? Can they be re-arranged, or changed and refined?

I think it might have been Dr Joseph Murphy or Emmett Fox who wrote that we could indeed grow back an amputated hand or leg, but that our imaginations and our faith would probably fail us. To that, I would add the affect of the collective mind. However, in the mind of unlimited potentiality, anything is possible. When Laurence Gardner wrote of superconductive magnetism, where superconductors have no resistance to the flow of energy, he was writing rather more prosaically for physicists. Yet, metaphysically, we can tap our imaginations along the same lines. The fields of energy, he writes, become very powerful indeed, and that intense heat can rearrange the atomic structure of gold - and other particles. These in turn unleash superconductor properties. Why not our own particular particles unleashing their superconductive powers? Indian yogis have been able to change particle structures simply by the powers of their mind. Many have been able to sense other dimensions, manifesting their thought forms out of apparent thin air.[6]

The youthful Yogananda wished that such a power "were possessed by the starving millions of the world." He subsequently realised that Gandha Baba had, through years of spiritual discipline, attuned himself to the pranic force, and was thus "able to guide the lifetrons to rearrange their vibratory structure and to objectify the desired result."

In The Tao of Physics, Fritjof Capra explores the parallels between modern physics and Eastern mysticism. He believed that both quantum theory and relativity theory, the foundations of modern physics, share a world view with the Eastern religions of Hinduism, Buddhism and Taoism. He further stated that pronouncements about the properties and interactions of subatomic particles where all matter is made, could as easily have been made by Eastern mystics from these religions as by physicists. However, since these mystics "tell us again and again that all things and events we perceive are creations of the mind", you can breathe a sigh of relief. In the pursuit of unlimited thinking, no-one will require you to change your current personal credo. By understanding the subatomic world of your own mind, you have more pieces to play with, more elements to refine, and can therefore set your timescales accordingly.

> *"Time is the lens through which dreams are captured."*
> *Francis Ford Coppola*
> *
> *"Time is God's way of making sure everything doesn't all happen at the same time"* Anon

---

[6] The Autobiography of a Yogi: Paramahansa Yogananda

PART 3: UNLIMITING YOUR MIND

For most mortals, time is the space between conception of a thought, and its manifestation. "I have to go to the office" is a thought. Getting there is its manifestation. Anyone who has been stuck in a traffic jam, or missed a train, or had a sick child change priorities, will know that things happen to Time. If traffic jams are a regular occurrence, you will be programmed to anticipate this "problem", and build it into your time planning. But is our understanding of time that cut and dried? God took six days to create the world – but they were probably "infinite" days. God had and has no need for beginnings and ends, being both Alpha and Omega. The limited human mind, unfortunately, does need timescales – and generally the sooner the better. Yet imagine taking a jigsaw out of its box, and tipping it out, in the expectation that it will fall perfectly into place? Even a child's version, with very few, large, pieces, involves moving one at a time. It involves matching them into their appropriate place in the picture's overall scheme of things. Not unlike "real" life.

> ".. time functions differently for each individual, and our perception of time is altered, or coloured, by the train of events that occupy our lives." Murry Hope[7]
>
> *
>
> "The stream of knowledge is heading toward a non-mechanical reality; the universe begins to look more like a great thought than like a great machine" Sir James Jeans[8]

Reality is what we experience from moment to moment based on our predominant thoughts and emotions. Linear time could therefore be predicated by

---

[7] Time The Ultimate Energy: Murry Hope
[8] The Mysterious Universe: Sir James Jeans

emotion. Non-linear time is unlimited. Conquering time is a secret to success.

It could be assumed that illusion is the opposite of reality. But *maya* is the ability to create illusion. In that illusion, we can experience reality, and what we can experience mentally, we can create and manifest. Thus illusion becomes reality. Not its opposite but a parallel force. We need to bring emotions into force though in order to turn one type of illusion into another type of reality.

I read once of a golfer who quit playing for several years. From usually playing in the nineties, he returned to the course and shot a "sparkling 74". During the seven years of abstinence, he had not had one golf lesson. Moreover, his physical condition had seriously deteriorated from spending time in a cage measuring approximately four and a half feet by five.

He had been a Vietnamese prisoner of war but his mind was unlimited by prison bars. Every day, despite physical deprivation, he saw himself going around the course, playing eighteen holes of perfect golf. When he eventually stood on a "real" golf course, with a physical club in his hand, his mind simply mirrored his illusionary experiences. The powerful emotions created by war and suffering fuelled those visions into perfect manifestation.

There is absolutely no doubt that setting yourself some goals can direct your life and provide enhanced direction. However it has never ceased to amaze me how many people achieve staggering levels of success with scant ambition and a minimal sense of direction. Questioned further, some said it felt right or they followed their heart. Yet others, like the Cuban musician Ibrahim Ferrer, after struggling for over fifty years with disappointments and broken promises, eventually closed off his heart. He vowed never to sing again. Yet one day, presumably out of the blue, he was

PART 3: UNLIMITING YOUR MIND

offered the chance to use his gift of song once more. He refused, but was persuaded with, for him, the big promise of "50 bucks" and his star finally ascended.

There are thousands of self-help books and courses which dogmatically dictate the way to train your mind and achieve your bliss life. Some are even slightly threatening, foreboding ill if you do not follow their instructions to the letter. Yet this is but one of many personal experiences that confirm to me that metaphysical principles do not necessarily work in ways that we can understand. You have to be totally open-minded to profit from unlimited thinking. That particular man continued to have his unsung talent whatever his circumstances. One day, someone needed that talent, and he was ready. More or less. To truly unlimit one's self, you have to push your mind into uncharted waters. You will also have to explore areas you may have been wary or critical of.

There are a number of intriguing and sometimes contentious topics which can enable us to assess our self-limitations and inner motivations. These include numerology, astrology, feng shui, colour therapy and much more - some of which I have already covered in previous sections. It is not a question of whether one believes in them or not. They provide a point of reference for the mind, that is all.

To put all your imagination's eggs in one basket, even if it is a new and interesting one, also defeats the point of limitless thinking. Discovering yourself means checking out everything outside of your normal frame of reference. However, if you genuinely think these "ologies" are rubbish, or if your faith precludes you from belief, then just treat them as passing exercises. Enjoy what they might teach you, while striving to keep your mind open to the elements that do resonate with your own truth. Try to be surprised. You will be.

PROFIT FROM UNLIMITED THINKING

TOOLS TO EXPAND CONSCIOUSNESS

> *"We live in the midst of invisible forces whose effects alone we perceive.... In this mind-side of nature, invisible to our senses, intangible to our instruments of precision, many things can happen that are not without their echo on the physical plane."* Dion Fortune

What is intuition? What does it mean to have psychic ability? Do we all have psychic powers? If so, how then can we test our own psychic powers - and what tools can we use? How does our intuition talk back to us? Obviously I would not have written all those questions if I did not believe there were acceptable methods for "tuning in".

Although I have been greatly blessed with a foundation faith as a Roman Catholic, and still have a deep fondness for it, I am nonetheless aware that the shadow of occultism does still cloud people's thoughts on anything remotely to do with what might be perceived as darker arts.

Occult derives from the Latin *occulere* - to hide. It has come to signify the esoteric and mysterious, as well as the magical and supernatural. If something is unexplainable, puzzling, transcendental and recondite, it is occultist. These definitions are a lot more acceptable to most, and provide a positive lumen to the next section.

TASKS
!**Set your intuition a task**
!**Log any reactions or actions you are prompted to take**
!**Follow through with any prompts you get**

PART 3: UNLIMITING YOUR MIND

> *"Each soul is a portion of the Divine, and that is the psychic or soul force which is a manifestation that cries as it were for expression."* Edgar Cayce

According to Edgar Cayce[9], "psychic ability is inherent in each of us". Intuition and imagination are subsets of our psychic abilities, and also of our limitless creativity. It is the limitless creativity of the soul, or psyche. Like most mystics, Cayce felt that by developing spiritually, psychic abilities would naturally evolve: "Pursue rather spiritual development; this is of the psychic nature, yes, but find the spirit first - not spiritualism, but spiritually in thy own life."

Perhaps a more acceptable term to most people is "sixth sense". It conveys extrasensory perception, without any - to them - perceived negative connotations. Our sixth sense is our intuition. Maybe both terms smack too much of old witches, because Dr Ronald Rensink of the University of British Columbia has a new name for it - 'mindsight'. Whichever word is used, for most people, intuition tends to protect and guide. Yet it can do far more.

Intuition can help us to discover more about ourselves and dig out buried talents. Intuition can help us to realise our potential - and even follow our bliss. "By awakening your sixth sense, you can learn to fulfil all the elements of your life.[10]"

> *"You can no more force intuition than you can force someone to fall in love with you. You can prepare yourself for it, invite it, and create attractive conditions to coax it, but you can't say 'Now I shall have an intuition'"* – Philip Goldberg[11]

Intuition, according to Albert Einstein, is the "really valuable thing". Intuition is the "divine voice" (Socrates), and the source of seemingly hidden

---

[9] Be Your Own Psychic: Doris T Patterson & Violet M Shelley
[10] Sixth Sense: Susie Johns
[11] The Intuitive Edge: Philip Goldberg

knowledge. Intuition is non-rational, spontaneous, mysterious. Intuition provides possibilities while allowing us the free will to accept or ignore it. Intuition fits into our current frame of reference and is therefore acceptable to our general mindset.

Goldberg says there are various elements (many faces) to intuition: discovery (Eureka), creativity (workable), evaluation, operation (guidance), prediction and illumination. But we must not, he says, doubt it in any way, this divine voice.

We must expect it to share, anticipate its inspiration and guidance, even though we don't know when or how often it may appear, or even how it makes itself felt. We must be confident in it, and make it feel welcome. So that's the occult bit then?! Seriously, despite those schizoid shadows of another voice, it is actually your own, rather powerful self you will be hearing or sensing. Dualism has long been philosophically argued over, but it is easier to accept if we treat it as a higher dimension of our own consciousness.

> *"Psychic exploration is best undertaken with a spirit of adventure."* Sonia Choquette[12]

The relationship with intuition is not one-way. While there is an element of the chicken and egg about it, goal-setting can direct our intuition. Learning prompts intuition - even learning a new word each day. In return, it can trigger off a wave of ideas... courtesy of intuition or the psyche.

Creativity feeds intuition. An earlier section is devoted to the benefits of writing: write a screenplay of your life – as you would like it to be; keep a diary of your thoughts; write a personal profile. In time, you will find yourself writing about things or getting ideas

---

[12] The Psychic Pathway: Sonia Choquette

PART 3: UNLIMITING YOUR MIND

that come from a deeper part of yourself, which could be the catalyst to a much more fulfilling life. Or simply a solution to a problem.

> *"We must be indulgent to the mind, and from time to time we must grant it the idleness that serves as its food and strength." Seneca*

Intuition likes spontaneous idleness. After all, how can you sense - or hear - if you are constantly in mental fifth gear? We modern creatures have so much stimulation in our lives that we barely give our intuitions airtime. Small wonder that those with serious spiritual intent, tend to live in splendid isolation, far from the madding crowd. To these holy men and women, we are the insane ones!

> *"Intuition attracts those who wish to be spiritual without any bother..."*
> EM Forster

Laura Day's tasks for exercising our intuition are very similar to goal-setting and journalling.[13] The key to success comes from accurate questioning, and being able to understand intuitive signals and messages. She defines intuition as a "nonlinear, non-empirical process of gaining and interpreting information in response to questions." So start listing those questions you want answered now. As you do, ideas will start to float into your mind - not necessarily immediately. Do not force them, and do not be over eager. Both will block the flow. However, it is imperative to catch and capture all ideas and thoughts on paper, even if they seem fairly meaningless to your current way of living.

Generally, handwriting can slow the process. However, the very act of "setting down" will make you magnetic to yet more, as it enhances the flow of ideas. As someone wise once said, "those ideas that come

---

[13] Practical Intuition: Laura Day

PROFIT FROM UNLIMITED THINKING

uninvited are commonly the most valuable and should be secured because they seldom return."

> *"The basic thing, whether in art or life, is 'presence of mind'. 'Presence of mind' is unpredictable. Our so-called will does not control it. We are controlled by 'presence of mind' which reveals reality as an absolute mystery." Rene Magritte*
>
> *
>
> *"If the soul has a natural knowledge of all these things it does not seem possible that it should so far forget this natural knowledge as to be ignorant that it has it at all." Thomas Aquinas*[14]

An Advent Calendar contains a series of pictures, hidden behind doors, all contributing colour and detail to the complexity of the whole. Providing, of course, that you open the doors. Our minds also have hidden doors which must be opened in order to enjoy added colour and detail in our lives. In fact, behind those doors is a veritable cornucopia of ideas and knowledge just waiting to find expression. Because our minds are not restrained by our physical bodies, almost anyone can have access to this unlimited storehouse. The only block or hurdle is limited or unexpanded thinking.

If what we desire to be, to have or to know is already pulsating in a higher frequency dimension, then to attain its like, we have to be sensitive to its other-dimensional vibrations. Like attracts like. We can do this through the expansion of our consciousness, and thus our ability to sense new and untapped frequencies.

> *"It would appear that a great many people don't believe in fortune-telling but are very anxious to have their fortunes told!" Francis X King*

There is nothing new about the human urge to consult oracles. From Delphi to present day horoscopes, despite our gurus telling us we can create

---

[14] Aquinas on Mind: Anthony Kenny

PART 3: UNLIMITING YOUR MIND

our own realities through positive thinking, we do seek confirmation and certainty. There is some self-validation in perceived certainty, even before the end result is realised. But oracles such as the Tarot, Runes, numerology and astrology are merely tools to be used to assist the process of mind expansion. They should only be used as a means of communication with your intuition and inner wisdom.

Because we live in linear time, we are often too preoccupied to notice when good or bad events seemingly materialise in our lives. We may think everything is hunky-dory in our jobs, only to be slapped with what appears to be a sudden redundancy notice. Our marriages may appear to be sound, yet one day you wake to find your spouse has called time on your union.

When I received similar warning signals from my choice of oracle, I did not want to believe them because things were going so well. Positive thinking bought me a bit more time, but my intuition was trying to warn me that unbeknown to me – and despite my hard labours – playing in this pitch was almost over. If I had been wiser, I would have asked better, less whiney, self-pitying questions. I would have asked for guidance and inspiration. Instead, I got cross and threw the cards away, despite their accurate warning.

The message therefore is to be ready to hear some truths and to ask for help. Redundancies, divorce, financial loss, ill health, death... however painful the issue, it is possible to bounce back with minimal bruising, if you ask the right questions. As an added bonus, you will also develop great inner strength and resilience.

I would advise caution, however, about the addictive nature of these oracles. When you develop a rhythm and trust in the answers, it can be tempting to use them too frequently. The same applies if you choose to use a human intermediary. Except the human variant also has the additional issue of expense.

Are the answers always accurate? In my experience, yes they are, as long as you do not overdo the questions. There is also another point to consider. Your intuition may be extremely keen to share something with you, preferring to give that information rather than an answer to your question. Experience and a growing self-understanding will usually sort out the relevant data.

One other piece of advice: if your emotions are on overload - you may be having some lusty thoughts about someone in the office, for example - your results will reflect those emotions, and will not necessarily be an accurate reflection of what will actually manifest. Logically, thoughts plus emotions could make it come to pass. But would you really want it to? Check out all the angles first. Your intuition may simply be warning you that you are expending a lot of energy in a lost cause.

> *"The only way to predict the future is to have the power to shape the future."* Eric Hoffer
>
> *
>
> *"The future enters into us in order to transform itself in us long before it happens."* Rainer Maria Rilke
>
> *
>
> *"As Above So Below"* Hermes Trismegistus

From time immemorial, people seem to have been interested in checking the entrails so to speak. We may not want to know our exact futures, especially if there is discord or hardship, but we would like pointers along the way. This is especially true if we have clear goals. If the answers strike a chord, or find agreement, we have no problem in believing. So whatever the oracle you choose, it is simply confirming something you may be thinking, desiring or feeling. It can help to allay doubts. It can force you to acknowledge actions to

PART 3: UNLIMITING YOUR MIND

take, or it can signal a warning - as indeed mine tried to do.

> *"Astrology, if explored from a psychological or scientific level, has nothing to do with belief. It's practical. It has to do with gaining knowledge and doing experiments." Jan Spiller*[15]
>
> *
>
> *"Astrology illuminates the secret corners of the self, provides a key to understanding others, contributes a useful method of scrutinising relationships, and even offers a glimpse into the future." Rae Orion*
>
> *
>
> *"Millionaires don't believe in astrology. Billionaires do." J P Morgan*

Astrology probably started about 5000BC, or even before, as the phases of the moon and planetary positions became vital in sowing, reaping and harvesting. Then, as associations formed, possibly coincidentally, astrology became a tool for guidance and potential. The movements of the planets were indicators of energy patterns, reflecting on Earth. They were not thought to make people behave in a particular way nor to cause events beyond our control.

To many, astrology is viewed as the first science, with such luminaries as Isaac Newton, Pythagoras and Nostradamus among its followers. The Mesopotamians believed, as do many current faiths, that everything in the universe was connected. The Kabbalah, an ancient Jewish mystical system, contains astrological references, with the Zohar describing an astrological chart as an expression of Divine Will[16]. Both the Old and New Testaments make reference to astrology and astrologers.

Since the earliest times, astrology specifically explored the relationship between Earth and the heavens. By studying the planets and the stars, and plotting their movements, the magi could predict the

---

[15] Astrology for the Soul: Jan Spiller
[16] The Complete Idiot's Guide to Astrology: Gerwick-Brodeur/Lenard

future, and observe the possibilities of human behaviour. In fact, astrology was deemed worthy of university study till well into the 1600s. Now, however, astrology enjoys mixed blessings. On the one hand there is the nonsense that is in the papers, avidly read by millions. On the other, are serious practitioners who genuinely provide excellent character assessments and personal guidance, as well as serious studies, which inform as well as provoke[17].

> *"The fact is, astrology's main purpose is to help man to chart his way out of dependence on any external influences - to become a free soul, guided only by the light of truth in his own heart.*[18]*" J Donald Walters*

There are the charlatans who sloppily use software to compartmentalise thousands of individuals into a few key patterns; and there are equally those who can pinpoint someone's star sign in the first few minutes of meeting them, providing a character analysis on the hoof. In fact, I was once blessed with that skill, although it has long since disappeared since it was only ever used as a party-trick and served no great purpose.

The correlation of star signs and star sign characteristics has been confirmed many times by the likes of Gauquelin, Eysenck, Ertel, Roberts, Seymour et al. But statistical accuracy is less fascinating than the likes of Linda Goodman[19], and quite how she got her reasonably accurate data for all those in-depth personality profiles. I have to say "reasonably" as she makes no concession to Asian, African and Oriental Aquarians for example. In her analyses, hair is likely to be blonde, sandy or light brown...... Obviously, these things can only be vaguely accurate, since we are more

---

[17] The Message of Astrology: Peter Roberts
[18] Your Sun Sign as a Spiritual Guide: J Donald Walters
[19] Linda Goodman's Sun Signs; Star Signs; Love Signs

PART 3: UNLIMITING YOUR MIND

than just our sun sign. The sun placement, to me, is the backbone for the other planets and aspects to flesh out. The Rising Sign, the Midheaven, the North Node, multiple conjunctions and aspects are some of the elements that differentiate you from any other Scorpio or Leo or Capricorn.

Thankfully for me, the Internet has solved the problem of learning how to cast a horoscope, with all its symbols and mathematical calculations. If you surf around, you will be able to get a reasonable character profile, plus chart positions, free of charge.

There are twelve houses governing all areas of a person's life: your purpose, finances, marital prospects and much more. What planetary activity may or may not be in each of these houses can bring hours of glorious navel-gazing. Luckily, there are also plenty of sites offering detailed information relating to those positions, also free of charge. If that does not appeal, or if your computer skills are nil, then check out the papers to find an astrologer to suit. However, this is a course in unlimited thinking, so do try and do some of the work yourself.

> *"Remember, the infinite intelligence and boundless wisdom resident in your subconscious mind is all-wise, knows all, and sees all, and you are simply using an ancient but simple mathematical process of receiving a true answer." Joseph Murphy*

The I Ching, also known as the Book of Changes, is one of the world's most ancient texts. It is a great Chinese classic, and is also a foundation of Taoist and Confucian philosophies.

The I Ching was brought to Europe over three hundred years ago, by the Jesuits. Leibnitz, the philosopher and mathematician, was an early follower. Because it is brief and clear - there are just 64 hexagrams - it can provide incredible insight and wisdom, and is regularly used by many, including

Western businessmen, for guidance and direction. Purists will probably stick with the acclaimed Wilhelm/Baynes[20] translation. However, because of the references to symbols and metaphors relating to Chinese life of 3,000 years ago, more modern versions are now available. Not only are there guides specifically for lovers, or for business, I have also got a battered copy of Joseph Murphy's Christian version[21] where the trigrams have been converted using New Testament truths, married to a modern metaphysical interpretation. Murphy does however suggest that the Wilhelm/Baynes translation should be used in parallel with his version, as it is "the most excellent of all books on the I Ching", adding that he uses it himself.

Within our subconscious minds are the answers to everything we need to know. The I Ching, like other methods mentioned in this section, can not only tell you about the state of your thoughts and emotions, it can also offer some very wise guidance and answers. If you don't fancy throwing coins or sticks, just think of a question or something that is a challenge in your life, and then open up the page at will. It will provide you with an appropriate answer to ponder. As Carl Jung wrote in his foreward to the Wilhelm/Baynes translation: "This great and singular book does not offer itself with proofs and results; it does not vaunt itself, nor is it easy to approach. Like a part of nature, it waits until it is discovered. It offers neither facts nor power, but for lovers of self-knowledge, of wisdom - if there be such - it seems to be the right book."

If the I Ching is good enough for some well-known businessmen to acknowledge publicly - probably because the language seems very masculine

---

[20] I Ching: The Richard Wilhem Translation [tr Eng: Cary F Baynes]
[21] Secrets of the I Ching: Joseph Murphy

PART 3: UNLIMITING YOUR MIND

and indeed businesslike - then it may be worth exploring.

> *"Deep in the collective unconscious of humanity – and perhaps at its very heart – lies the desire to worship a revealing God who will disclose to believers everything they need to know for living a full and productive life*
> *Ralph Blum*[22]
>
> *
>
> *"The Viking Runes are a mirror for the magic of our Knowing Selves. In time, as you become skilled in their use, you can lay the Runes aside and permit the knowing to arise unfiltered, just as some dowsers use only their bare hands to find water." The Book of Runes*

Runes are multilevel symbols of creation, life, death and rebirth. Initially similar to mantras as sounds to communicate with the divine, runes then became associated with specific messages and concepts. They now serve as a symbolic language between the conscious and unconscious minds to be interpreted to suit the physical, mental or spiritual need. Although there are archetypal associations to all of these systems, in time, your subconscious will endow each symbol with personal meaning and you will have a highly-individual message just for you.[23]

A burgeoning interest in spiritual esoterica, allied with the modern desire for quick results, means that there are plenty of easy-to-understand packages available today. You can opt for the traditional rune stones or buy card sets, all neatly presented with a convenient self-paced guide.

Runes are used for meditation, divination and healing, as well as magic - if that appeals to you. For the purposes of unlimited thinking though, runes can help to uncover solutions to problems. They can throw light on influences around us and even predict future events. According to Sirona Knight "When you use

---

[22] The Rune Cards Sacred Play for Self-Discovery: Ralph Blum
[23] The Little Giant Encyclopaedia of Rune: Sirona Knight

runes, you increase your self-awareness, relieve stress, gain a sense of personal empowerment, heal and clear out blockages in your life." Wow... definitely worth exploring.

> *"..the Tarot is an excellent method for turning experience into wisdom. At its essence, the Tarot deals with archetypal symbols of the human situation, symbols we can relate to our own lives that help us better understand ourselves."* Anthony Louis

No-one is exactly certain when the Tarot was first popularised, although the Castillian King Alphonse X1 did issue a proclamation in 1332 forbidding their use. The Roman Catholic Church was also not overly fond of it, calling it the "Devil's Bible[24]".

It is true that the Tarot can definitely put the frighteners on – especially if you pick the Death or Tower cards. No matter how many books you might read saying those cards only mean change or end of one phase, and upheavals or chaos, the images are so stark and uncompromising that your first reaction tends to stay.

There are seventy-eight cards in all. The twenty-two cards of the major arcana depict universal archetypes. They are a sequential representation of the individual's search for enlightenment, starting with The Fool and ending with The World. The minor arcana of fifty-six cards includes all four suits with the court cards.

If you do choose to explore your inner potential using the Tarot, I would recommend you do not use an intermediary. Even an instructive book is shaded with the views and energies of the writer, and the main objective is to hear what your own still, small voice is trying to tell you. Having said that, it is helpful to start with an instructive book that resonates with

---

[24] Tarot Plain and Simple: Anthony Louis

PART 3: UNLIMITING YOUR MIND

your way of thinking, if only to fully understand the symbolism and meaning of the images. After all, if you pick, say the four of cups, you may not know what your subconscious is trying to tell you.

The Tarot can inspire very strong feelings - not always in its favour. Many poets, philosophers, scientists and psychotherapists have been drawn to its compelling imagery and hidden messages. Jung believed that the Tarot images "distantly descended from the archetypes of transformation", whereas T S Eliot seemed to have been simultaneously fascinated and repelled.

I indicated earlier that it is easy to develop a compulsion for these forms of divination. Reading the cards for yourself can be very therapeutic, as I have discovered many a time, and it is not difficult to keep returning to such havens. Despite that, I did have a major clear out of the many Tarot books and cards I had bought over the years. I felt I was putting my faith in them, and not in my inner wisdom, even though it was a mechanism for that inner wisdom to communicate with me. I put them all in one of those charity bags, for the Salvation Army or something similar.

Later, when I realised where they went, I wryly imagined someone praying fervently for my soul to be saved. Well, it certainly made me smile. Later, I bought fresh sets with less provocative images: an Angel Tarot and a beautiful one with golden Tsarist biblical icons.

Please do not be put off. It is not some extrasensory spirit invading your thoughts, but a hidden dimension of your own mind being tapped. If you dip into them from time to time, they can provide a very informative, symbolic conversation with your subconscious. They can increase your intuitive powers and help you to develop a greater spiritual awareness[25].

> *"My own mind is the direct revelation which I have from God and far least liable to mistake in telling his will of any revelation."* **Ralph Waldo Emerson**
>
> *
>
> L *divinus - divus* **godlike; divination - *supposed insight into the unknown gained by supernatural means;* supernatural - *force above the laws of nature***

Whether there is any validity in astrology, the I Ching, the Runes, Tarot or indeed any other method of divination, is neither here nor there – they are simply tools for self-discovery. However, the point of this exercise is not to build up the reputation of a particular esoteric art. It is to discover something further about yourself, and, if there are traits which are pleasing, to build them up further. If not, dismiss them.

Part of the problem as I said earlier is the association with the occult. The very word does have a slightly chilling resonance but, again, it simply means hidden, esoteric, mystifying and unexplainable. Another challenge is getting to grips with the idea that far distant planets and star formations can have characteristics that dictate who and what we are or can be. This is especially true for Aquarians, like me, whose ruling planet changed once another one was discovered...! Presumably then, so too did elements of our personality. But, logic and pedantry aside, it can be a valid form of inner awareness. While astrology provides character definitions and potentiality, the I Ching and Runes are more geared to thought patterns, and can even be predictive.

It is believed that the universe is constantly trying to share messages[26] with us. We are told that we

---

[25] How To Read The Tarot: Sylvia Abraham
[26] Signposts: Denise Linn

PART 3: UNLIMITING YOUR MIND

are surrounded by signs that can direct us and help us to understand better our motivations. Any one of these divinatory methods can help the process along. And, best of all, you can maintain control.

> *"Numerology is a method of linking the microcosm with the macrocosm. ... Numerology is not a complete science. It is just one branch of the predictive sciences" Harish Johari[27]*

Numbers have always fascinated me, contrarily, since I did not even get CSE maths! In my long sales career, I found numbers also intrigued my customers - numerology specifically. Where astrology was found to be a tad yin, and a women's pursuit, it seemed entirely acceptable to men, to express interest in personality assessments derived from numbers. Perhaps that is due in no small part to Pythagoras.

Pythagoras, the Greek philosopher and mathematician of theorem fame, is credited with being the founder of numerology. The Pythagoreans believed that everything could be expressed in numerical terms, and that everything reduced to numbers. The principle numbers were given specific characteristics, with one through to nine, encompassing the flow of life - similar, in principle, to the Tarot's major arcana. (The Hebraic system operates differently, believing the number nine to be divine.)

Numerology has been in use in several ancient cultures, many pre-dating Pythagoras, including China and Egypt, so it is definitely not a 'New Age' fad. It would be insulting to its complexity, and to numerologists, to try and summarise every number[28] with a few words, but, for brevity, and with thanks[29] to Julia Line's excellent workbook, I am.

---

[27] Numerology A Key To Human Behaviour: Harish Johari
[28] www.sun-angel.com/numerology
[29] The Numerology Workbook: Julia Line

PROFIT FROM UNLIMITED THINKING

1:innovate, achieve, original, intolerant
2:emotion, receptive, understanding, self-conscious
3:versatile, energetic, artistic, outspoken
4:practical, efficient, calm, dull
5:adventurous, resilient, clever, restless
6:loyal, reliable, creative, complacent
7:intellectual, philosophical, impractical
8:materialistic, tenacious, tough, ruthless
9:humanitarian, successful, spiritual, conceited

There are also other important numbers to consider. But that can be your research homework. Basic numerology makes use of the numbers in our dates of birth, and our names, to analyse character and potential.[30] Something as simple as the day we were born can guide us to a more fulfilling career path[31]. For example, if your birth date reduces to three, it suggests a career as a writer, artist or musician. If it reduces to two, then how about politician or teacher? It can also explain any mysterious longings: the executive (4) who longs to be a homemaker (6), or the financier (8) with selfless humanitarian desires (11).

It is a practical and, some say, a scientific tool in understanding hidden aspects of our nature and desires. Through even a cursory play with it, numerology can help you to uncover talents and life goals, and possibly any opportunities and challenges.

Numerology is an excellent self-help tool for the logical as well as the more esoterically-inclined. By at least being made aware of the talents we possess, we can then choose to take different paths in life[32]. Each day is also supposed to have a numerical vibration. To be in harmony with the day's vibration is to gain winning tendencies. To find out a day's frequency, add

---

[30] www.webnumerology.com
[31] www.numberquest.com
[32] Numerology: Sonia Ducie

PART 3: UNLIMITING YOUR MIND

the day to the month and then to the year and reduce it to a single number[33]. The exceptions are eleven and twenty-two.

1 positive opportunities action start something be assertive
2 receptive cooperate observe study thoughts not mind
3 express go for it smile make others smile be out and about
4 do routine work
5 be active investigate analyse be enthusiastic chances
6 consolidate business interests social love reconciliation
7 meditative seek peace and quiet
8 executive day organise drive big business tangible results
9 be philanthropic give generously
11 listen to inspiration share enthuse inspire
22 reach for the sky dreams can materialise

What if you were adopted and do not know your date of birth? What if your name has changed?

Most of us have a healthy curiosity about our past. We all want explanations for those whispered desires and longings. With few exceptions, we all want to add substance to our self-awareness and self-value. These feelings are probably reinforced in those without birth parents who can, or will, shed further light.

While it may not be ideal, one way of addressing these issues is to treat your "new" date of birth as the start of the new you. Additionally, you may find the other exercises in Profit From Unlimited Thinking might provide you with answers that will fill in the gaps. For you other adventurers in time and space, the future is indeed unlimited. Today could be the first day of the rest of your life!

---

[33] Numerology Made Plain: Ariel Yvon Taylor

> *Latin: oraculum; from orare, to speak, to pray: the answer of a god to an inquiry respecting the future. Brewers*

Angel cards, playing cards, dice... Oracles, whatever form they might take, are never as good as developing your own self-discovery cards. It is not as difficult as it may seem, and it can be enormous fun. Unlike the shop-bought versions, you can create and remove cards at will, to retain freshness, or because you have been inspired to do so.

By creating your own card divination system, you will be immediately identifying the path you would like to take. You will also have a totally free hand to write whatever words of encouragement, warning or advice that you wish. You can write about progress or regress, or standstill - these things do happen to all of us, however positive an outlook we may have. In fact, sometimes, we need to take steps back to consolidate or clarify our position. No movement, or standstill, is also not as undynamic as it may appear.

You can segment your cards into work and play. You can create suitable affirmations and suggestions. The choice really is unlimited. Just remember, the purpose is to discover what your subconscious is trying to tell you. In any case, whatever you do write down will probably be a prompt of some sort pre-generated by your subconscious.

Ideally, the cards should be small enough to shuffle. There is also no limit to how many you should use. Aim for about twenty to start with, and add more as situations arise or change. This will give your intuition more leeway as symbols or words can have multiple meanings. Each card should have either a word, phrase or statement written on it. Try to write down something relating to every aspect of your current situation, your hopes and desires, your fears and your doubts. Write motivational sentences. Create

PART 3: UNLIMITING YOUR MIND

cards for your fantasies and secret wishes. Create instructional cards. If you prefer, use symbols and pictures.

The most important thing is to regularly use these oracle cards so that the intuitive area of your brain improves and strengthens, allowing you discover your own inner language. As these cards will be your handiwork, there will be less of an addictive kickback attached to working with them.

The 'cards' do not have to actually be cards. The last set I created for myself were stars made from luminescent coloured cardstock, which I had bought from a high street stationers. They were certainly bright enough, with the positive associations of stars, and could be purchased in different sizes. So now the stars that reigned at your nativity[34], can be in your control... unlimited indeed!

> *"May my book teach you to be more interested in yourself than in it - then, in everyone else more than yourself." Andre Gide*

Bibliomancy is the ability to foretell the future by analysing a randomly chosen passage from a book. Bibliotherapy is discovering a healing message, also from something read in a book. In theory, any book could be used with adequate results. Practically, Shakespeare, the Bible, poetry or even a dictionary might provide greater scope. Or you might have a favourite novel, with a hidden subtext - rather like the Bible Code.

Many years ago, I picked up Marcus Aurelius' Meditations[35], looking for guidance during a particularly rough period. The passage my finger pointed out was verse twenty-nine in Book Five. Not exactly the most uplifting words, when my then world

---

[34] Dr Faustus
[35] Penguin Classics: Marcus Aurelius Meditations

was collapsing around me, although I had asked a pertinent question. Perhaps my finger slipped, and I should have read of "unsavoury armpits and bad breath" instead. After all, it is very difficult to feel doomy and gloomy when you are laughing. Since I am still around to tell the tale, however, no doubt that was just a warning.

As a precaution, if you do get any fatalistic or distressing messages when your emotions are being rocked, *please try to get some other form of help at once*. The message may just be reflective of the state of your mind. The call to action is to *talk to someone who can help* - and *not* to follow through with whatever the message might be saying.

Final words to Marcus A: "Many of the anxieties that harass you are superfluous: being but creatures of your own fancy, you can rid yourself of them and expand into an ampler region, letting your thought sweep over the entire universe..."[36]

> *"So I awoke and behold it was a dream."* John Bunyan
>
> *
>
> *"All men dream: but not equally. Those who dream by night in the dusty recesses of their minds wake in the day to find that it was a vanity: but the dreamers of the day are dangerous men, for they may act their dream with open eyes, to make it possible."* T E Lawrence

The earlier quotation from Marcus Aurelius is probably quite apt for this section on dreams as well.

Dreams can prove an interesting way of looking into your subconscious[37]. They converse with you, the dreamer, in subjective symbolic language. While there are archetypes common to all, your subconscious has its very own dictionary of symbols and language, which it can be fun trying to decode.

---

[36] Book Nine: Verse 32 Meditations Marcus Aurelius
[37] The Dream Workbook: Jill Morris

PART 3: UNLIMITING YOUR MIND

Some of the best scientific and artistic ideas have come from dreams, as have many money-making schemes. For the spiritual, it is a way of communicating with your Higher Self, without the anxiety of hearing voices. Yet your subconscious does have a voice, and it does want to communicate with you. The only problem comes from trying to decipher the message. Added to the complexity of dreams in general, it is small wonder we can barely remember them let alone understand them. "Dreams often condense several different ideas and impressions into a single compact image..[38]".

As your subconscious likes to reinforce its important messages to you, it is a good idea to log whatever comes through, whenever you manage to remember it. Many dreams can be a variation on a similar theme, and you will begin to recognise patterns and characters, which then become part of your unique dreamer's dictionary. Through your dreamer's dictionary, it is then possible to decipher your own secret code.

An interesting piece of dream research found that people with large egos were much less aggressive in their dreams, while artistic types are the least likely to have sex in theirs! Dreams can flag up any concerns or anxieties which have been ignored in your waking life. They may go as far back as childhood, forcing your conscious mind to work through them. They also can represent hope and ambition, drawing your attention to unfulfilled potential, so it is definitely worth making the effort to log and understand them.

The first step is to buy a notebook and label it My Dream Diary. Then, every morning, immediately on waking, turn to a fresh page, date it, and log your mood and any immediate feelings and characters. If

---

[38] The Dream Game: Ann Faraday

you can recall your dreams or even snippets of them, log those too. Over time, you will find they are passing on different forms of messages, or the same one with different symbols and characters.

It may not always be possible to remember anything for weeks and months at a time. But we do all dream. Most of us cannot remember our dreams, or they evaporate as soon as our eyes start to fully open. We may even suppress them for fear of what they remind us of. Yet it is possible to recall between three and nine dreams and possibly even more each night.

I once, foolishly, made a dream pillow from selected herbs. Having conscientiously placed it under my head, I fell asleep, only to wake up virtually on the hour every hour with one mini dream adventure after the other. After three dreadful nights of multiple dream recall, when I "woke up" that following day, I promptly binned the pillow.

Crystals can be used to achieve more measured recall. A piece of jade or smokey quartz or a green sapphire placed under your pillow will enable you to recall some of your dreams more gently.

Most dream recall is an amalgam of several dreams, but since it is the association that is important, every element can convey something useful. Colours, peripheral images, people, anything and everything has a meaning. Be assured that if your subconscious wants to convey something truly important or life-changing, you will get a very clear dream, not once, but several times.

Prophetic dreams usually occur at three o'clock in the morning, and are repeated each day for three days.

I was blessed just the once with such a series of warning dreams, but unfortunately misinterpreted the message, to then embark on a troubling love affair. It was hugely traumatic and life-changing. But, on the

PART 3: UNLIMITING YOUR MIND

plus side, in seeking answers, it also ultimately aided spiritual growth and knowledge.

TASKS

!Buy or make a dream diary
!Make or buy cards that can be easily shuffled
!Write down anything that concerns you
!Write down what you think might happen
!Write down what you would like to happen
!Write down motivational words and phrases
!Transfer each one to a separate card
!Open a book at random; log the first sentence that catches your eye
!Choose one of the above 'oracular' methods and investigate it

MIND & SPIRIT BASICS

> *"In the life of the spirit there are no facts, but only life, as it appears to us in one form or another."* Pirandello
>
> *
>
> *"The spirit is the true self, not that physical figure which can be pointed out by your finger."* Cicero

According to Francis Crick "You, your joys and your sorrows, your memories and ambitions, your sense of personal identity and free will, are in fact no more than the behaviour of a vast assembly of nerve cells and their associated molecules."

I love the confidence displayed by scientists. Truly. It is so all-encompassing that we lesser mortals believe, unquestioningly, every word. In fact, Crick is probably right at one level. But new developments and personal understanding nearly always change, and so too do scientists' pronouncements.

Unlimited thinking is accepting that whatever we know today, may only be part of a truth or reality. Unlimited thinking is living for today, with today's rules, while being alert to the potentiality of the unknown. It is not carelessly dismissing ideas because they are intangible or not yet personally experienced.

> *"Education is a progressive discovery of our own ignorance."* Will Durant

A post-mortem study of brains has shown that the more education a person has had, the greater the complexity and number of dendrites on the neurones in the language area of the brain. This is good. Education and other forms of mind training keep the brain active and exercised, helping to protect it from strokes and other brain-induced illnesses.

PART 3: UNLIMITING YOUR MIND

Education, as an aside, is knowledge gained from systematic instruction. Universities are not the only places in which to be systematically instructed. Many people are indeed quite unsuited to the mores of higher education via a university or college. However, that would not preclude them from gaining knowledge systematically.

Dr Graham Rawlinson[39] has his own method of brain-training. His supposition is that there is a parallel processing mechanism within the brain. His 1976 thesis posited that skilled readers can understand the correct order of letters even when the middle section is jumbled. Since a high proportion of dyslexics achieve high levels of fame and fortune, he might have a point. Brains recognise the patterns of words just like we can understand the essence of language without necessarily being able to define individual words.

Brains, minds, psyche, consciousness, thoughts, spirit, subconscious - these are some of the components of our physicality, and our spirituality. Still, this is not a religious treatise. It is an exploration into unlimited thinking, with overviews of those elements most obviously concerned with mind and thought expansion. Apart from those who view the world as physical events explained only in physical terms, most subscribe to a perspective of dualism - that there is a causal interaction between mental and physical events. I think, therefore I am, or, in religious parlance, on Earth as it is in Heaven.

Unlimited thinkers subscribe to the latter, and thoughts, as far as we know, happen via the mind. The relationship between the brain and the mind is a little more complex. Philosophers felt that it worked on behalf of the mind, connecting our experiences with

---

[39] How To Invent (Almost Anything): Dr Graham Rawlinson

our very existence, thus retaining a spiritual dimension.

The scientific approach gives the brain itself more authority, with groups of neurones having special functions and purposes. In essence, the current view is that the brain is an intelligent information processor. By contrast, our conscious mind is altogether more mysterious.

> *"Consciousness stands alone today as a topic that often leaves even the most sophisticated thinkers tongue-tied and confused... there are many who insist - and hope - that there will never be a demystification of consciousness." Daniel Dennett[40]*
>
> *
>
> *"Consciousness... what I mean by it is actually just sensation, experience, sentience." Colin McGinn*

What gives us our sense of self? Awareness is one element and consciousness is a state of awareness, a sensation of being aware, or alive. According to Arthur Reber[41] "consciousness is one of the fundamental defining features of our species: that to be human is to possess not only self-awareness but the even more remarkable capacity to scan and review mentally that which we are aware of". As an aside, the faculty of self-awareness is supposedly only possessed by man and not by animals. What makes us so sure of this? Is this not limited thinking? Pavlovian responses by animals may be just a fraction of the sensory perception of both men and animals that we are aware of. Indeed, study of feral children shows a quite different level of awareness by animals that is definitely on a par with compassionate-consciousness - which takes us firmly into the realms of the spirit or inner divinity.

---

[40] Consciousness Explained: Daniel C. Dennett
[41] Penguin Dictionary of Psychology

PART 3: UNLIMITING YOUR MIND

Many philosophers believe that consciousness belongs to the realm of the spirit. Plato felt that consciousness was part of our non-material soul surviving the death of the physical body. For Descartes, consciousness worked hand in glove with free will and rationality, and that was the soul. He believed the material and non-material interacted within the pineal gland – known in eastern mysticism as the third eye.

Consciousness will forever continue to fascinate as we seek to find answers to those eternal questions: "Who am I?" What am I part of?" Mystics have answers. But scientists are quite rightly more rational. They need to compartmentalise unlimited concepts within the boundaries of human limitation. They cross and re-cross philosophical and scientific bridges, trying to fathom an endless whole through the minutiae of its known parts. Those with mystical perspectives are swept aside by materialists such as Francis Crick.. Consciousness to Crick, as co-discoverer of the double-helix shape of DNA, is nothing more than the effects of oscillating brain cells. To Dennett, consciousness is an illusion – but then that is what Eastern mystics have been saying for a very long time. Dennett however believes that consciousness can be created using Artificial Intelligence. What? Pleasure and pain in a tin can? Who knows? Even Sir Martin Rees believes at some point in time that humans may have to give way to intelligence that started life in a circuit board. Possibly, if enough of us think that way.

Mystics, with a greater respect for infinity, would stop short of wishing the trials and tribulations of human existence onto any other life form, however it may be created. Scientists, predictably, have no such fears. They live for the consciousness of today. Unlimited thinking is awareness of our self within a much greater macrocosm.

PROFIT FROM UNLIMITED THINKING

> "If you happen to have a wart on your nose or forehead, you cannot help imagining that no-one in the world has anything else to do but stare at your wart, laugh at it, and condemn you for it, even though you have discovered America." Dostoevsky

So consciousness is awareness, and self-consciousness is a concept of self. Consciousness knows "I" exist. Self-consciousness says "Who am I?" According to Roger Scruton and David Chalmers[42], higher forms of consciousness include our individual responses to hearing a sublime piece of music, or even a sense of smell. Awareness of the sounds or the smells contribute to our sense of self.

As well as having a consciousness of music and smell, we can have a prosperity consciousness. In similar vein, it is our individual response to this prosperity vibration that predicates our wealthy or impoverished self. Like music - and ideas - abundance and affluence are all around us as invisible substance – whether we are in tune with them or not. It is our choice to have it flow to us or away from us by conscious awareness of our positive thoughts. Therefore it is our thoughts, through our awareness of self that keeps us from, or guides us to, whatever it is we desire.

> "The highest possible stage in moral culture is when we recognise that we ought to control our thoughts." Charles Darwin

I make no apologies for throwing out precursory questions. It is just throwing the interactive ball back to you! This question is: 'What is a thought?' What does a 'thought' mean to you?

Writing simplistically, a thought is the product of thinking. Thinking is an inward dialogue, either conscious or involuntary. It can be reflective or deliberate. It can reason or meander.

---

[42] The Conscious Mind – David Chalmers

PART 3: UNLIMITING YOUR MIND

Humans presume that no other species can think, although animal cunning is a form of thinking. While other species could be directed to think about changing patterns of behaviour, humans, generally, can be taught to think in a higher, more creative and intellectual fashion. The resultant action reflects the degree of learned thinking. That action resonates and vibrates in harmony with the energy of its parent thought.

A thought, metaphysically-speaking, has tangibility and puissance, despite being invisible and, usually, unsensed. A thought, or thought-form, can be very real to the thinker. Ask any voodoo practitioner. These thought-forms are believed to exist on another, as yet, scientifically-undiscovered plane or dimension. As ever with the law of balance, higher-minded thinkers attempt to fill this thought-plane with ideas that will benefit the whole, or to transmute those less pleasant thought vibrations which we are all guilty of to some degree. Equally, on a thought-plane, but no doubt vibrating rather lower, are the pop-mind views regarding soaps, celebs and reality shows. This thought-plane would be the equivalent of a tube train in the rush hour. A not very happy experience.

An idea, or tune, or storyline could be floating around waiting to be picked up by musicians, writers, scientists and other creatives. The successful artist is usually sued further down the line for plagiarism when in fact the idea was open to not just those two protagonists. The differentiator will always be individual experience and perspective. How many of us have had ideas, only to let them fly off as the baby's nappy needs changing or you miss your monthly targets and the boss starts to harangue? Meanwhile, someone else, taking advantage of the law of creative idleness has bagged it, and made it a bestseller. Life's a bitch as they say... or is it?

PROFIT FROM UNLIMITED THINKING

> *"If your mind is obsessed by thoughts of insecurity and inadequacy it is due to the fact that such ideas have dominated your thinking over a long period of time."* Norman Vincent Peale[43]
>
> *
>
> *"Few people think more than two or three times a year; I have made an international reputation for myself by thinking once or twice a week."*
> George Bernard Shaw

Thoughts are the foundations of our conscious acts. Everything that ever was or will be, starts with a thought. So it makes sense that positive thinking should be consciously ingrained into our mind habits[44]. We should be conscious of every thought, and make sure they are positive, because they have the power to create and destroy.

Thoughts have a habit of springing up in response to the many stimuli of the modern world. Who can watch the news without having a mental or verbal comment? Regrettably, I have been known to yell at the TV when various politicians share their consciousness - to the detriment of my spiritual evolution! My free will is engaged, of course, thus I take full responsibility for the resultant effect. Which current celebrity has not had the benefit of your observations and wit?

Despite the barrage of information received, we have to take responsibility for what our minds choose to retain - or comment on. We can think whatever we want to think. Unless we have allowed ourselves to be brainwashed, no-one can direct our thought processes[45].

Thoughts repeated over and over again, which we have allowed in, become beliefs, and beliefs manifest in time. Your passing thought may have been about the fifteen-minute celebrity, but the kickback

---

[43] The Power of Positive Thinking: Norman Vincent Peale
[44] The Power of Thought: John Algeo & Shirley J Nicholson
[45] The Basic Ideas of Science of Mind: Ernest Holmes

PART 3: UNLIMITING YOUR MIND

will, in time, relate to you. Our fears can also manifest in time, as Job so pungently noted: "Everything I fear and dread comes true.[46]" But then, so too can our desires come true. We can energise whatever we choose. Thoughts are potential-energy waiting to be realised through our desire-energy and intent.

> *"Energy is Eternal Delight." William Blake*
>
> *
>
> *"Energy: modern term for the forces of life at work throughout creation... unseen forces and the vibration of the environment... collectively labelled 'energy'" Rev Carol E Parrish-Harra*

Energy is the capacity for activity, the force or drive, or capacity to do work. Phrased that way, energy does not seem particularly delightful, unless you are a physicist, although it has roughly the same meaning in life as in physics. Work results from a force moving an object. Energy provides the capacity.

In physics, there seem to be endless types of energy: atomic, binding, chemical, electric, potential, gravitational, internal, kinetic, magnetic, molecular, nuclear, vibrational and wave for example. Many of these also apply in spiritual metaphysics.

> *"There was neither non-existence nor existence then... There was no distinguishing sign... one breathed, windless, by its own impulse... The life force ... arose through the power of heat."*
> *Rig Veda 10.129 Creation Hymn*

The universe is pulsating and vibrating with energy. Every atom, electron, photon, proton and neutron has its own vibrational intelligence and energy, transmitting and/or receiving in continuous unsensed melody. Apologies to physicists for my slapdash synopsis.

In mystical terms, everyone and everything has its own unique tone with its own electro-magnetic

---

[46] Good News Bible Job 3:25

frequency, its own singular tune. Including you. At its most seemingly invisible levels, everything has an interconnected vibration or sound. In essence, therefore, radiate in harmony with your melody, and your life should be a bowl of cherries. Life, though, is rarely that simple, even with an understanding of the nature of universal thought and energy.

> "..the human energy field ...carries with us the emotional energy created by our internal and external experiences - both positive and negative."
> *Caroline Myss PhD[47]*

Within the human body, there are hundreds of energy centres. They are whirling masses of energy or power centres through which we receive, transmit and process life information. Quantum physicists confirm as much, though rather more pragmatically. Human DNA not only has a quantified vibratory level, it also has been shown to have a melody. So once again science is able to prove centuries-old mysticism. All very well and good, but how can that unlimit our thoughts and minds? And how could that affect our health and wealth?

Our bodies have a three-layered energy or etheric field - physical, emotional, mental - extending way beyond our tangible selves, from top of the crown to toe, and beyond our outstretched arms. Each organ too has its own energy field and frequency, as indeed does each particle that comprises the self we can see and touch. Through this etheric field, the energy within us is extended, to merge with the energy around us, and surrounding us. As like attracts like, or repels unlike, then these intelligent particles attract and repel, all the while sharing and retaining information in their databases. It is not unlike morphic resonance or

---

[47] Anatomy of the Spirit: Caroline Myss

PART 3: UNLIMITING YOUR MIND

Mesmer's "subtle fluid" associating all things in "mutual intercourse".

In computer parlance, our seven main chakras, or energy locations, are similar to hubs in distributed processing. They are centres of electro-magnetic activity exchanging energy between the other main chakra/hubs and the twenty-one minor chakra/spokes, as well as the universal energy field. Then there are all those memories, experiences and impressions from beyond immediate space and time. That is a lot of information processing and stored records which may now be superfluous to needs. Some of it may even be damaging to future requirements. I am not a great fan of counselling or shrink-wrapped advice, as I believe it has a tendency to focus on the negative. However, in some cases, it may be necessary to get help to identify, and possibly clear out, this unwanted "data".

> *"...illnesses and health problems result from disturbances to the flow of prana[48] through a network of power centres, passageways and energy fields that interpenetrate the physical body."*
> Master Stephen Co & Eric B Robins MD[49]

Blockage of the energy centres and energy fields does not just result in ill-health. It can seriously impede manifesting goals and desires, and, of course, unlimited thinking.

There are a number of ways in which we can get our energy flowing freely again: yoga, acupuncture, meditation and chanting. Colours can also be used to stimulate or calm our chakras. Wearing yellow can help to stimulate the digestion. Blue is healing and sedative and can reduce stress or overflow of energy. Sluggish flow can result in obesity and more serious viral diseases. Too forceful a flow is just as harmful.

---

[48] energy
[49] Your Hands Can Heal You: Master Stephen Co & Eric B Robins MD

Understanding the flow of energy within ourselves can be incredibly helpful in self-healing.

Unsurprisingly, every organ in our body is made up of multiple particles - all with a unique intelligence and frequency. The wave frequency of colours can be sensed across all systems of the body[50] and used to heal and harmonise. Angela Wright in The Beginner's Guide to Colour Psychology tells us that each one of us has an "absolute" genetic colour code. While I am a firm believer in the power of colour, in unlimited thinking, nothing is absolute. It is only absolute in terms of our current understanding. However, should you tend to favour specific shades, then their particular association to you, if positive, will provide benefits.

Shades of red can provide a boost to your self-confidence, for example. They can enable you to be more assertive as well, but, equally, can be draining, or provoke aggression. The effects of blues can vary from increased mental effort, to having a healing presence, to projecting dignified authority. Think IBM suit-blue. Green can mean restful, as well as love. It is also associated with jealousy. Yet it is also the colour of abundance.

Yellow is sunlight and confidence. It stimulates and opens up the mind. As both yellow and blue are keys colours of www.floreo.org, I have chosen not to reflect on their negative associations! Violet relates to our higher self, contemplative and spiritual. Purple is royal but also deluded if used in too much quantity. Pink is the colour of unconditional love but also has a soporific influence. It is not a colour to wear if you wish to be taken seriously in the business world.

Orange assists success and hails the extrovert, while brown is earthy and reliable. Conversely, it is a

---

[50] Color Medicine: Charles Kotsche

PART 3: UNLIMITING YOUR MIND

background colour lacking in assertion. Taupe and beige might be quiet and classy but are also background colours. Black might be a favourite of fashionistas but it absorbs the light. It is a barrier colour even though it is undeniably elegant. White, ostensibly the colour of purity, can also separate the wearer from reality.

Colours, whether worn as clothing or your choice of decor or even eaten - red peppers, purple aubergines, spring greens - can seriously influence your life. Even insurance companies can price up or down the fees you pay for your car. Silver cars are apparently the safest on the roads, while black cars are more likely to be driven by risk-takers[51]. Our energy centres are also influenced and characterised by colour.

> "..each level of consciousness is a basic vibration... The whole principle of this flow of changing vibrations is often known as the Tattwic Tides."
> Peter Rendel[52]

There are seven major chakras (wheels) within the body which correspond to different levels of consciousness. They control the physical condition of the body[53] and have their own individual characteristics and functions. Each chakra is marked by one of the seven colours of the spectrum.

Chakras are doorways through which energy, be it emotional, mental or spiritual, flows into physical expression. This related energy flows through the chakras and is distributed into our tissues and cells and organs. Chakras also act as major receivers and transmitters for the electro-magnetic frequencies which are being sent out every second of every day and every night. These EMFs oscillate and resonate and

---

[51] British Medical Journal 2003/University of Auckland research
[52] Introduction to The Chakras: Peter Rendel
[53] Journey through the Chakras: Klausbernd Vollmar

flow with the energies and frequencies of the Universe. They attract their like into our lives, and they are predominantly controlled by the power of our thoughts. As we have the power to control our thoughts and thus our EMFs, we can also, in theory, control our destiny.

> *"No man is an island, entire of itself; every man is a piece of the continent, a part of the main." John Donne*

We are not separate from the Universe and our microcosm can affect not just our bit of our personal world. We also affect the bigger picture too. Nothing is unconnected even though it may appear to be so. Any progress or regress that you encounter, will help or hinder others even if they have no obvious connection.[54] Obviously, the reverse also applies.

Our thoughts and attitudes have a much more lasting resonance than we either realise or can conceptualise. Thoughts and emotions can vibrate across time and space in ways we can barely comprehend. For most of us, whether we believe in afterlives or other lives, feeling in control of this life is challenging enough as it is. But if you cannot control your thoughts, you will never feel in control of any of your lives!

What do you want? If you can resonate or vibrate with its frequencies, you will have what you want. How? The vibration of your desire sends frequencies out into the universe resonating with identical frequencies. Like attracts like. Similar circumstances, people and opportunities will appear within your reality in direct ratio to the power of your focused thought, and ability to receive.

Visualisation and affirmations work in a similar manner. Your images and sounds are

---

[54] Space, Time & Medicine: Larry Dossey

PART 3: UNLIMITING YOUR MIND

reverberating through the cosmos, tuning you into similar images and melodies. A more poetic way, perhaps, of saying you get back what you give out. Too often though, there is a core vibration that is repressed and far more powerful than whatever you may be chanting or visualising. You may have been reinforcing inner behavioural patterns by loose thinking or actions which negate all these new efforts. You may be thinking unconsciously about your fears - and what you do NOT want. You will have to dig out the roots of these negative thought forms with self-hypnosis, working hard in changing to new thought patterns that counteract previous mind and cellular conditioning.

Train your conscious mind to ponder on quality thoughts that build the foundations of what you do want and allow these to become firmly imbedded within your subconscious mind. Let them become your dominant vibration. Create a vision of what you desire and focus your energy on manifesting it. As you almost tangibly feel this "imagined" reality in your mind, your subconscious will believe it to be "physical" reality. It will then task itself with confirming it. It will attract the circumstances, the people, and the opportunities you need to bring about the vision you have created.

Do you believe me? Whether you believe this is rubbish or not, you are actually creating right now. You are just unaware that you are doing so. You are an unconscious creator and also an unfocused one, so you are probably creating a whole lot of stuff you do not particularly want in your life. You are probably also counteracting all the things you do want. Conscious creating means you are in charge of the creative process and can learn to manifest at will.

Act "as if" - use the fake-it-till-you-make-it action plan. Act as if you had the essence of what desire. How would you think? How would you feel? What would you do? Well, do it, feel it, think it, now.

PROFIT FROM UNLIMITED THINKING

Just make sure your finances can handle your more extravagant desires. This will ensure that your dominant vibration is in harmony with all that you desire – and that your subconscious mind is fully aware of it too.

Psychologists are generally agreed that to achieve peak performance it is vital to achieve a state of semi-hypnosis, as if on auto-pilot. This state of being is not just for athletes either.

When I first went into technical selling, I found myself frequently working on autopilot – to great success. It came from a combination of tiredness after a lot of driving and also possibly a little fear. When parts of the brain shut down from stress, provided previous knowledge is already in place, another brighter, sharper part can take over. I was certainly amazed at my own ability to deliver the appropriate technical and marketing case for a wide variety of potential end-users.

Most of us do not realise that we use a mere fraction of our brain power. We probably have incredible intelligence and experience already programmed into our cells. Even Dr Roger Sperry might agree with that, up to a point. He believed that the brain's circuits are hardwired, with each nerve cell having a fixed, non-modifiable functionality.

Unlimited thinkers would prefer the views of his professor, Paul Weiss, who believed that experience and learning influenced purpose. However, if cellular intelligence works beyond time and space, then it is conceivable that functionality would appear to be fixed. But not necessarily hardwired.

PART 3: UNLIMITING YOUR MIND

> *"We've got this interesting little thing we all subconsciously do", says Golly, "we tend to look up to top right when we're trying to remember something visual, we look top left when we try to remember words, and we look down when it's something conceptual.*[55]*"*

Most of us favour either the left brain, making us better at logical, analytical tasks and decision making, or the right brain which is creative, visual, imaginative and intuitive. However, by stimulating one or more of the four quadrants to the brain - front and back of the left and right sides, each with its own characteristics - it is possible to develop whole brain activity.

To develop the left front, and your logical, analytical and critical thought faculties, learn a complex game like chess. The left back controls discipline and attention to detail. Are your finances in order? What is your timekeeping like?

The right front stimulates the imagination. Daydreaming is an excellent tool for stimulating the right front brain. Right back brain controls emotions and intuition and can be stimulated by music or artistic endeavour or even by watching something sentimental like Bambi!

> *"You must realise by now that your conscious mind is the "watchman at the gate", and its chief function is to protect your subconscious mind from false impressions." Joseph Murphy*[56]

Every year, science provides confirmation of ancient beliefs about mind powers.

A few years back, it was revealed how rats could control a robotic arm through the power of thought alone. This would pave the way for telepathic power around the home: turn on the TV, get the Hoover going all by thought power alone – and some

---
[55] Please could a reader help me with attributing this quotation?
[56] The Power of Your Subconscious Mind: Joseph Murphy

PROFIT FROM UNLIMITED THINKING

electricity of course. For now. One day, possibly in Sir Martin Rees' human-free world, our minds will figure out a different way of harnessing energy.

It is believed that there are several levels within the mind. We know of the conscious and un- or pre-conscious minds. We also know of the subconscious mind. For most levels of mundane human living, they are quite sufficient to be getting on with!

The unconscious mind is also known as the inner, subliminal or subjective mind, or the id. We can usually be made aware of the processes of this mind dimension.

The subconscious mind is viewed as having programmable, mechanical properties. In Psycho-Cybernetics, Dr Maxwell Maltz states that the subconscious mind works in a similar manner to a computer. Since computers are still advancing hugely, it is probably fair to say that the subconscious can also reason, up to a point.

As a rule, we are not aware of the reasoning and actions of our subconscious minds. Imagine how chaotic even blinking or lifting an arm would be if we were! It would be rather like that exercise of rubbing your stomach with one hand while patting your head with the other.... multiplied a gazillion-fold. By contrast, the conscious state is one in which our existence is conditioned by our sensations and feelings, and thoughts and actions. Self-consciousness is a step higher in awareness, but the real repository of knowledge and unlimitedness is the subconscious.

In Part 5, I have included more details of the various processes and mind states involved in self-programming, or self-hypnosis. Through self-hypnosis, we can interact profitably with our subconscious minds. Not only can we tell it what improvements our conscious minds would like, we can also receive in

PART 3: UNLIMITING YOUR MIND

return, symbolic messages of hidden and useful knowledge. I have also included a sample hypnosis script which can be amended to suit individual needs. Use it as a skeleton script for your own creative endeavours.

> *"Man has three ways of acting wisely. First, on meditation; that is the noblest. Secondly, on imitation; that is the easiest. Thirdly, on experience; that is the bitterest." Confucius*
>
> *
>
> *"Meditation is really the mind thinking of the Soul, just as Activity is the mind thinking of the world." Paul Brunton*
>
> *
>
> *"Whoever here among men attain greatness, they have, as it were, part of the reward of meditation. ...He who reverences meditation as the Supreme - as far as meditation goes, so far he has unlimited freedom."*
> *Chandogya Upanishad*

I confess to having a prodigal-son approach to inner education: off on mundane or materialistic trips, I pay lip service to still and silent listening. Yet when I do, and it can be for mere seconds, I am greatly rewarded beyond my deservability. In fact, probably like most mere mortals, I am awed by what I could receive, and thus switch off.

A lot has been written about meditation. What happens to our consciousness during the process? Devotees of meditation swear it transports them into a new realm of consciousness. Others are relieved of stress, or gain an exceptional energy charge. Creativity is enhanced and obstacles have been known to "miraculously" disappear.

Research has shown that a deep meditative state does result in a reduction in metabolic activity, with increased cerebral blood flow. The characteristics are directly opposite to those of a stressed state. Brain wave patterns differ from those in the sleeping state. Yet despite the alertness, the meditator experiences a calm restfulness. This is described as transcendental consciousness.

> *"Meditation is as simple as breathing."* Greer Allica
>
> *
>
> *"The road of meditation is not an easy one. The first shock of surprise comes when we realise how undisciplined our mind really is..."* Lawrence LeShan[57]

If you are anything like me, lengthy meditation can frequently make you twitch and fidget. Thankfully, I discovered my One-Minute Meditation can work almost as well - at least for my current capacity to receive. It certainly shoos away any negative thoughts and allows me to feel a sense of directed confidence.

The usual instructions for meditation are to sit comfortably and let your mind relax into a state of restful awareness. For a successful meditative session, it is important that one's physiological functions slow down. Unfortunately, if you have just stepped out of a sales meeting, or are in the middle of prospecting, to meet end of quarter quota, you will have neither the time to relax your physiology, nor an understanding sales manager. Ladies' loos are usually prime gossip-spreading meeting rooms and, short of finding a solitary park bench opposite a large lake, they can provide the necessary aloneness for the OMM. Men are advised to stick to their own WCs.

Close your eyes, hold your breath and let the only image be of infinite nothingness. Don't gulp a minute's worth of breath, or hold in your stomach. Just stop, and sense the infinite within you. As you do, even in those seconds, you will feel as if the sides of your mind and body have merged with this infinite nothingness. Yet, as you do, you will be aware of an enormous potentiality about it.

---

[57] How to Meditate: Lawrence LeShan

PART 3: UNLIMITING YOUR MIND

Even those short seconds can give you an extraordinary sense of self-belief and power. Small wonder I have called my autobiographical essays Delusions of Divinity?[58] It feels almost like overhearing a conversation, or peeking inside someone's windows on a Sunday stroll, yet, at the same time, being a part of it.. You probably will not be aware that you are actually still breathing, albeit slowly.

Do apply some commonsense to practising this exercise if you have asthma or any other respiratory disease.

> *"The essence of meditation is nowness... (it) is not aimed at achieving a higher state or at following some theory or idea, but simply, without any object or ambition, trying to see what is here and now."*
> Chogyam Trungpa
> *
> *"The holiest name in the world, the name of the Creator, is the sound of your own breathing."* Arthur Samuel Joseph
> *
> *"Empty yourself of everything, let the mind become still."*
> The Book of Tao

Meditation is now generally accepted as a worthwhile method for controlling stress. Indeed one recent guru advised a form of meditation while driving. This is not at all a good idea! Listening to soothing music is far better, and may even attract ideas or solutions to problems. The key is diverted attention.

> *"In the Meditator's worldview, God isn't separate from the world, but is the consciousness out of which everything is formed."* David Harp

While Eastern chanting, and yoga predominate, there are in fact many forms of meditation.[59] One of my favourite books on the subject is a Teach Yourself - Meditation by James Hewitt. It is intelligent and informative, as well as practical. It is

---
[58] Delusions of Divinity?: Euphrosene Labon (not yet published)
[59] The 3 Minute Meditator: David Harp with Nina Feldman

particularly telling that the only line I have highlighted is "Desire for results as you meditate in fact robs you of results." Ah, plus ça change!

> *"It seemed to me that the Yoga exercises produced in us a certain silence favourable to contemplation, the approach of God and personal contact with the divine Persons." J-M Déchanet OSB*

Yoga is a physical form of meditation. Obviously not one for the ladies' loo! I well remember when it was said to be contrary to Christian faith to practice yoga... till I discovered one of the better books on yoga was written by a Benedictine monk.[60]

The most important demand from unlimited thinking is to learn to quieten your mind at least once a day, and one of the best ways is through meditation whichever practice you choose to adopt. The result is not dissimilar to runner's high. However, during transcendental consciousness, the mind is enhanced, without borders, and is able to consciously receive and create.

Through still and silent meditation, one achieves perfect equilibrium. Isn't that a beautiful word? A state of mental and emotional balance... in these moments of deep mental and emotional balance, previous creative efforts are usually rewarded.

While it is possible to achieve moments of similar equilibrium in a busy world, "moving meditation" can be distracting. Dogs' calling cards, other people passing by and traffic are just some of those distractions making demands on our subconscious energy. Thankfully the one-minute meditation (OMM) can not only still and focus your thoughts, it will also rebalance your EMFs[61].

---

[60] Yoga in 10 Lessons: J-M Déchanet OSB
[61] electro-magnetic frequencies

PART 3: UNLIMITING YOUR MIND

> *"Too much meditation could create hypersensitivity and nervousness in certain persons."* Paul Brunton[62]

While I may not be very good at lengthy meditation sessions, I do have an enhanced self-awareness which tells me when I must still my mind. By and large, I obediently take time out to tune up. When the benefits emerge, as they invariably do, I always wonder why I do not practise more devoutly...!

> *"...those will survive whose functions happen to be most nearly in equilibrium..."* Herbert Spencer

Finding balance, whether emotional, mental or spiritual, in our frantic and materialistic world can be incredibly difficult. Hip gip can affect even prime time players in our struggle to match our worldly needs with the cries of our souls. Even as our bodies flash painful warnings, it is possible to re-align our auras, and, in effect, to begin a self-healing. For those with serious illnesses, please make sure you follow your medical practitioner's advice as well.

> *"An aura is a collection of electro-magnetic energies ...exiting from the physical, vital, etheric, mental, emotional and spiritual bodies.. (which) are suspended around the human body in an oval-shaped field.*[63]*"*

Start by breathing naturally. There is no need to take great swooping breaths or to count down with each inhaled or exhaled breath. Just bring your hands into the Albrecht Durer position - that is as if in prayer. Still clasping your hands together, raise your arms upwards, till just above your head. Then, spread your arms out, into a full circle, bringing your hands back into the Durer position. As you do so, you will be re-aligning your aura, and you will sense all those

---

[62] The Notebooks of Paul Brunton: Vol Four, Part 1 Meditation
[63] You and Your Aura: Joseph Ostrom

intangible particles of electro-magnetic energies re-balancing perfectly.

> *"The reciting of mantra a given number of times, combined with concentration, opens our mind instinctively to supernormal powers and insights." Lama Thubten Yeshe*[64]

In the beginning, whether from the "OM" of Eastern mysticism, or the "Word" - Logos - of Western spirituality, all things were created through sound - that is, vibration. Although mantra is a Sanskrit word with several interpretations, including "divine speech" or "tool of the mind",[65] as well as "mind protection"[66], all of the major faiths have several mantras. These include: 'Lord have mercy' and even 'Jesus, Mary Joseph', 'La il'ha, il'alahu and 'Avinu Malkenu'. Nam-Myoho-Renge-Kyo enjoyed fashionable popularity with actors and singers.

Kotodama is a symbolic sound technique used in Reiki. The syllables are similar to bija or mystic seed mantras[67], and can be extraordinarily powerful: for example ho-ku-ei meaning focus, ho-a-ze-ho-ne for connection.

Buddhists and Hindus have many mantras, some of enormous length and complexity. They tend to be focused on particular aspects of the divine: strength, abundance, healing, love and so forth. Sadly, the mantra "Jesus Christ" is now more widely used in more derogatory circumstances, even by those professing to be Christians. There is nothing to stop you, though, from re-energising its original, more compassionate light.

A mantra is a vibratory sound formed from a word or series of words. It is used like an affirmation,

---

[64] Mantras and Mudras: Lillian Too
[65] Healing Mantras: Thomas Ashley-Farrand
[66] The Relaxation Response: Herbert Benson MD
[67] Meditation and Mantras: Swami Vishnu Devananda

PART 3: UNLIMITING YOUR MIND

repeated regularly and hypnotically. As you chant, you will resonate with its particular frequency. With the Buddhist and Hindu mantras, you will be resonating with the power and benefits of centuries infused into its vibration, yet bringing unlimited awareness right to the present moment and beyond. Sometimes it is useful to fool the mind by repeating seemingly unintelligible words. Your intention is to power up one thought and energise its essence, and to then manifest it in your life. If you are mentally arguing with a thought, it will cancel itself out – or worse – manifest what you do not want. This is where Sanskrit comes into it own - unless of course you are already a scholar. If you really cannot get your tongue round strange languages, just remember that Ramana Maharishi said "every word is a mantra."

Breathing keeps energy and blood flowing. It is possible to breathe and not think, therefore "I am" becomes a supremely powerful mantra of being. When mantras are linked to breathing patterns, the act of breathing becomes the first stage of mystical experience - discovering the real "I (unlimited) am".

Yantras have long been associated with mystical experiences. Christian saints, gazing upon images of Christ, have written of their ecstacy, and of how they were transported to realms of indescribable glory. Although traditionally a yantra is a diagram or complex pattern of interlocking circles, triangles and squares, it means 'instrument' in Sanskrit. A painting of Christ has the power to transform consciousness as much, if not more, to many meditators. It is the instrument of the mind's transcendence.

A mandala is a circular yantra. It is believed to represent the Absolute Principle, having no beginning or end. Diagrams and pictures can be contained within the mandala. Eastern mandalas are amazing works of art. Our Western world has opted for computer-generated yantras and mandalas, which can then be coloured in as a form of therapy. Constructing your own yantra can be taken as an act of meditation, a profound contemplation which expands consciousness and unlimited awareness.

> *"The thumb is symbolic of cosmic (divine) and the index finger is symbolic of individual (human) consciousness." Gertrud Hirschi*

I am ashamed to say that hands really only became fascinating to me after I was in a car crash and suffered very bad lacerations and broken fingers on my left hand. I was convinced that they would be in perfect order once the cast came off so it was a massive shock to see the mess and open wounds on the back of my hand.

Scar tissue meant that bending my fingers was practically impossible. I chanted specific healing mantras and tried all sorts of potions and exercises, once again expecting immediate results. Then one morning I woke early and found myself picking out another book, and opening it to read "Sometimes healing is expected too quickly and we give up before it can take place. Not all healing can or should be instantaneous."[68]

Mudras are generally viewed as hand positions, used in yoga, to focus the mind. Specific positions can lead to its associated state of consciousness. By crossing, bending or extending one's fingers, both the mind and body are engaged. When linked with sound, the action triggers off unseen frequencies of power and resonance.

Catholic priests link thumb and index finger, while praying the Mass. The same gesture is used while in the lotus position. The Albrecht Durer position is also the Atmanjali Mudra or gesture of prayer. It

---

[68] Mantras: Words of Power: Swami Sivananda Radha

PART 3: UNLIMITING YOUR MIND

creates harmony, balance and peace. In India, it is used as a greeting - Namaste. It greets the God within fellow human beings. It is a calming mudra, stabilising and strengthening the mind.

The British rugby player, Jonny Wilkinson, became as known for his hand positions as for his 2003 World Cup winning drop goal. It seems similar to either the Linga Mudra or upright mudra, increasing one's powers of resistance, or the Ganesha Mudra, for overcoming all obstacles. [69]

Essentially, mudras aid concentration. With PalmTherapy, the exercises will allow the mind to follow up a proactive action plan.[70] Moshe Zwang states that there is a connection between the creases, mounts and lines of the palm and fingers. The subtitle of his book is Program Your Mind Through Your Palms. With specifically-addressed stimulation, he believes that our personality and well-being can be re-shaped for the better. "You can also use it in daily life situations when you need that extra energy... the mental abilities to perform, to react and to achieve."

As I am still trying to reduce the adhesions in my left palm, I am unclear precisely what I am programming my mind with, but I have found palm massage to be very helpful generally.

---

[69] Mudras: Gertrud Hirshi
[70] PalmTherapy: Moshe Zwang

> *"Without silence being taken daily, there is little chance of meditation becoming effective."* William Bloom[71]
>
> *
>
> *"In the stillness and silence of meditation, we glimpse and return to that deep inner nature that we have so long lost sight of amid the busyness and distraction of our minds."* Sogyal Rinpoche

Philip Larkin, a professed atheist, wandered into a church and said "It pleases me to stand in silence here." While the church obviously had something to do with it, the key element is silence. That holy place warranted high praise - his silence. In the beauty of silence, his other senses could take over. In the spiritual silence of a holy place, maybe he sensed eternity.

The world can almost be divided into those who fear silence, and those who are driven to distraction by its lack. Such is the value of silence in this noisy age, to the latter, that a Professor Selwyn Wright has even developed a Silence Machine. Those who fear silence may have a recollection of Rousseau: that absolute silence equates with death. Unless you are already six feet deep, silence nowadays is never absolute. Even in a remote desert, keen ears could hear the shifting sands.

Silence is giving a chance to your unlimited senses to make themselves known.

I do advise caution, however, for those who suffer from depression or other forms of mind illness. Choose the silence of nature, if you must, since that will provide light for those darker moments. Remember also to empty wanton thoughts onto paper. The exercise will not only help to lift any mental loads, it will also be your silent friend.

"God" is a name for the source and supply of all unlimited potentiality. However we may define our

---

[71] Meditation in a Changing World: William Bloom

PART 3: UNLIMITING YOUR MIND

god, as Mother Teresa said, "he cannot be found in noise and restlessness. God is the friend of silence". It makes sense, therefore, to take time out to discover what that might be for you.

> "He is never alone that is accompanied with noble thoughts." Beaumont & Fletcher
>
> *
>
> "When you have shut your doors and darkened your room, remember, never to say that you are alone; for you are not alone, but God is within, and your genius is within." Epictetus

Antonia Byatt once said that solitude and separateness define her existence, that without them she would cease to exist. Monasteries have perfected the art of silence with togetherness, but for the rest of us, silence is best developed in solitude. All the great teachers "discovered" their god during their aloneness, and since their god set them on the path of great world potential, some profitable solitude should go well with your silence.

Most people would rather chase a frantic and stress-inducing social life than spend time alone. To be alone is to admit personal defeat. "I am alone, therefore I have no friends", or, "I am not liked that is why I am alone." This is untrue. We make choices. Many choose to be alone because their creativity demands it. As an aside, if you are alone and have not chosen to be, then doing something about it should have figured high on your list of goals in Part 1! For more social bunnies, there is no need give up the whirl and razzle. You will just need to make time to be alone. You may even find you like your own company.

Many years ago, I had a personal motto: "If you do not like your own company, don't inflict it on others." My social life, at that time, was particularly manic and I craved those solitary moments. I did not seem to achieve much in terms of creativity or spiritual insight. It just made me feel good about myself, without necessarily having anything to show for it. Gaining something for almost nothing cannot be bad.

While I agree with Andre Gide, that solitude is bearable only with God, that is scant comfort if you are an atheist or agnostic. References to a divine being[72] may even annoy you, but please persevere. In Part 5, I will show you how to create your own unlimited guru, or god. As it will be part of your imagination and yourself, it should not conflict with any intellectual or spiritual ideals.

> *"Achieved that stillness ultimately blest..."* Hart Crane
>
> *
>
> *"Alone... The word is life endured and known It is the stillness where our spirits walk And all but inmost faith is overthrown."* Siegfried Sassoon

Speaking about the death of his father, Ziggy Marley said "It was like a *stillness* had clouded my world. It felt like nothing existed. Nothing mattered. I just went very quiet. I didn't feel sad. Just stillness."

Eckhart Tolle[73] writes: "When you lose touch with inner stillness, you lose touch with yourself. When you lose touch with yourself, you lose yourself in the world." Stillness is not just physical inaction. It is also mental quietude. You discover a sense of formlessness where all physical barriers simply evaporate. Stillness can be enjoyed in the presence of others – although you might get some bemused looks. Animals seem very wary of stillness, dogs especially. Perhaps it is because they have got so accustomed to hectic humans? Animals are more in tune with senses that are generally untapped in humans. By creating an inner stillness, the human is effectively switching off an understood

---

[72] Domine, indulge mea
[73] Stillness Speaks: Eckhart Tolle

PART 3: UNLIMITING YOUR MIND

transmission. No doubt, to a dog, the 'phone line has been cut, or the frequencies are like a foreign language.

The act of stilling both the mind and body, paradoxically, seems to make others tune in. In metaphysical terms, shutting down the known senses, allows the unknown senses to open up. One of these is the link to the collective mind, the realm of unlimited thought. This is the ultimate aim of stillness.

TASKS
List your key impressions after a session of meditation
Describe how do you feel about silence?
How long can you keep still?
Find out the Sanskrit names of the body's main energy centres
List ways in which you expend your energy
Write your own mantras

INTELLIGENCE: IQ EMOTION SPIRIT

Intelligence does not always seek expression in commonplace ways. What is intelligence anyway? It is generally agreed to be a measurement of understanding: the ability of a sentient being to learn and work things out. It could even be a sense of responsiveness.

According to experts, there are four basic types: rational, intuitive, relational and practical. Well that's lucky then - something for all of us!

> *"What was good was to have intelligence and yet not understand. It was a strange blessing like experiencing madness without being mad." Clarice Lispector, Brazilian novelist*

It never ceases to amaze me how IQ tests can really measure understanding and responsiveness. Probably because I am not very good at them! Commonsense is a sign of intelligence. Yet many

PROFIT FROM UNLIMITED THINKING

people, gifted with commonsense, probably do not have even a CSE to their names.

We learn something new about the mind almost every day. Take our earlier example of an Alzheimer's sufferer. Previously, they might have been sympathetically dismissed as past usefulness. Now, some forms of "empathy carework" are confounding expectations.

Those with short-term memory and information processing problems, are finding new and beautiful ways of creative expression. A researcher, working with hospices, found poetry to be the natural language of dementia because it allowed feelings to be expressed powerfully. The Alzheimers sought understanding through the language of hidden emotions.

Registering emotional quotient is rapidly paralleling the tried but tired IQ format. In fact, emotional intelligence is being assessed as an important part of regular interviewing techniques.

Daniel Goleman, the psychologist who coined the expression, believes that how we control our emotions and understand the feelings of others will be key to rising to the top of the pile. Emotional Intelligence is, as he says "the capacity for recognising our own feelings and those of others, for motivating ourselves, and for managing emotions well in ourselves, and in our relationships."

We are being emotionally unintelligent when we have feelings of self-pity, insecurity, jealousy and helplessness. Our emotions are controlling us when we are angry, impatient and lack focus. Our EQ[74] is based on our resilience and positivity in any situation. It is our ability to rise above criticism or anything that triggers high levels of negative emotion.

---

[74] Spiritual Intelligence: Danah Zohar & Ian Marshall

PART 3: UNLIMITING YOUR MIND

High EQ people are not overly concerned by what others think or say about them. They know their emotional peaks and troughs, and manage to bounce back from life's setbacks and upsets. Optimism is a sign of EQ. It is also a mark of the unlimited mind

Charge your thoughts with optimistic emotion, and those high frequency vibrations will magnetise better circumstances into your life. Being a good person, being thankful and being joyful, all fall into the higher frequency category as well.

Happy people tend to be more creative; miserable people are more logical. Or at least that's a theory some psychologists have come up with. Personally, I would not have classed Van Gogh as a happy person. Those psychologists further added, that happiness has the same effect as brain damage.

There is contentment, happiness, and ecstatic happiness, and they are no doubt referring to the latter, as strong emotions do have a tendency to distort perceptions.

In unlimited thinking, creativity is not stunted or enhanced by good or bad emotions. The world is peopled with many grumpy, but creative, actors, musicians and artists, whose grumpiness is often on public display. However, the knock-on effects of their grumpiness may not be the kind of creativity we would desire in our own lives!

Those higher frequencies are part of the intelligent, creative, magnetic force within us. We have huge powers to magnetise into our lives whatever we desire and must learn to override any low, negative frequencies instantly. Then, the knock-on effects will be happiness - with creativity and fulfilment.

> *"Clarity of mind results in clarity of passion..."* Blaise Pascal~

Emotional intensity is very powerful indeed. Passion is a major driving force, and is not confined to horizontal activity. Many of the world's billionaires were passionate about their products and services when their bank balances were pathetically low. A high EQ could and should include passion.

What are you passionate about? Far too often, most people go through their entire lives with not even a spark of passion. Emotions can be distracting. However, it is possible to transmute passion so that its force is fulfilling and prospering, and not depleting or destructive.

Anger, although a "deadly sin", can be transmuted into a positive expression of passion. Righteousness can give anger a moral dimension which can be a catalyst for positive action. Anger, with love, is a passionate emotion, an EQ qualifier. Rage, on the other hand, is destructive and is based on hate. Aggression is positive only when it creates driven action. Then, of course, it is assertive action.

There is power in the emotion of gratitude as well as in the power in a smile. Appreciation is another powerful energy raiser and EQ qualifier. No matter where you live, there are natural things to look at and appreciate. Rainbows, fluffy clouds and blue skies, the fresh smell of ocean air, the warmth of spring sun, the coolness of a breeze, or a rain shower on a hot afternoon are all things we can appreciate and enjoy.

More prosaically, we can appreciate having a home, somewhere warm to shelter. Look around most cities and you will see people whose homes are cars, cardboard boxes, bridge underpasses or "shelters". Many people take their own basic comforts for granted.

Though many people have found themselves totally alone, most of us do have a friend or two to

PART 3: UNLIMITING YOUR MIND

appreciate. If you have a friend, and even kind neighbours, you are better off than many people, which is surely worth the EQ of appreciation. As is living in a democratic society.

Politics aside, many people live in countries where they have no rights, such as being able to vote, or having the freedom to worship, which those living in democratic societies can take for granted. Education is freely available for us, as is health treatment, even if there is usually room for improvement!

Generally, in the western world, there is abundant food to eat. We can choose from a huge variety of good, healthy food to buy from numerous sources at any time. The down side to positive appreciation of food is gluttony. Greed, by contrast, could be turned into an EQ qualifier.

Sometimes we set our satisfaction limits too low. Having more houses or cars might appear greedy to those without. To the housekeeper, mechanics and others involved in their sales and service, they are a source of income. The art collector can be construed as greedy. Not to the artist, or the gallery owner.

Greed, according to Philippe Gigantès, [75] created the superpower states. He calls these greedy people "Grand Acquisitors". The "Grand Acquisitors" probably did not focus on greed for greed's sake - accumulating materials goods or power - but on the end result.

> *"All you have to do to diminish your fear is to develop more trust in your ability to handle whatever comes your way!" Susan Jeffers*[76]

Fear, unrestrained, is like ink seeping into blotting paper. But fear is just an emotion. Not a very nice one admittedly, but it can be controlled. Fears can

---

[75] Power & Greed: Philippe Gigantès
[76] Feel The Fear And Do It Anyway: Susan Jeffers

PROFIT FROM UNLIMITED THINKING

even have a positive resonance. Fears can tell us what we actually want. So, odd though it might seem, when fears can be so debilitating, we really ought to be thankful for them. They draw our meandering attention back to positive action and affirmation.

When you write down a fear, you will have the basic words to create the affirmation for a specific desire to counteract the fear. By applying some mental discipline into focusing on the desire, and not the fear, you can then change your attitude and, in turn, what happens next. Wasn't it Job who focused so much on his fears that they came to pass? That is what we want to avoid!

Worry and anxiety are just as counter-productive as fear. They induce heaviness of spirit and can result in poor health. In order to raise frequencies, it is important to face the problem. What is the worst that can possibly happen? Be prepared to accept the worst, without actually dwelling on its possibility. Remember Job! If you know your job is on the line, carry on working to the best of your ability while brushing up your networking skills, and updating your CV. Focus on being successful, whatever happens.

If your relationship is suffering, you can choose to either mend it or walk away. If you are in debt, further retail therapy is not going to help! With both relationships and debt management, there are supportive organisations that can help you to focus on turning the negative emotions of fear and anxiety into positive action plans.

Dire money problems as well as thwarted love can create powerful and destructive emotions. Sometimes the emotional energy is so strong, it can trigger irrational behaviour which feels very rational at the time - I speak from embarrassed experience! But, as Teresa of Avila once said, "Everything passes....". And, so it does. So too do the wretched memories and

PART 3: UNLIMITING YOUR MIND

sensations, leaving behind wry smiles, and a feeling of relief, even if the journey out of Hades was very long and torturous. Everything does indeed pass.

It is important to transmute and re-direct this energy into a plan of action that progresses rather than hurts. When the pain has gone, shame, indifference or even humour will take its place. Focus on humour and make it part of your EQ portfolio.

A word on indifference: it is not an emotion to cultivate since it is the opposite of love - and even the opposite of hate. However, sometimes it can help to re-balance the senses. It can bring a relative calm to a troubled mind. The neutrality of compassionate indifference, if practised for a short time, could help to restore emotional equilibrium.

We all will have difficult times and experiences. It is part of the cycle of spiritual evolution and personal development. We can break into a new cycle of unlimited living though. We have exceptional inner powers which have to be discovered, nurtured and developed. Adversity is a tough teacher, but the lessons learned can make us leapfrog out of our current limits.

If you really are one of life's worriers, then let it be about something that is beyond most mundane lives, like an asteroid dropping on the South Coast. Neither you nor I will be around to worry about the results, except in infinite time and space. Then we will have a whole new set of challenges!

If something untoward is going to happen, it will, and you would be better served energising your thoughts on building up your inner resources, or visualising a positive outcome of some description. The effect of an energised positive image is to counteract and balance. Work on your self-esteem, and the effect of the event will be minimised.

The worst form of worry is about the past. Why? It has already happened and you cannot undo it, so move your mind forward. Many counsellors make a healthy living by getting their clients to focus on events that happened in the past, sometimes in a past beyond our current comprehension.

This form of therapy is perfectly acceptable if it enables us to better understand our current patterns of behaviour. It is not advisable to relive those hurts or sufferings though. By accepting that they have contributed to personality and outlook, it is easier to create a preferable alternative, or at least to be more forgiving of faults.

> *"It is the disposition of the thought that altereth the nature of the thing."*
> *John Lyly*
>
> *
>
> *"The day you recognise PMA for yourself is the day that you will meet the most important living person! ... Why, the most important living person is you..." Napoleon Hill & W Clement Stone*

PMA grabbed me by the jugular many years ago, in a direct sales conference.

Of course we all know that a positive mental attitude contributes to hope, expectancy, good health, abundance and much more. To me, at that stage in my life, however, it meant aggressive selling tactics and a desire for huge levels of wealth and material goods. Neither appealed overmuch.

The words failed to register their true message with me simply because I was associating them with a lifestyle I did not aspire to. Being positive in a bullish kind of way seemed to ride roughshod over everyone else - or so I thought at that time.

To have a positive mental attitude is much more than setting goals and targets. It is a way of life. Having a positive mental attitude means trying to find the silver lining even if your life is a pea-souper. It

PART 3: UNLIMITING YOUR MIND

means forgiving your enemies - certainly not wasting any energy on trying to get even. It means accepting others, because you will not be able to change them. It means changing your attitudes and perspectives because the change in yourself WILL result in a different reaction. which may ultimately effect what you want for the better.

> *"Annual income twenty pounds, annual expenditure nineteen nineteen six, result happiness..." Mr Micawber/DavidCopperfield*
>
> *
>
> *"The definition of happiness of the Greeks... is full use of your powers along lines of excellence." John Fitzgerald Kennedy*

Happiness is not just an EQ qualifier. It is also a sign of spiritual awareness. We do not have to walk around like grinning minnies to be happy. Eric Hoffer said that if we had certainty we would be "impervious to fear". Possibly. Happiness comes from believing in your own certainty.

> *"Optimistic people are successes not only because they see themselves as problem solvers but also because their minds hold an arsenal of alternatives." Alan Loy McGinnis*[77]

The "science of wellbeing" is taken very seriously by scientists. Happy people are more popular, more successful and healthier, according to research. So what is the secret of this happiness?

Many psychologists and sociologists[78] believe that people are born happy, that it is in our genes. Yet others have flown the flag for marriage, family and friends, voluntary work and faith. Intelligence and financial security, as well as beauty and health are also excellent reasons for happiness, or maybe even to create it.

---

[77] The Power of Optimism: Alan Loy McGinnis
[78] Journal of Happiness Studies: ed Prof Ruut Veenhoven

PROFIT FROM UNLIMITED THINKING

Professor Martin Seligman, [79] a leading figure in the field of theorising happiness, posits that there are three kinds of happiness: having a pleasant life, or a good life or a meaningful life.

So-called 'mid'-life crises are happening much earlier as happiness eludes. Many careers may be lucrative and glamorous, but they frequently extract their pound of flesh. Increasing income does not generally produce a corresponding rise in wellbeing despite the obvious material advantages.

So, happiness is relative. Happiness is generally experienced from moment to moment, rather than as a continuous unlimited sensation. But it is possible to expand and increase those moments. The mind and body can be taught good and bad response mechanisms.

Learning how the mind works and where we fit into the bigger mindset will help us to re-pattern our thoughts and thus our mind, to be happy more often. We have to learn to be in control of the inner parts that release the flow of feel-good chemicals – and it can be as simple as telling ourselves that we are in control.

We are in control of our lives, and our happiness, when we discover what pleases us, what makes our hearts "leap for joy".[80] Quite a few of us know what these heart-leaps are. But the battle with monthly bills usually ensures that we shove them back where they come from. When we re-discover them, the circumstances are not always conducive to immediate action.

One of my heart-leaps came late at night, sitting in a freezing Canadian airport lounge. When I read Kehoe, I was a cold and unhappy bunny, but I did make a note to do something proactive as soon as I

---

[79] www.authentichappiness.com
[80] The Practice of Happiness: John Kehoe

PART 3: UNLIMITING YOUR MIND

returned home. That simple action was an acknowledgment to the source of the heart-leap that I would be following up all leads; that I would be finding a way to "follow my bliss" at some time. By indicating this plan of action, although aimed at an unquantifiable point in time, I had foiled the use-it-or-lose-it mindset.

> *"SQ is the necessary foundation for the effective functioning of both IQ and EQ. It is our ultimate intelligence." Danah Zohar and Ian Marshall*

According to Robert Holden, "Happiness is not in things; it is in you. Happiness is your inner light that has no "off" switch." [81] The inner light could be another way of describing our spiritual intelligence or SQ.

Zohar and Marshall state that SQ gives us the ability to discriminate, our moral sense. It allows us to be creative and to "envision unrealised possibilities".

Those with high levels of spiritual intelligence want to use their talents to help the wider world. They have a higher vision and want others to share it as well. The rest of us find it a struggle helping ourselves. We generally live our lives by a fine moral code, but things get in the way of bigger deeds, if indeed we feel any inner prompts.

If you are reading this, chances are you have been feeling the odd prod or two from your higher nature. While you may not want to start a new world religion, or become a statesman, you may want to take a more active part in your local world. You may want to "stand up and be counted".

In Part 5, I will show you how to discover and nurture the source of your true spiritual intelligence, and find out how to step up to the plate.

---

[81] Shift Happens!: Robert Holden

T+E+V=M

Most of us are familiar with the old verité of positive thinking. But how many of us have a quality thought, and then try and chase it into conscious reality? In our impatience to speed the process, that luminous affirmation darkens, and, quite often, manifests just the reverse.

> *"Man is made or unmade by himself; in the armory of thought he forges the weapons by which he destroys himself.." James Allen[82]*

Thoughts take form on an invisible plane. So we need to understand what makes a thought, and its life cycle, in order to better handle those inevitable moments of invisibility. Thoughts plus energy plus vibrating equals manifestation or T+E+V=M. Work with me on this. After all, this book is about unlimited thinking!

Everything in this universe is composed of subatomic particles, all vibrating or resonating at various frequencies. That includes you and me. All sentient beings have their own individual tune or 'divine melody'. We can either resonate up, to a more refined dimension, or down to mass mind and below. Where there is similar resonance, we attract, and become part of that larger mass. And all with the vibration of our thoughts and senses.

A Dr Luca Turin believes that hearing, sight and smell are also 'vibrationary senses' and that they too have vibrationary[83] frequencies. What this means in practical terms is that what we speak, or listen too, or see, all add to, or detract from, our inner, personal frequency. The thoughtforms we then attract are drawn to these accumulated frequencies.

---

[82] As A Man Thinketh: James Allen
[83] also referred to as vibrational or vibratory

PART 3: UNLIMITING YOUR MIND

> *"If you were to be suddenly handed an enormous sum of money without adequate preparation, the vibration of the money would be out of balance with your vibration. "Sanaya Roman & Duane Packer[84]*

Some years ago, I affirmed for abundant wealth. "As above" happened quite quickly for me. I felt an enormous weight flow around me, which I instinctively knew was great wealth. I haven't the faintest idea how it would have manifested for me, but I had a sure sense that it was around me, ready to be realised. Except I could not bear it. I actually knelt down and prayed for it to go! All the more inexplicable as my house was being pulled away from me by the recession, and my debts were piling high. I seemed then to prefer the trauma of severe financial loss to the unacceptable weight of huge wealth.

This is not so unusual. Many people make millions for others, yet get by on substantially less. They enjoy the pleasures of abundance, but at arm's length.

These days, while more open and ready, I am constantly aware of the responsibilities that are indubitably attached to largesse.

> *"The choices we make in thought, word and deed inevitably return to us in kind." Taro Gold*

Thoughts are continuously vibrating in some unsensed dimension, each with its own energy pattern, waiting to be attracted into our reality. When we resonate in co-operation with a thought's wavelength, we attract its essence to ourselves, for better or worse. We have tuned into that particular vibrational frequency, which for want of a better description, is a thoughtform.

Visualising and affirming power up the energy of a thoughtform. A million people thinking of peace

---

[84] Creating Money: Sanaya Roman & Duane Packer

will add enormous power to the vibrational frequency of a thoughtform for peace, for example. Whether we achieve peace would be dependent on how many people equally preferred the chaos and disorder that brings them personal power and wealth. A thoughtform could almost be said to be a heavenly see-saw, forever seeking perfect balance; its frequencies in blissful repose. Except for we constantly demanding sentient beings!

Thoughts may be invisible and intangible, but their vibrational frequencies are nonetheless still making their presence felt. Sensitive people can be particularly affected, and many avoid large gatherings. Writers, musicians, scientists, philosophers and artists usually prefer seclusion in order to be inspired.

We all post thoughtforms, as well as receive them, every minute and every second of the day. Daydreaming posts thoughtforms up there too. Where else do ideas come from? There is a whole dimension of thoughts, good and bad, being powered or defused, all the time.

Some years back there was a big rumpus over the copyright of Shirley Valentine. A tale with a similar plotline and characters had been written across the pond but came to light only with the huge success of the eponymous film. Was this plagiarism, or was it two creative minds tuned into the same plotline frequency?

We are interconnected. Of course we will share ideas and views if we are resonating at similar levels, with similar outlooks. In that particular instance, they were both writers working in a similar genre, in the western world. It is how we flavour and colour our presentation that provides its unique perspective, not a string of words in the same sequence, and certainly not a plot.

Interconnectedness works with all of life. Some limited minds need science to prove something before they will accept it as fact. And that's a fact! Well, science has affirmed that animals and plant life can transfer or transmit information to their fellow life groups. Monkeys have been shown to pass on newly-acquired skills, such as washing food in sea water to improve its taste, to fellow monkeys on another island. There are many more confirmations of the interconnected resonance of species. Rupert Sheldrake calls it morphic resonance.[85]

While we may have been born with a personal vibration, the circumstances of life, plus our individual actions and thoughts, can and do change it, resulting in what we manifest - and how. Fear, for example is a lower vibration. If there is an innate fear within the core of your being, which you may not be consciously aware of, then that will be your predominant vibration. No matter how enthusiastically or positively you may affirm and visualise, if you do not address that core vibration, you will only enjoy limited achievements.

Some people seem to effortlessly manifest success and wealth. They have their core vibration to thank, although that too could change. Greed, for example, would eventually dull the core, attracting adverse experiences.

Philosophers and scientists, and possibly mystics, may get a kick out of pondering the nature of thought and how it manifests. You and I have desires and anxieties, and we want to be able have more of the former and negate the latter. There is an easier way.

---

[85] A New Science of Life: Rupert Sheldrake

> *"And God said, 'Let there be light...'"* Genesis
>
> *
>
> *"One clear, unchanged, and universal light,*
> *Life, force and beauty must to all impart,*
> *At once the source..."* Alexander Pope

In case you had forgotten, Part 3 has been all about unlimiting your mind. We have stepped away from the familiar and ventured into the less commonplace. While for some, many of the topics may be just a fresh slant on something you already know, to others, it is either claptrap, or even worse. If one thing angers our fundamental creed, it is easy to dismiss everything. But despite any provocative elements, my intention has never been to offend.

We can greatly enrich our lives, and indeed our faith, by tapping into higher, unlimited dimensions. This book simply provides tools which are both practical as well as esoteric. Indeed some have been used by the world's greatest scientists, philosophers and mystics.

> *"You fancy this world is permanent of itself And endures because of its own nature, But really it is a ray of light from the Truth And within it the Truth is concealed."* Sa'ad Al-Din Mahmud

What is light? Scientifically-speaking, there are quite a lot of definitions. The one that partially suits my purpose is "electromagnetic radiation capable of inducing visual sensation". In fact, metaphysically-speaking, light is a lot more complex and all-encompassing: light is a component part of realisation or manifestation.

Many years ago, I had an unusual near-death experience. I was not hospitalised, nor was I ill. In fact, I was working on some notes of a home-study course, and felt a little tired. As soon as I lay down, I was asleep. It was about three o'clock in the afternoon. It felt like hours, yet the whole incident took barely twenty minutes.

> *"Angels are waves of energy."* Cynthia Rose Young

In the NDE, I was immediately in the presence of what felt like three beings, although it looked like a very bright light. An enormous loving warmth and wisdom seemed to emanate from these three beings, in one bright light. Much later, I started to call them lumiels (lum from the Latin lumen, meaning light, and el, meaning of God) - and that has now stuck.

They moved aside to reveal a massive, awe-inspiring darkness. In those seconds, I felt a wise fear, as if I was in the presence of an almighty power, that must be treated respectfully. Having said that, from this distance, I would now describe the fleeting scene in more science-fiction type terms: a huge, endless, pulsating, raw - yet intelligent - energy. But there was also this blessed feeling, this love and belonging that was so strong, I wanted to stay.

Resentfully, I awoke. Although I sensed that the lumiels had given me a choice, I felt mildly resentful in making it. It was a resentment borne of a complete confidence that I was totally loved, no matter what. They were completely unjudgmental. Make of that what you will. What is important is the relationship of light and darkness. Light comes from the omnipotent darkness - and that is this element of unlimited thinking.

There is a Taoist[86] contemplative exercise which uses light to create whatever is required. If you are in need of a job or money, health, love - whatever - you simply imagine, or tell yourself, that the light entering your head IS the job, money and so forth.

---

[86] Burn Disease Out Of Your Body: Stephen T Chang/Richard C Miller

PROFIT FROM UNLIMITED THINKING

The light can be sun or moonlight. It could be the light of a candle or the North Star. According to Chang "It is unimportant that you are using only your imagination to practice this exercise - it works." Chang says that by facing the North Star as you practice the exercise, it will be easier for your body to receive the electromagnetic energy flowing from the star. It brings a whole new meaning to wishing on a star!

If you really want to "see" the light, borrow some of the imagery from the film 'Ghost'. Mentally see yourself capturing the stream of light particles, not your spirit moving up with them! You are here to stay and do something useful with your life, which of course is why you are reading this book.

An interesting result of doing this exercise is discovering if you are out of balance, or if there is a blockage stopping you from receiving. Once again, use the light to clear it. As for re-balancing, Betty Shine, the medium, used to physically shift the light, or aura, around herself if she felt out of balance. She would smooth down the space around her head, arms and body, juggling the invisible, unsensed energy, till she felt better aligned.

We turn on the light when we want to feel comforted. Angels, the "progeny of light",[87] are generally seen as protectors, comforters and messengers. If my NDE is anything to go by, light illuminates and assists our potentiality. It brings a message of unlimited power. Only we can complete the transition.

TASKS

!How would you define intelligence?
!What time do you give to your spiritual life?
!Do you have to work at being positive? If so, how?
!What have you ever felt fearful about?

---

[87] John Milton

PART 3: UNLIMITING YOUR MIND

!What did you do to overcome it?
!What do you think is your primary vibration?
!Is it reflected in the circumstances and people in your life?
!Keep a thought-diet log for a day
!Do your thoughts reflect what you think is your primary vibration?
!What would you use the light exercise for today?

PART 4 - MANAGING CHANGE

> *"One must have chaos in one's self in order to give birth to a dancing star"* Nietzsche
>
> *
>
> *"Within you is a limitless, unborn potential of creativity and substance, and the present experience can be your great opportunity to give birth to it. Thus, if you will, the tragedy can become a blessing, the disadvantage can become an advantage, the failure an opportunity.£"* Eric Butterworth
>
> *
>
> *"A certain amount of opposition is of great help... Kites rise against, not with the wind."* John Neal
>
> *
>
> *"Prosperity is a great teacher; adversity a greater."* William Hazlitt
>
> *
>
> *"There is no excellence without difficulty."* Ovid

THINGS HAPPEN

For most of us, seeking our bliss can definitely be a bit like walking a tightrope, frightening and not without perils. But the end results will be worth it. Both the poet and the philosopher more or less state that adverse conditions are a pre-requisite for reaching the heights.

Stretching your mind from its boundaries, whether through using a coach or even reading a book, will inevitably have some form of impact on your life. If you share your life with others, then they will have to make choices to expand with you - or not.

Whatever goals we set, they invariably trigger changes. The depth and chaos involved are generally in ratio to the end result, and to the factors involved, including spouse, children, family. To lose weight involves changing eating patterns, taking time out to exercise regularly, and to join a support network. Success or failure can hang on whether there is a supportive family. Their eating patterns may have to mirror yours. Your spouse may not like your "self-centredness" and the upsets to his or her status quo.

Becoming self-employed, and giving up a regular, reliable income might create discord if you are married. If you are single, the same situation might remove the social atmosphere of the office. Pursuing an artist's life may seem romantic, but he or she still has to be fed and sheltered.

Change, though ultimately rewarding, can be both extremely stressful and deeply frustrating. Self-belief has provided the fuel for the change. But, unfortunately, no matter how unlimited we may be in our thinking, we cannot control all the circumstances that accompany the process of change.

We cannot alter change. Change is a constant fact of life. But then so too is learning to adapt to it. We may not be able to control it, but we can manage our responses to it. Admittedly, the task is easier if we have purposely set the cycle in motion ourselves. Others involved, intentionally or otherwise, may not feel quite as enthused to start with - or ever. How we adapt, and react to change, can provide us with an exciting, fulfilling, meaningful life. Our emotions and character during moments of change will also affect, positively and negatively, those around us. So we need to make sure we adopt the right attitudes from the start. We need to be aware of possible fallout if others, understandably, prefer to stay as they are.

> "We cannot remain consistent with the world save by growing inconsistent with our past selves." Havelock Ellis
>
> *
>
> "All changes, even the most longed for, have their melancholy; for what we leave behind us is a part of ourselves; we must die to one life before we can enter into another!" Anatole France

Try not to resist any changes. See them as unlimited opportunities, with you firmly in control, and you will profit from them in some way. That is a given. We may not be in control of a redundancy notice, but we can be in control of how we view our potentiality and what we do with this unexpected opportunity. Shall I stay in the same field? Or should I make a fresh start elsewhere? How about a sabbatical to study new skills? Shall I fill some of my spare time with some voluntary work?

If change has been seemingly forced onto you, through negative aspects like ill health, divorce or death, your pit may well be a little deeper to climb out of. But you will, and you will build excellent spiritual muscles while you are at it. More than most, you will have to set down all the elements involved in your particular situation and set manageable action plans.

Once you have itemised and assessed your plans, you must make a decision and then act on it. You may even have to make series of parallel decisions.

If the pit really is horrendous and dark, you may have to ask yourself some more searching questions. Start with:

what is the problem or situation?
what caused it?
is there a solution in the problem
what would be the ideal solution?
or a realistic one?
do I have a fallback solution?

PART 4: MANAGING CHANGE

Even for deep matters of the heart, these same, rather antiseptic questions can turn up valuable answers.

Many years ago, I prayed for my soulmate. A soulmate to the Big E does not necessarily mean the same thing to you and me. Evidently, I needed someone, with time and space connections, to herald a spiritual sea-change. It certainly did that. I was on an emotional and financial roller-coaster for about nine years, well after the so-called soulmate was even less than a dim memory! What kept me going was an instinctive need to find the positive in the situation, since the person evidently was not.

At the time, it felt like physical death and indeed there probably was a spiritual death in order to "resurrect" so to speak. Any flippancy now, by the way, is contradicted by my journals of the time. However, these things pass, and with their passing comes inner strength and deep spiritual insight. I feel that even an atheist would be intrigued by that!

> *"Chaos often breeds life, when order breeds habit."* Henry Adams

Unlimited thinking, without a single doubt, heralds change. Since we cannot generally avoid change, then why not at least pre-empt it with unlimited thinking? Pre-emptive change is easier to feel in control of. However, the more self-aware you are the better you will feel, and the better you will cope with change.

If you have been creating your own exercises around the themes and topics in the earlier parts of Profit From Unlimited Thinking, you should, by now, have a very good sense of self-awareness.

> *"Nothing in the world can take the place of Persistence.*
> *Talent will not;*
> *Nothing is more common than unsuccessful men with talent.*
> *Genius will not; unrewarded genius is almost a proverb.*
> *Education will not; the world if full of educated derelicts.*
> *Persistence and Determination alone are omnipotent." Anon*

I am not sure who said the poem at the start of this section. I have credited it to the ubiquitous Anon. It was Adam Faith's favourite aphorism, and he needed it more than most as his fortunes soared and swooped, then soared and fell again. He never forgot though that the key was perseverance.

The positive attitude of perseverance ensures that when success inevitably comes, it will be all the sweeter and more abundant. J K Rowling is a perfect example of this. She may not have envisaged multi-millions in the bank, but she did persist, and she believed in herself and her talents.

Spencer Johnson[1] uses mice in his parable of coping with change, where ultimately an individual's attitude dictates whether he or she will grab an opportunity, or be lost and disillusioned in the process.

Apart from perseverance, some other primary attitudes are courage, humour, determination, compassion and forgiveness. If you bear a grudge against your employers for handing out that redundancy notice, you will be stopping fresh opportunities from coming your way.

Another key attitude is to discover your enthusiasm. Even in tough times, if you have something you are enthusiastic about, it can be not only a beacon of support, it can guide you towards your true potential.

---

[1] Who Moved My Cheese: Spencer Johnson

PART 4: MANAGING CHANGE

> *"What a day may bring a day may take away."* Thomas Fuller MD

Courage is a primary attitude which we discover by accident - sometimes in both senses of the word. Incidents on the journey, for some of us, are not always easy to accept. Things happen which aren't always pleasant, and certainly not pre-empted. Courage provides extraordinary willpower and strength.

I can categorically state that I was less than happy with my God for a bad car crash which, after two general anaesthetics, left me with broken bones and bad scarring in my left hand – as if I didn't have enough imperfections already! However, as Catherine, my lovely neighbour pointed out, I would not have otherwise met so many different people or experienced another side of life. People also wanted to give, and I had to learn to receive.

We can shape our attitude thus by believing that this change – good, bad or indifferent – is going to result in something better. A good change is marriage, or maybe having a baby. It should be pleasant, but what of those sleepless nights? (That's the baby, not the new husband..!) And, that change is usually forever. The new child brings a whole series of other changes... as indeed does a new husband.

One secret to handling change is to address what you have in front of you. Manage effectively what you are currently experiencing. Another way is to create mental images of the results you would like to see - and then focus on them.

There is also a school of thought that believes that all change is good. Pedantically, I believe that the results of the change are good, not the change itself. Heather Mills McCartney may well have found spectacular love and a high-profile value sequentially, through the loss of a limb. But the loss itself was not good, no matter how brave and feisty a person may be.

Sitting on a cloud outlining our next incarnation, we may happily say that for recognition and rewards, we will sacrifice a leg. The earthbound reality, for a time, may well be somewhat different, as our idea of physical beauty rapidly changes and as we go through the pain and discomfort of learning to walk again, and possibly also in learning to deflect pitying glances.

Mills McCartney undoubtedly has a feisty, even abrasive character that thankfully fuelled her progress and positive outlook. From the beginning, she adopted the attitudes of a winner. She used her misfortune to help others, and subsequently has scaled measurable heights in both public service and emotional satisfaction.

Change does lead to better outcomes, but we have to be prepared for some not-so-pleasing and even painful detours on the way.

TASKS

!What episode in your life, if any, has been so dire, you have felt like giving up?
!How did you get the better of it?
!How do you feel about it now?
!Did you make a conscious decision to mentally move on or did time and other experiences simply make the original episode fade into the background?

> *"A person of bourgeois origin goes through life with some expectation of getting what he wants, within reasonable limits. Hence the fact that in times of stress 'educated' people tend to come to the front."* George Orwell
>
> *
>
> *"Stress is the state manifested by a specific syndrome which consists of all the non-specifically inducted changes within a biologic system."* Hans Selye

Stress is a much-abused word. Although stress actually indicates a build-up of energy, not in itself a

PART 4: MANAGING CHANGE

bad thing, its associations have firmly tied it to less than pleasant experiences.

Many long-term employees take days and weeks off, citing stress. What their employers should be doing is identifying the causes of this build-up of pressure and how it can be transmuted. Their jobs may not provide adequate outlet for their talents, for example. They may be bringing their personal problems into the workplace, and might have to adopt flexible working patterns. The effort expended will be rewarded in increased productivity and harmony.

With a stifling compensation culture, it is difficult to currently assess valid stress at work. However, there have been increased reports of bullying bosses and colleagues, increased workloads and the inequities of the work/home balance. Fear of losing a job can not only exacerbate negative stress, it can also be a self-fulfilling prophecy. But stress is a component part of managing change and our ability to use it fruitfully will lead to better and more suitable conditions.

Paradoxically, although stress relates to energy, it can manifest as apathy. It is still a build-up of energy but it is a stagnant mass. While an adrenaline rush is positive, lethargy and mental overload are not. To release or transmute the former would require silence and stillness, while the latter would probably benefit from some sort of physical exercise. Stress often feels like a pressure cooker. We build up a head of steam which, used positively, can be the basis of a very fine dish. Unfortunately, because it rarely feels very pleasant, stress management consultants believe no stress is positive. But then, of course, that is what they are paid to believe.

TASKS
!Do you agree that stress can be positive?
!In what ways do you relieve your stress?
!Do you find you do more when you are stressed?
!Which is more stressful, your home or your working life?

> *"All the adversity I've had in my life, all my troubles and obstacles, have strengthened me. You may not realise it when it happens, but a kick in the teeth may be the best thing in the world for you." Walt Disney*

Pressure is an ideal marker for assessing your limitations. Pressure also works differently for each person and, often, different trades. Most salespeople, for example, thrive under pressure. Ends of quarters have produced amazing results when bosses have been on the rampage. Journalists frequently produce copy to tight deadlines. One can feel the steam building, and equally feel it being released as targets are met and a fresh quarter begins.

Where stress turns negative is when linear targets apply and there is no let up. Doctors suffer negative stress as their fellow human beings expect them to be on constant call. Having a vocation does not mean allowing your needs to be submerged by the aches and pains of others, however serious they may be.

Based on the paradigm of cumulative energy mass, creativity too can also be stressful. A successful playwright once wrote that he felt an enormous physical burden prior to writing. He could not get the words and character analyses down fast enough and they were hanging over him with an almost tangible physical presence. Once they had been recorded, he felt quite lightheaded!

Steam – or stress – has to be released. Steam building on steam produces volcanic effect – and that's not pleasant for anyone. As part of managing change,

PART 4: MANAGING CHANGE

we have to learn to handle the inevitable energy fluctuations that will occur. We should be conscious of our pressure levels and create time in our busy lives to re-balance them.

Having a support structure, who can be good sounding boards, is vital. They do not necessarily have to be your family or friends. I have often had spontaneous and useful conversations with total strangers. As there is no risk of preconception or embarrassment, you can be as free as any inhibitions will allow. You may even get valuable advice in return.

> *"The degree and kind of a man's sexuality reach up into the ultimate pinnacle of his spirit."* Nietzsche

The process of change, as well as stress generally, can sometimes play havoc with relationships on a physical level. Men in particular can experience a sexual downturn when business problems are particularly pressing. Accept that your libido may take a brief holiday and ignore those who live by the "use it or lose it" dictum! Your libido will return when the time is right, and your stress levels are contained. If you are with the right partner they will accept that. However, it is important to talk to and take time out with your partner. Relationships are more likely to founder in the desert of silence than of physical restraint.

There is power in stress. The energy of stress can be monitored through the increased growth in our nails and hair when we are under pressure. Adrenalin speeds up our metabolism, heartbeat and even cell growth, although the calibre may not be that special.

Learn to be in control of this stress-energy through breathing techniques and healthy eating. Avoid excess alcohol and caffeine and take regular exercise. Take time out to watch a funny film or read something inspiring.

PROFIT FROM UNLIMITED THINKING

Unlimited thinking is not just about unfettered flights of the imagination. When you hit Planet Earth again, there must be a sound foundation to contain your dreams.

The first point of contact is you, and your ability to capture and build on the thoughts and ideas that come to you. If your energies and thoughts are dispersed, then so too will your dreams be. If you let circumstances and stress dictate anything more than immediate responses, then it is unlikely you will ever achieve any of those hidden desires. However, turn the situation around and use it creatively.

Try not to wallow in the dubious pleasures of stress and chaos. People do! How many people do you know who preface every conversation with a catalogue of their woes or problems at work or home? Or their deteriorating health? Do not be one of them.

At a sales conference I once attended, Robin Fielder advised something along the lines of heartily shaking the hands of the misery, and saying "Excellent", before making a swift departure. Perhaps that might be a bit harsh and lacking in compassion, but he has a point.

If you are aware that you are like this, please do not repress the urge to talk. Just make sure you speak to the right person or persons who are qualified to help. If you are not aware of this unfortunate habit, fast retreating backs will soon make sure you are.

PART 4: MANAGING CHANGE

> *"Bliss in possession will not last"* James Montgomery
>
> *
>
> *"We ...get possessed by our possessions"* Max Lerner
>
> *
>
> *"He that hath nothing is frightened of nothing"* Thomas Fuller MD

Most of us know the aphorism about nature and vacuums, and possibly also Big Daddy's reply[2]. However, there is far more to owning - and clearing - possessions than simply filling or creating a vacuum.

Like humans, possessions also have electro-magnetic frequencies. They also resonate and attract energy. Many possessions have emotional energies locked into their particle structure. A gifted empath can sense personality and history from items of clothing or other personal possessions. In my time, I too have picked up sensations from biros as well as photographs, but did not really enjoy the sensation. All these EMFs are sharing your space with you, whether you are aware or not.

Karen Kingston, an expert in Space Clearing says: "Whenever I meet someone who tells me they are stuck, I know that if I visit their home I will almost always find lots of clutter." However, if an item is too precious, either financially or sentimentally, then try to cleanse it[3] and re-invest it with more progressing and prospering vibrations.

In our homes, we have countless memories and paraphernalia, all with memories and associations. I am not advocating a complete clear-out, unless you plan to live the next phase of your life as a hermit. However, an intelligent dispersal of some of the items can provide a tremendous sense of release - and maybe even a boost to the family income. [4]

---

[2] From Cat On A Hot Tin Roof: Tennessee Williams
[3] Creating Sacred Space with Feng Shui: Karen Kingston
[4] Spirit of the Home: Jane Alexander

Many families keep a room dedicated to a departed child or spouse. The comfort derived from this is both valuable and unquantifiable. Yet, the soul has to move on too. As we cling to the past, we stop their spiritual evolution on another dimension.

Make some time today to see how your possessions and memories may be limiting you and maybe your loved ones.

TASKS

!How do you feel about your possessions?
!Do you hang on to things in case they 'come back into fashion'?
!Do you feel a sense of loss when giving things away?

> *"How use doth breed a habit in a man!"* William Shakespeare
>
> *
>
> *"Habit with him was all the test of truth, 'It must be right: I've done it from my youth."* George Crabbe

We are all, by and large, creatures of habit. If you disagree with that statement, shift your kitchen tools around, or move the lounge furniture, and then check how often you reach for something that has been moved. Or count the times you bump into a chair that has found a new home.

Just as automatically lighting up after eating is a bad habit, waking up each morning speaking a positive mantra would be a good habit to engender. As well as being the skeleton of addiction, habits can be an excellent form of mind discipline. So, how can we make or break a habit?

Mindfulness. [5] Most of the time, we live our lives on auto-pilot. For the best part of each day, our behaviour is totally automatic. Even highly complex

---

[5] Mindfulness: Ellen J Langer

PART 4: MANAGING CHANGE

actions like driving a car are completed with virtually no conscious awareness.

A task repeated over and over again is soon learned and moved out of the conscious state. Listening to the radio while driving is a classic example.

It can take from thirty to forty days before "change" becomes a "habit" – and that includes avoiding the moved chair. The easiest way to break a habit, is to replace it with another. For example, if you wish to give up smoking, replace the post-prandial cigarette with a glass of water. Sip it slowly, making each sip a physical affirmation of intent.

In this case, "avoiding the moved chair" would be sitting in a non-smoking area, asking smoker friends not to offer you one of theirs or creating a reward scheme with your cigarette money. For example, two packs equals a new CD or DVD, twenty packs equals a new shirt or dress. If you are feeling particularly confident, you could create a special holiday.

If you have inner habits, like worry, fear and doubt, then you will need a habit-buster before you can replace them. Your fears may be entirely valid, or a warning signal to do something constructive. If you are on a subsistence wage, then it is normal to feel worries about your income. However, a habit-buster would start by identifying whether you have a closed mind towards your current source of income, whether you could take another job or change your current job.

A habit-buster would identify whether you are able to receive more. Worry, fear and doubt, and also guilt, usually stop the process of receiving and that includes inspiration and guidance. The new habit would be to allow your mind to find alternative solutions to your income problem.

Once there is mental consensus, the new habit would include affirmations as well as more practical activity such as budgeting, holding car boot sales to clear clutter and gain some income, and also getting another job. Even if you are stuck at home, there is always something more you can do to bring in extra cash.

Many people have developed the habit of running several jobs simultaneously. Some years ago, I had three and thought nothing of it. I needed the money and one job alone simply did not provide it. However, my three jobs kept me interested enough to ensure my energy or enthusiasm never flagged. I also had developed the habit of seeing the bigger picture, which in this case was a required income. In time, I found one job providing that same income and more, but I had broken through the barriers to receive.

Monday mornings are a bad habit for some people. Instead of being thankful for a way of making a valuable contribution, Mondays are now 'moan' day with a significant rise in the number of heart attacks and other stress-related diseases. If you feel tense and irritable because of your job, you are either in the wrong job or the right job but the wrong place. Your habit-buster should be to see the good in your current situation first before you can go on to change it. The Law of Crummy Returns will invariably bring you more of the same in another position if you do not.

Change could involve part-time or flexible working or getting a transfer to a more amenable location. It could involve increasing your skills by taking further education or going on a management programme. Your boss may even fund you if it makes life easier for him or her.

Habits can be so ingrained we do not even notice them. Even our family and friends accept them as being part of us, as we do their tweaks and twitches.

PART 4: MANAGING CHANGE

If you are unsure of your habits, keeping a diary log might help to identify them.

Without knowledge of them, how can you change them? If you are feeling particularly bold, ask someone you value to help you. The effort will eventually be well-rewarded.

Once a particular habit has been identified, we can start to replace them in various ways with more favourable ones. Universal habits, which I hope we all share, such as cleaning our teeth and washing our hands, are ideal mechanisms for conjunctive affirmation.

Try using the shower to wash away negativity or even to feel positive energies flowing down on you. I prefer the latter and feel enormously lifted despite my non-power shower!

Change the internal mantra that goes with your morning coffee, or the traffic jams to and from work. And if you do not know by now what it may be, then you should return to the section on keeping a personal journal!

Probably the best regular activities to ally with positive mental thought-building are those we generally dislike. Cleaning, washing dishes and dusting rate up the scale with me of annoying tasks, simply because there is no end to them. Weeding and shopping come close. Yet, when I spruce up even a small section at a time, there truly is a clean energy that gives impetus to other work or personal creativity. Because of the time involved, I gave up on mowing the lawn and created a zen garden instead. Now, even the weeds have a sort of isolated green beauty in a sea of pink gravel. Habit-busting can take all forms with unexpected delights in return.

As you start to stretch your creative processes in culling and replacing your habits, a strangely marvellous thing will begin to happen. Even as you begin to knock on the door marked "creative possibilities", ideas will pop into your mind. Please do not dismiss them. They may not relate to your immediate crisis, but they will eventually play a part in your unlimited evolution.

> *"No problem of human destiny is beyond human beings."* John F Kennedy
>
> *
>
> *"Probable impossibilities are to be preferred to improbable possibilities."* Aristotle

It is said that the seeds to a solution lie in the actual problem itself. Not much help if the problem has landed you deep in manure of course. You might have to just trust that those seeds are doing something worthwhile, unseen - and wait for a first sighting of green shoots. Alternatively, dragging the metaphor a little further, one could search for the seeds first and then plant them more knowledgeably. For example, you may be hanging on to your job by the thinnest of threads. It would be easy to blame a short-sighted management team, as indeed I have before now! How could they have not seen my potential? Why do they just want to pigeonhole me in this task, when I am capable of doing that one? That sort of thing.

Track back and ask yourself a number of searching questions, from your viewpoint, and from those of the management team. If you have taken the job just to pay the bills, then you will constantly have issues of "fitness to the task", no matter how experienced and skilled you are.

The seeds of the solution lie in finding a close fit, and you ought to be able to do your sowing while still in PAYE situ. Enough of gardens, weeds and seeds! Whether in the home or at work, you can develop good habits for problem-solving.

PART 4: MANAGING CHANGE

A major metaphysical law is to think of what you DO want, and not what you do NOT - because we tend to create what we focus on. However, for accurate problem-solving, we do need to clearly identify the components of what we perceive is the problem.

First of all, clear your mind of everything except those elements relating to the immediate issue. List each element in the order of its emotional importance. Remember, emotion fuels effects, therefore, you will want to make sure the effects are moving in the right direction. As an example, you may have an income crisis. You may also have emotional issues to address. Is the emotional issue the source of your income - either a job that distresses you or a spouse? Or is the partner getting in the way of your own income creation? Be clear about the parameters before attempting to solve the problem.

Affairs of the heart can cause unbelievably crazy actions and reactions. Believe me, I have been there and am still shocked that the results reverberated for so long and so many years, simply because I did not address each element with enough tight discipline. But then who does, when the physical pain of thwarted love blocks out common sense?

Self-love, through self-respect, can also come a cropper in our working environment. How many colleagues do you know who have taken redundancy or dismissal very sorely, and then spent months in retributive action? Pursuing vengeance in any sphere of activity is not problem-solving, and you may miss opportunities through your blinkered obsession.

Of course, not all problems are earth-shifting. However, even relatively straightforward ones can seem dire if there are a number of elements involved: end of work targets, awful boss, sick child, unhelpful partner or no partner at all...

PROFIT FROM UNLIMITED THINKING

If a problem arises, make sure you have all the facts - then address the most important element immediately. Be organised. Delegate if you can. Use a support network - and if you do not have one, then make that a goal to start or join one.

Be enthusiastic. It is much easier to wallow but if you can summon up the genie of enthusiasm, despite yourself, you will find the situation turning in your favour. That is a promise!

Problems are opportunities to our feistier, more confident, colleagues. Small problems usually herald inevitable bigger change waiting in the wings, so far better to turn a small problem into an opportunity than wait for a big challenge. Too often, we ignore them and then have a big problem to address instead. Either way, they are really prompts to take creative action, not reaction.

Problems and disappointments should nurture our drive and ambition. If we turn over each problem to our unlimited minds as a challenge, we will find the effects will be altogether more fulfilling and sustainable in time.

> *"If a soldier or labourer complains of the hardship of his lot, set him to do nothing."* Blaise Pascal
>
> *
>
> *"Arrears of small things to be attended to, if allowed to accumulate, worry and depress like unpaid debts...If we attend continually and promptly to the little that we can do, we shall ere long be surprised to find how little remains that we cannot do."* Samuel Butler

To manage change effectively, plan effectively. Plan every day. Complete your daily plan before you go to sleep so that your subconscious can be working overnight on your behalf. You will wake up motivated and inspired. Instead of spending half the day working out what you want to do, you will be focused and energised on particular tasks and actions.

PART 4: MANAGING CHANGE

Results come in stages. Use your personal journal to log them down, or create a special success diary. Success for most of us comes through taking small steps which build the correct foundations. Don't expect to log down securing that big contract the day after making your first visit, though stranger things have happened!

Goals give clarity. They help define and flesh out desires with detail and required actions. With goals, you know what you want, and what you need to do to achieve them. But goals cannot provide mental discipline.

There will be times when you wonder why you are following a particular route, especially when it is full of twists and turns. Try reading about someone who has been through similar challenges. Let them be your guiding light if necessary.

Very few people have achieved their goals that easily. You are not jerry-building; you are building the means for your desired life and that takes some effort, especially if several elements are involved.

Those who do appear to achieve rapid fame and fortune, with no firm foundations, invariably see it all turn to dust not long afterwards. While we may have unlimited powers, as humans, we generally operate within a limited framework.

In unlimited thinking, there is no such thing as being lucky. "Luck is where opportunity meets the prepared mind". Jung called it synchronicity. As we expand our minds through unlimited desires, keep our thoughts generally positive, and persevere with our goal action plans, we will resonate with people and events that appear to make us lucky.

Dr Richard Wiseman's research in The Luck Factor showed that lucky people created their own good luck from having a positive mental attitude. He reckons there are four principles to being lucky.

PROFIT FROM UNLIMITED THINKING

Lucky people follow up opportunities. They listen to their gut feelings. They expect good fortune and they make something good out of a bad experience. Although we cannot alter the reality of constant change, we can learn to manage our response to it. Change is a fact of life and the ability to turn chaos into order will be one of your greatest assets. By looking at change as an opportunity, your attitude is already proclaiming that you are open and more than capable of being and doing anything you want to be or do.

Seek out kindred spirits. They will help you to keep the dream alive. Families and close friends rarely offer the level of support you will require if it forces them out of their own comfort zones. But no man is an island to quote the poet.

Take advantage of the many Internet-based networks that are springing up. Develop and maintain your own network and support team. And remember to take time to nurture your spiritual self. There is an invisible support team longing to be asked!

Learn, and make it a priority to keep learning. Mental care is vital and there is no better way of feeding the mind than through learning. That in turn will help to keep change within manageable proportions.

Keep your mind focused on where you are going, and not on past mistakes, or even past glories. If you can manage all of that, then you are definitely in control of your change management.

TASKS

!Review the earlier sections in Part 4
!Create your own set of Tasks
!Describe where you are now in terms of self-awareness

KEEPING TABS ON YOUR THOUGHTS

> *"You Can't Afford the Luxury of a Negative Thought"* John-Roger and Peter McWilliams
>
> *
>
> *"If you could read my mind, what a tale my thoughts would tell..."* Gordon Lightfoot

If our thoughts could be heard we'd be very shocked indeed. Even without big issues like politics and religion, we unconsciously meander from one thought to another, as our inner computer registers and processes everything that passes through its wavelengths.

It's said that the mind can only hold one thought at a time. This may be true of the conscious mind. The subconscious or unconscious mind, by contrast, has multiple thoughts and reactions perpetually beeping in and out like electricity signals at the National Grid.

We would be driven to distraction if we were consciously aware of all of these thoughts. However, some persist - and increase in frequency: where am I going to insert that newspaper article to the left of my laptop; there is bright light streaming through the window on the right - I'd rather be outside; is my lunch date going to be a meaningful encounter; I must type like a pianist with raised hands to lift the pressure on the underside of my wrists; sit back, twitch legs to avoid DVT...

Every one of those thoughts, given attention, could take on a "life" of its own. By life, I mean other inter-related thoughts would attract and attach to it. With DVT, there is the issue of air travel and now sitting in traffic jams. Traffic jams could then attract thoughts of cars and work - and work pressures and so on.

PROFIT FROM UNLIMITED THINKING

These thoughts can be endless, looping, evanescent, monotonous. However, they are generally just friendly signals to and from our subconscious minds, to take action or remember something.

There are even more that we will rarely discover, signalling body and brain functionality. Meditation does at least slow them down so that the inside of your head does not resemble Piccadilly Circus in high season!

The thoughts we are conscious of are the ones we should be paying close attention to. If I am conscious of the need to move my legs, I must not ignore it. I must get up and walk around. If I am conscious of the need to raise my hands, I must do so. Failure to comply will only result in sore wrists.

Our self-conversation is affected by our moods and our current world view. Read the newspapers too much, and the self-conversation is frequently liable to be gloomy or mundane in the extreme. How many thoughts are wasted on fictitious soap characters?

We have a re-run in our heads, long after the programme is over. Then there is another try-out before discussing it over lunch with friends. The gossip columns continue the theme, and soon our wonderful unlimited minds have been looped into endless maunderings about, well, not very much at all!

> *"Conscience: the inner voice which warns us that someone may be looking." H L Mencken*
>
> *
>
> *"The voice of the intellect is a soft one, but it does not rest till it has gained a hearing." Freud*

Contrary to what the men in white coats may think, it is not madness to sense voices.

Hearing is a sense, but thankfully very few of us actually hears another voice. What we "hear" are aspects of our own personality. These inner voices are

PART 4: MANAGING CHANGE

dramatis personae of our own life script – the joker, the critic, the judge, the flirt, the fearful and wimpish, the angry, the lusty and so forth.

Most people talk out loud to themselves. Although this habit is exacerbated if you live alone, even people living with another, mumble away, having imaginary conversations with themselves. Madness presumably is when the conversation becomes "real". A mumble and grumble is an acceptable form of sane self-conversation.

Self-conversation, or self-talk, [6] though, is not just thinking aloud. Self-conversation is the patterns of thoughts and views that have coloured your life so far and will continue to do so, unless you choose to change them.

Make a habit of self-observation. By watching what you think, you will in time be aware that every event in your life has been manifested through some thought or belief. Paradoxically, this can bring a sense of control and should be a welcome task.

Thoughts, or unconscious self-conversation, repeated over and over again become a belief. That belief, in turn, will become a reality. Only by understanding our thoughts and beliefs can we begin to change them.

Since our self-image is coloured by our thoughts and beliefs, this is a major exercise to undertake. In his perennial bestseller, Dr Maxwell Maltz, a plastic surgeon, wrote[7] that unless the scarring within was healed, then physically changing one's appearance would have minimal effect.

---

[6] What To Say When You Talk To Yourself: Shad Helmstetter
[7] Psycho-Cybernetics: Dr Maxwell Maltz

> *"Because people who 'talk to themselves' are thought to be crazy, nearly everyone has an injuction against listening to the voices in his head."* Eric Berne

If you keep in mind that your voices are just aspects of yourself, then it will be much easier to listen to your inner dialogues. They are there to guide and protect after all - even the voices of worry and fear. For the vast majority, they are not some demon about to take possession of your soul. That said, a demon voice is the ability within each of us to receive darker signals. By letting mental dialogues come to the surface, you will soon learn to distinguish the prospering from the detrimental, with sufficient warning for replacement therapy.

A demon voice can be, for example, an obsession with internet porn. What may start out as prurient curiosity could be nipped in the bud if healthy mental dialogue is also allowed a hearing. If the former signals are much stronger, then I hugely doubt that you will be reading this book!

Unlimited thinkers have learned to keep their minds healthily curious. Unlimited thinkers have learned how to use self-conversation to build mental discipline, because curiosity can be a temptation.

Self-conversation can and should be used to help in changing habits. A little self-conversation is invaluable in developing the habit of positive thinking, for example. You can tell the voice of doubt to go away because you are doing the right things. If it hits back with more fears and doubts, you can talk it down again either through affirmations or revisiting a past success, or remind it of your action plans.

The self-conversation in this section is concerned with thought awareness and replacement. It

PART 4: MANAGING CHANGE

is not Tevye[8] talking to his God - which we will cover in Part 5.

Changing the way you think and feel about yourself - that is, your self-conversation - can make you attractive without the need to resort to the knife. Audrey Hepburn's image remains one of everlasting beauty. Yet she had to will herself to feel sexier than her curvier peers. She once spoke of standing by the entrance to a party, telling herself that she had more sexual attraction in her nose than the bevies of busty beauties already there. She had already learned the art of positive self-conversation.

TASKS

!Be honest - do you talk to yourself?
!What do you "hear"?
!Are you too busy talking at people and not listening to yourself?

> "One of the things that NLP represents is a way of looking at human learning... it's more appropriate to describe NLP as an educational process. Basically we're developing ways to teach people how to use their own brains." Richard Bandler[9]

Neuro-Linguistic Programming[10] was a term coined by Richard Bandler and John Grinder in the 70s as, he says in the quotation above, an educational process. Roughly, it provides a foundation for assessing our subjective experiences, how we take in information, what we find important and how we respond to it. More importantly, it allows us to change any experiences that hamper us in anyway. It achieves this through sensory and linguistic re-programming of perceptions and thoughts.

---

[8] Fiddler on the Roof
[9] Using Your Brain for a Change: Richard Bandler
[10] Richard Bandler & John Grinder: Reframing: NLP and the Transformation of Meaning

PROFIT FROM UNLIMITED THINKING

Although widely used in most fields of personal development and therapy, Bandler himself prefers its wider remit of tasking the brain to expand its functionality. NLP helps to identify beliefs. In theory therefore, it allows us to regain our potential to be in control of change.

NLP is based on very similar premises to mind mechanics, self-hypnosis and visualisation. However, its language is more yang than psychotherapy. It tends to business-science-speak such as "submodalities" and choice of associations, as well as subjective responses to experiences. By veering towards the business framework, it has been accepted much more readily by people who are turned off by New Age-speak or who are nervous of Eastern mysticism.

I would definitely recommend NLP for those of a more pragmatic nature, as esoteric practices, while much more fun and easier to accomplish, do require taking a greater leap of faith.

UNDERSTANDING METAPHYSICAL PRINCIPLES

> *"Many people settle for and actually practice their limitations. They practice them so constantly and for so long a time that the limitations become habits." Norman Vincent Peale*

If the first principle of unlimited thinking means you have to break free from mental limitations of what can be and has been, then it stands to reason that there are some other laws to be aware of.

Socrates wrote of the law of Causality or cause and effect, Emerson of Compensation. In fact I have discovered that there are shedloads of metaphysical principles .... laws of destiny, mind, recording, nature, resonance, affinity, control, concentration and

PART 4: MANAGING CHANGE

correspondence... all no doubt created to back up the message the guru wanted to impart, and why not[11]?

Most humans like breaking laws though. The more there are to break, the more we can start challenging ourselves to create our own laws. How about this lot for a start? The laws of request, attraction, resistance, reflection, projection, attachment, attention, flow, abundance, clarity, intention, prosperity, manifestation, success, balance and polarity, karma, reincarnation, responsibility, discrimination, affirmation, prayer, meditation, challenge, frequency or vibration, miracles, healing, purification, perspective, gratitude, blessings, decree, faith, grace, one - phew![12]

Seriously though, from pre-Socrates to the present day, very few of these metaphysical principles differ over much. They are all valid if they help achieve an objective, and merely present a perspective of wider spiritual truths.

Unsurprisingly, unlimited thinkers also have a few principles to be aware of. They are the Principles of Vibration, Attraction, Imagination, Desire, Flow, Substitution, Balance, Now, Accumulation, Belief, Smiling and Thankfulness.

---

[11] Universal Laws of Success: Brian Tracy
[12] A Little Light on the Spiritual Laws: Diana Cooper

> *"The spiritual dimension is the energetic basis of all life, because it is the energy of spirit which animates the physical framework."* Richard Gerber[13]
>
> *
>
> *"Vibration is the action of thought; it is vibration which reaches out and attracts the material necessary to construct and build."*[14] Charles F Haanel

Scientists agree that all things vibrate at their own unique frequencies. Ancient wisdom states that all things were created through the vibration of sound. What we think and what we speak vibrates throughout the universe, and indeed throughout the time and space continuum.

I have my own particle theory of time and space resonance and intelligence, but we are concerned with this here and now, and how we can discover either our resonant or even core vibration. There is a subtle difference between the terms. The first relates to the frequencies we reflect and project, based on current experiences, emotions and desires. The second, or core vibration, relates to our more profound selves - specifically down to particle level.

If you have been thorough in following up the sections on self-understanding, you will by now have a good perspective on your resonant vibration. By having goals and desires, you will also have identified the vibration of those desires. Do they make you feel lighthearted or heavy and burdened? Angry? Happy? Fearful? Compassionate? The energy of these will either add to or subtract from your core vibration which in turn produces your resonant vibration.

Is it important to know our real core vibration? Unless you choose to live as a hermit mystic, then probably not. Regression therapy has its place where the loop of traumatic experience needs to be

---

[13] Vibrational Medicine: Dr Richard Gerber
[14] The Master Key: Charles F Haanel

PART 4: MANAGING CHANGE

identified and broken. However, the soul is infinite and it would be ill-advised to pursue the past out of curiosity. Therein lies the pursuit of madness.

In The Dice Man, Luke Rhinehart writes that the human personality is legion. Mark 5: 9 writes 'The spirit told him, My name is Legion, there are many of us...' So it is reassuring to hear that when a soul is reborn, the Goddess of Memory blesses us with a clean slate - or at least a dominant personality. Perhaps not so clean, as many inexplicable talents, phobias or instinctive bonds link us back to past conditioning. They are echoes from our core.

For the spiritually-inclined, the Christ light is the dominant personality, a state of ultimate being and demon-chaser par excellence!

The Unlimited Thinker's Principle of Vibration should assume a state of mind synonymous with lightness of being. Past thought patterns can be transmuted or deleted through visualisations and affirmations of the highest kind.

By having a clear vision of what we desire, unfettered by negative associations, we then ensure the right vibratory frequencies to aid manifestation.

This law enables us to develop our inner magnetism. If something crops up en route to Utopia, deal with it. It may be related to past thought patterns or it just may be a necessary experience to build up the correct vibration to match with your chosen desire. You may want to be a high-flyer in the company you have long served, or to get married to your live-in lover. Instead, you are made redundant or are ditched by your partner.

It is quite possible, the energy in those life scenes, while not exactly stagnant, was not sufficiently fresh and freely-flowing to vibrate with the chosen desire. Perversely, the anger, frustration and pain has built up a volcanic power which, correctly directed, can

PROFIT FROM UNLIMITED THINKING

bring exactly the right, high-frequency, conditions for the chosen desire. Vengeance, however tempting, is not correctly directing your power! It is based on fear and hatred, which are low-frequency vibrations.

If you are still fairly cynical about the power of the Principle of Vibration, in an Edgar Cayce Newsletter [#45], there was a piece about the Fauna Institute in the United States. In experiments, they showed how to measure vibrations in bones. Apparently cats purr on the same frequency that heals them – the bones that is. In repeated (unscientific) tests, the purring of cats has helped towards healing sick patients. Nature's ultrasound?

If you are already thinking unlimited, just imagine that every one of the particles that gives you your complete self, has its own individual intelligence and power, its own memory. You are the great processor, controlling and keeping everything together. That should give megalomaniacs something to build on!

Jokes apart, in theory, you should be able to self-heal or even to shape shift and metamorphose. In practise, very few of us are so doggedly single-minded. But it is somehow reassuring to know that we can call on an unlimited ability that is desperately under-utilised.

> *"Without contraries is no progression. Attraction and repulsion, reason and energy, love and hate, are necessary to human existence." William Blake*
>
> *
>
> *"Many people believe that they are attracted by God or by Nature, when they are only repelled by man." William Ralph Inge*
>
> *
>
> *"If man conformed to the divine law, his word would make things instantly." Charles Fillmore*

In straight physics, two likes (poles) create the effect of repulsion. Contrarily, two unlikes (poles)

PART 4: MANAGING CHANGE

attract. A magnetic pole seeks its own. A freely-moving north-seeking pole will always point in a northern direction. The same applies to the south. Clear as mud. But then I am no physicist!

What is metaphysically important is the area of influence around the source of magnetism called the magnetic field. We are the source of our own magnetism, and our magnetic field is influenced by whatever dominating thoughts attract and repel their like on a moment by moment basis, each and every day.

Add these teeming swarms of unconscious thoughts and signals to your core and resonant vibrations, and that is a very busy magnetic field! This field is the basis of your Principle of Attraction.

It is said in eastern philosophies, that this dance of life is just an illusory screenplay, where the characters have been created and projected by ourselves to highlight the need for some form of spiritual learning. The people and experiences around us are projections of our thoughts, fears, prejudices and past conditioning, including mass-mind thoughts.

If we really want to understand what signals we are receiving, giving out or repressing, then there is probably no better echo than the people around us. What we think of them, how we relate to them and how they relate to us, should give us a good view if we are unlimited enough to perceive it.

Sometimes if we are too obtuse to see repetitive behavioural patterns in ourselves, we attract an outside source to act them out in front of us – a friend, a stranger, a colleague or a loved one. The projected behaviour is usually an exaggerated response otherwise we would never notice it. Once we recognise the potential lesson - good or bad - within ourselves, we can choose what to do next.

The act of recognition serves to reduce or enhance our magnetism or attraction. A violently jealous partner, for example, may be an exaggerated projection of very mild possessiveness that nonetheless can reduce our magnetic field. Accepting it calmly in one's self could even free the partner from radical reactions.

Every single atom of our physical bodies has the power and intelligence of a magnet. We are constantly attracting and repelling through our predominant and deeper-seated thoughts. Small wonder there is a book entitled You Can't Afford the Luxury of a Negative Thought... worth the RRP for the title alone!

Thoughts are the fuel for what we magnetise or attract. The first commandment of the Principle of Attraction is to make sure our thoughts are as creative and as positive as the situation will allow. If we think suitable thoughts, hold on to them, charge them with emotion, they will attract their like, and the desired end result, within a given time frame.

> *"...and at each step I experienced that subtle thrill which anyone of imagination must feel when treading hitherto unexplored country.."* Eric Earle Shipton
>
> *
>
> *"It would be a bitter cosmic joke if we destroy ourselves due to atrophy of the imagination."* Martha Ellis Gellhorn
>
> *
>
> *"let us chase our imaginations to the heavens, or to the utmost limits of the universe; we never really advance a step beyond ourselves, nor can we conceive any kind of existence, but those perceptions, which have appeared in that narrow compass."* David Hume

If you are anything like me, your imagination can create such a crescendo of positive expectancy that you fully anticipate results to come with the next morning's post.

PART 4: MANAGING CHANGE

Natural law, however, prevails. Other people are usually involved. Other elements play their part in the gigantic jigsaw puzzle that forms your desire. If you want to be on any best seller lists, you not only have to write your chef d'œuvre, you also have to write a proposal, find an agent and a publisher, get it printed, then distributed - and finally you have to market it!

Of course, none of that guarantees best sellerdom. The Principles of Imagination and Self-Belief have to play their parts too. Where the previous mental image once provided the words, and the energy to capture the words into cohesiveness, new mental images have to be formed and energised, around the essences, or frequencies, of success and acclaim.

Patience and determination are natural supporters of disciplined imagination. The only result of keeping a daily checkout for results is in frequencies plummeting faster than a scalded cat.

The Principle of Imagination works on the premise of step-by-step actions. Fulfil one step, and you are lead on to the next one, and so on and so forth. This generally applies, no matter what your desire may be.

You want a job? Step one, write or tidy your resume, Step two, network, contact agents and jobsites. Maybe even companies directly. Interviews follow. Another step.

At the very beginning, you should have had a mental image of actually being IN the job, which is absolutely correct in terms of visualisation technique. The energy of the image will resonate with ideas and guidance letting us know what to do next. But in our human dimension, it is unlikely that we will step directly from our mental image into the job position without undertaking at least one or two of the steps.

A cynic would probably say there is no law of imagination in play here but a steady follow-through of an action plan. True enough. But we should be chasing our imaginations to the "utmost limits of the universe". The Principle of Imagination exists to stretch our boundaries and capabilities. Too often, we plod through life with mundane dreams when with a little imagination, we can raise our game a little higher.

If we can imagine it, or "conceive it" as the saying goes, then we can receive it. "Fantasy is our unique capacity to give ourselves, through our imagination, everything we desire that is missing in our lives.."[15]

> *"A strong passion for any object will ensure success, for the desire of the end will point out the means."* William Hazlitt
>
> *
>
> *"It is hard to fight against impulsive desire; whatever it wants it will buy at the cost of the soul."* Heraclitus
>
> *
>
> *"Some desire is necessary to keep life in motion..."* Samuel Johnson

The Principle of Desire is a two-pronged fork. On the one hand, desire keeps us alive and moving in the direction of our dreams. On the other, granted wishes very rarely resemble the lightness and brightness they had in our imaginations. Does that mean we should give up on our desires?

Absolutely not. Perhaps if we call it the Principle of Passion then it would take on a finer resonance. Passion is strong enthusiasm. It is deep feeling and eagerness. Passion, correctly directed, can change the world for the better. But it needs Desire to set it on its way in the first place.

The Principle of Desire or Passion finds all of us in one way or another at some time. Desire starts

---

[15] Creative Breakthroughs: Jill Morris PhD

PART 4: MANAGING CHANGE

with small steps. Desire comes from those niggles that can defeat us or provoke us into action.

In Britain, desire for a fairer old age has galvanised the passion of pensioner-power. Eighty-year olds are prepared to go to prison in their desire to make sure their voice is heard. Many more have joined organised protests over wide-ranging issues, where once they might have tut-tutted at the television screen, feet up with hot cocoa in hand.

To brave the elements and test an exhausted body for the sake of principle is passion indeed.

Wayne Dyer writes[16] that an Indian holy man told his devotees that to try to manifest what you want from life without passion is like dressing up a corpse. From the outside, it might look the part, but inside it is dead. "To be dead inside is to be without passion."

Unfortunately, both desire and passion have accumulated bad reputations. Inaccurate interpretations of intuition, or following the wrong line, can lead to darker events. Ultimately, the Principle of Desire is secondary to the Principle of Free Will. Our desires may make us shudder with temptation and pleasure, but Free Will controls the next step.

If it feels good, do it, in the words of Millie Jackson. But our feelings should always take into account the greater whole. After all, feelings are subservient to thoughts. With effort, we can transmute or substitute a feeling through the power of our thoughts.

Unlimited thinking invariably revolves around macrocosm thinking. Good desire also gives one a sense of lightness of being, and that has to be a good yardstick for action.

---

[16] There is a Spiritual Solution to Every Problem: Wayne W Dyer

> *"'Tis sufficient to say, according to the proverb, that here is God's plenty."*
> John Dryden
> *
> *"how bountiful, the hand of Heaven."* William Wordsworth

The Principle of Flow is interesting and challenging. It is something most of us will probably never really sense and yet our language is full of terms partially relating to it.

We might feel flat. Or we need to re-charge our batteries. 'Lighten up', is an everyday expression to chivvy along a gloomy friend. Yet the Principle of Flow is much more than a synonym for electricity.

Flow is the movement and creative abundance of the Universe. We move and flow within this great unsensed Creative Intelligence. It is constantly sending and receiving signals which we process or ignore on a subliminal level. What we receive, or process, is based on our primary frequency. So it is vital to raise it - or lighten up - to get into the correct flow.

We do not stop receiving just because we are in Pauper City or emotionally bereft. We are actually receiving more of what is our predominant vibration - poverty consciousness. To feel alone and unloved is a sign of poverty consciousness as is to feel that you will never find a job. This is not the same as being unemployed, which is a temporary state.

In a similar way, income ebbs and flows and, as long as we can retain a steady concept of wealth consciousness, it will come back in full measure. That is a guarantee. Equally, since the Principle of Flow governs and links everything in the Universe, how can we possibly be alone? By an ironic twist, we are in fact in complete harmony with a million other lonely, sad souls! We are just not aware of it, nor using our innate knowledge to climb out of the dark pit - and, correspondingly, to help each of those other lonely, sad souls as well.

PART 4: MANAGING CHANGE

Since you have taken the trouble to read this far, then you are already half way out of the pit and you can use the Principle of Flow in a more positive, enhanced, manner. Even a small change will start to trigger unseen benefits.

Vacuum-creation is not just about clearing clutter from our cupboards. We have address books which are chock-a-block with names that have passed their sell-by date. We could and should cut a scythe through any one-way relationships - whether in business or in our personal lives.

How else can we create room for the Principle of Flow to provide more and better ones? Those who are meant to be in our lives will stay or come back in. The rest will evaporate into the fog of past tense.

For most of them, a simple delete stroke will do the trick. For others, if the hand of friendship has been rejected, a blunter approach may be called for. Only you can set a value on yourself and increase your Principle of Flow.

If your health is under par, then you will need to use specific tactics to raise your frequency, in parallel with following normal medical advice.

Music therapy, for example, is an excellent lightener provided the lyrics are also upbeat. Many great pop tunes have dire lyrics "I'm losing my favourite game..". Even Tubthumping, [17] the floreo theme tune (for the essence of the chorus, and not as an advocate of alcoholic indulgence!), has one word in the chorus which I always change to "singing my life away". It invariably makes me chuckle, and humour is absolutely the best way to lift your resonance.

Only you can make that change. Not your spouse, nor your coach nor counsellor. The Principle of Flow will work for you only if you become its master.

---

[17] Chumbawamba

PROFIT FROM UNLIMITED THINKING

> *"How do you fight an idea? With another idea."* Massala in Ben Hur
>
> *
>
> *"If I say to you, 'Do not think of the Statue of Liberty', of course, you immediately think of it. If you say, 'I'm not going to think of the Statue of Liberty', that is thinking of it. But now, having thought of it, if you become interested in something else, say, by turning on the radio, you forget all about the Statue of Liberty - this is a case of substitution."* Emmet Fox[18]

Our conscious minds can only hold one thought at a time. The Principle of Substitution is basically 'fighting' or replacing one idea with another, one feeling with another, or one thought with another. By fighting, I do not mean engaging in a mental tussle. That will not work.

If you feel anger, throw its energy into positive action. Start a campaign, write letters. If you are feeling unrequited love, keep a journal and transfer your emotions and passion on to paper. You may even get a best-seller out of it! Sublimate with physical exercise. Cuddle a baby.

Rather than mourn the death of a loved one, focus on all the good times not on the loss. With death, the energy that flowed between you and the loved one has slammed back into your essence. That is why it can feel so crippling and disorientating. You are now carrying this earth energy for both of you.

It is imperative to transmute or release this energy. Use it to build a support network for others. While this may not exactly fit Emmet Fox's instructions, it will provide purpose and fulfilment to your grief.

The Principle of Substitution is primarily about raising our spiritual pitch. If we have negative or potentially destructive thoughts, they will decrease our inner value. What happens within will in time externalise in our everyday life. Or, as the saying goes,

---

[18] Around the Year with Emmet Fox

PART 4: MANAGING CHANGE

"On Earth as it is in Heaven". If we want heaven on earth, then we must make the effort to substitute those unheavenly thoughts.

> *"Every faculty which is a receiver of pleasure has an equal penalty put on its abuse. ... There is always some levelling circumstance that puts down the overbearing, the strong, the rich, the fortunate, substantially on the same ground with all others."* Ralph Waldo Emerson
>
> *
>
> *"Nature's universal balance is another device by which nature maintains a perfect balance of everything that exists throughout the universe..."*
> Napoleon Hill

Have you ever wondered why your life has so many ups and downs? According to spiritual teachers, this is the law of compensation, balance or even karmic retribution in action. As well as operating as a leveller, it is seen as a means for spiritual evolution.

Napoleon Hill[19] believed that nature made it "compulsory" for individuals to experience both the "bitter and the sweet experiences of life". He posited that this compensating device also provided the seeds of the solution. It compensated the individual for any adversity.

According to Hill, there are two kinds of life-affecting circumstances: those seemingly beyond our control and those which are in our control. In the former, 'mental attitude' with a directed reaction is in our powers. With the latter, we are in control, or at least we should be. Our emotions, our personal relationships and views are all elements and circumstances which can take on a different resonance, if we choose to let them. The choice being ours, we thus have control.

But the Principle of Balance is more than just a divine "book-keeping system". We, as spiritual beings, seek balance not from the perspective of our finite

---

[19] You Can Work Your Own Miracles: Napoleon Hill

vision, but from an inner infinite awareness. "All things are connected like blood which unites one family... Man ... is merely a strand. Whatever he does to the web, he does to himself."[20]

And there's the rub. The Principle of Balance may be operating in our lives for no discernible reason: the mother who questions the short life of her child; the clipped-wings of paralysis or mentally altered-dimensions. Compensation comes from learning how to fly in non-traditional ways. Stephen Hawking is but one example. The autistic artist Steven Wiltshire is another.

The Principle of Acceptance invariably operates with the Principle of Balance. Acceptance does not mean giving up. It means not berating one's apparent bad fortune. It means using the current status as a starting point instead of incessantly digging back, looking for clues. It is possible to be a winner, despite a poor hand, if the cards are played strategically.

With the Principle of Balance, nothing ever stands still. With every action, there will be a reaction.

> ~"..timeless state of intense conscious presence in the Now.." Eckhart Tolle
> *
> "The word 'now' is like a bomb through the window, and it ticks." Arthur Miller

In The Power of Now,[21] Eckhart Tolle teaches the mystical essence of being: "Being is the eternal, ever-present One Life beyond the myriad forms of life...".

True enough. But the Big E is rather pragmatic too! The Principle of Now also recognises the importance of stepping back to acknowledge where you

---

[20] Chief Seattle
[21] Eckhart Tolle: The Power of Now

PART 4: MANAGING CHANGE

have come from, what you have achieved and what you are trying to achieve.

To achieve those farfetched desires, your focus and mental energy must be in the still and silent present. It must be in the Now of potential energy - and that cannot happen if you are living with thoughts of either the future or the past.

There are quite a few practical ways in which you can check whether you are living for the moment. Do you worry about things that have happened or may happen? Do you still churn inside over past wrongs or arguments? Do you find yourself reliving them – the good scenes as well as the not so good? Are you impatient with life and the seemingly longwinded ways in which life allows you to achieve your goals?

We may not be able to change the past but we can change our attitude towards it. We may not be able to predict the future but we can build up happier vibrations by positive expectation. To do that, we need to find something good in whatever we are doing or wherever we are right at this very moment. If you are in a bedsit with substandard heating and you have just lost your job, that might be easier said than done. If the love of your life has just dumped you or you have lost a much wanted child, not only will that be difficult, it will also be emotionally draining. But it is not impossible to find something of cheer, if you can make that effort.

Release any sense of guilt or failure. Force yourself to grin at your face in the mirror and I guarantee you that the burden will soon feel lighter. You might feel a prat. You may even weep as you grin, but you will feel better. I promise you that. And that is what is meant by power being in the present moment. Your breath, your choice, your decision. You choose the current image and you can pat yourself on the back for such a stunning piece of self-discipline when all you want to do is crawl under the duvet with some cheap plonk.

Tolle, being more mystically-minded, talks of problems being illusions of the mind. It is true that our emotions, whether of love, fear or anger, invest these illusions with exceptional power. We feel deeply and therefore our 'now-ness' is utterly focused on the cause of this emotion.

Yet, if we can switch off these images and emotions, even for a second or two, and allow a more refined and purer energy an opportunity to get through, then we will experience that eternal, ever-present, One Life.

In this moment, the Principle of Now will give you what you need most.

> *"For unto every one that hath shall be given, and he shall have abundance; but from him that hath not shall be taken away even that which he hath."* Matthew 25: 29-30

To those struggling with very little, it is one of life's great ironies that those who are blessed with material abundance are frequently given freebies of one description or another. Suppliers bend over backwards to provide free meals, flight upgrades, clothes, cars and much else which the receiver could easily afford without even noticing.

A famous pop star was conned out of millions before chancing upon the withdrawals from his bank accounts. Meanwhile, he was never out of pocket and, presumably, never once felt poverty consciousness, as the money and other goodies kept pouring in and piling up.

By contrast, another world class pop star, while still mega-rich, has seen his life begin to show cracks. His poverty consciousness comes from his flickering self-esteem. This in turn has resulted in his cashflow problems.

PART 4: MANAGING CHANGE

The Principle of Accumulation is not class or celebrity-conscious. It works independently of who someone is and what they have achieved. It is quite a just law and is free to each and every one of us as it works in direct proportion to our predominant thoughts.

We get more of what we regularly think about. If we think of abundance, it will gradually start to accumulate in our lives. To think of lack and bad fortune will also accumulate.

Like a small savings account, the Principle of Accumulation is a gradual building up of regular deposits. Add the interest paid for many small sacrifices and unseen and unappreciated acts that we each are responsible for, and we have the makings of a healthy bank account.

Wonderful though they are, we can accumulate more than material goods and money in the bank. Our talents and our friends are signs of the Principle of Accumulation in action. Our success in our work is another, as is our good health. An unshakeable spiritual life is the best manifestation of the law in action. No matter what challenges may come our way, we merely bend with them, knowing that we have accumulated enough inner light to see past the darkness.

If we want more of something, whether a talent or more tangible prosperity, or even inner light, then we have to build up our mental capacity to receive. Ultimately, we can only be given what we are capable of receiving.

> *"Back of every creation, supporting it like an arch, is faith. Enthusiasm is nothing: it comes and goes. But if one believes, then miracles occur."*
> **Henry Valentine Miller**

H L Mencken said that faith could be defined as an illogical belief in the occurrence of the improbable. Krishnamurti was even more uncompromising: "The constant assertion of belief is an indication of fear."

Thank God for JC... Faith the size of a grain of mustard seed is quite sufficient to move even a mountain. Phew! It is certainly about as much as most of us can manage.

The Principle of Belief treads a fine line between calm certainty and Krishnamurti's constant assertion concealing fear. To need to feel belief does indicate fear, as true faith is a complete awareness of a particular reality whether we have tangible proof of it or not. We visualise and it is our belief in our visualisations at any moment in time that powers them into eventual realisation.

Calm belief or faith keeps us going despite the frequent hurdles on the way to manifestation and the perverseness of intangibility. If we are in tune with what we believe in, the energy is so powerful, it seems to magic our desires instantly into our lives, such is its power. Yet the end result can remain invisible for a long while. The Principle of Belief guides us into taking the many small steps needed to actualise the desired image.

Meanwhile, we literally have to have a calm certainty in the seemingly ultimate impossible becoming possible. Small wonder most self-help gurus recommend keeping desires hidden. How else can we explain the "things hoped for... evidence not seen"?

Whatever we believe in, good or bad, will become our reality. Calm certainty will ensure its outcome either way. Harbour any doubts, and you invite failure. The Principle of Belief is not blind. It is not hope. It is a genuine confidence - meaning 'with faith' - faith in your desire, and faith in your self.

PART 4: MANAGING CHANGE

> *"She gave me a smile I could feel in my hip pocket." Raymond Chandler~*
>
> *
>
> *"A smile is often the key thing. One is paid with a smile. One is rewarded with a smile. One is brightened by a smile. And the quality of a smile can make one die." Antoine de Saint-Exupery*

Busy Anon, has written that a smile costs nothing. That is debatable. But it does lift both the smiler and those smiled at, fostering goodwill, and creating a rippling moment of positive harmony.

We do not give enough importance to the many little powers we have. Who would credit a mere smile with power? Yet psychologists have discovered that facial expressions can create "marked changes in the autonomic nervous system.[22]"

A single smile can lift not just your spirits. It can make others feel good too. A smile can also increase harmony and productivity. In a work environment it can be motivational[23] helping to create a more productive environment.

Gurus in India have held laughter clinics for years. In the UK, Robert Holden has built a niche market around the power of laughter and smiling. Mark you, someone who smiles all the time, can either come across as an escapee from a lunatic asylum, or be rather annoying.

I once spent a day with a relentlessly happy person, a friend of a friend. No matter what the topic of conversation, it provoked wide smiles which seemed to debase any intelligent interaction. My mood veered between utter gloom and wanting to strangle her as I felt trapped with her company. In the end, my feet took action and, miracle of miracles, my smiles returned. As with everything, it is important to find the right balance.

---

[22] Paul Ekman & Wallace Friesen
[23] Robert Holden - Laughter The Best Medicine

Stumbling from your pit in the mornings, the last thing you may want to do is smile at yourself in the mirror. But to start off every day with a smile is a wonderful way of raising our consciousness. And, in raising our consciousness, we raise our vibrational frequency.

The Principle of Smiling can bridge the gap between trauma and happiness. Even a small smile. Smiling is not laughter, although that has its place too. "The world loved man when he smiled...[24]"

> *"Next to ingratitude, the most painful thing to bear is gratitude."* Henry Ward Beecher
>
> *
>
> *"God give you pardon from gratitude and other mild forms of servitude."* Robert Creeley
>
> *
>
> *"Be thankful f'r what ye have not, Hinnissy - 'tis th' on'y safe rule."* Finley Peter Dunne
>
> *
>
> *"And you must be thankful."* Dag Hammarskjold~

I have always had an internal argument about gratitude and thankfulness. Gratitude seems so Uriah Heep-ish. With apologies to Louise Hay,[25] indeed there are far more esteemed writers bemoaning gratitude than praising it.

No doubt, many will find me pedantic, but I love the word "thankful". Thanks, thankfulness - there is a much brighter, lighter resonance to those words than gratitude. Gratitude is thinking of the starving and the needy with almost a thank-God-it's-them-and-not-me kind of attitude.

Thankfulness is enjoying the process of shopping, cooking and eating. We are thankful for the vast array of colours, textures and tastes - and that they

---

[24] Stray Birds: Rabindranath Tagore
[25] Gratitude A Way of Life: Louise Hay

PART 4: MANAGING CHANGE

are available for us whenever we want or need them. It is counting our blessings without feeling the guilt.

Yet the Principle of Thankfulness is quite clear. We do have to be thankful for something in order to open up for even more of it in our lives.

There is always something for which we can be thankful, even when we feel as though our world is at an end. Thinking of things to be thankful for helps many people put their life into perspective, especially during tough times. So, no matter how difficult your life may be at this very moment, stop and try to identify at least three things that you may have been taking for granted. For a start, you can read - that is, if you are reading this! Power comes from knowledge. Read more. Become an expert in something. Be thankful that a source of knowledge is never further away than a library.

You may have a serious illness, but you are not yet dead, so get excited about your remaining potential. Be thankful for the time you continue to have left. You can still leave something of lasting worth. Choose to leave the best of yourself and your gifts. On this subject, I read once of a woman with a terminal illness wanting to do exactly that - leave something worthwhile. She got so involved in it, that her 'end date' came and went and, to the best of my knowledge, she is still alive.

If you have had a bad divorce, unable to see your children and left financially-blitzed, the last thing you may want to feel is thankful. In fact, hand-in-glove with this law is the Principle of Forgiveness. "..to give thanks is good, and to forgive.[26]"

Resentment and anger cause blockages which will automatically hinder any good things from flowing your way. It takes a superior soul to freely forgive, but

---

[26] Algernon Swinburne

then to forgive is divine. Thankfulness and forgiveness connect us with our higher natures - the source of potential magic in our lives. Why allow a negative moment in space and time to have endless repercussions?

Don't be too hard on yourself – it is limiting.

A metaphysical mystery is the need to give thanks before whatever we desire actually happens. We thank God or our inner guru in advance as a gesture of faith. On Earth as it is in Heaven.... As we give thanks for its heavenly realisation, so it eventually manifests tangibly for us on Earth.

The Principle of Thankfulness allows us to make faster progress, or at least fearlessly feel that we are on the right track. Thankfulness is a form of praise - and when we praise, we invoke the Principle of Accumulation.

This principle can even re-activate and re-energise the cells of our bodies. It truly is a wonderful healer.

A final word on the Principle of Thankfulness refers to my mythological namesake. The Three Graces, Euphrosyne, Thalia and Aglaia - personification of the sun's blessings - were also considered to be the goddesses of gratitude. Ah! I knew there was a lesson somewhere ...

TASKS

!What would your metaphysical principles be?
!List at least 10 things you are attracted to.
!List the close characters in your own life screenplay
!Are there any characters who play intermittent roles?
!Write down any recurring negative thoughts you may have.
!List at least 10 things to be thankful for.
!What would you like more of in your life right now?

PART 4: MANAGING CHANGE

PROBLEM SOLVING

> *"A mediocre idea that generates enthusiasm will go further than a great idea that inspires no one."* Mary Kay Ash
>
> *
>
> *"The thinker dies, but his thoughts are beyond the reach of destruction. Men are mortal; but ideas are immortal."* Walter Lippmann
>
> *
>
> *"No man can establish title to an idea - at the most he can only claim possession. The stream of thought that irrigates the mind of each of us is a confluent of the intellectual river that drains the whole of the living universe."* Maurice Valency

A problem, metaphysically-speaking, is an idea seeking its balancing solution.

Ideas exist on some unseen and unfelt dimension whether we take advantage of them or not. Perhaps they are seedlings from other more creative souls. Perhaps their time has not yet come - like electricity once was, for example, prior to Volta, Ampère, Faraday et al.

A problem exists in a particular state of mind. If asked to describe it in non-scientific terminology, you might say it was highly-coloured, busy, dark, foggy, as if a vice was gripping your brain and so on. Basically, there is no clarity, or even a vacuum for an idea to fill. Thus no solution can be found from the state of mind where the problem exists.

Step one is to stop thinking of the problem. Step two is to release some of that fog vibration with thoughts of positive potential. Just by assuming that ideas and solutions exist will automatically attract them to you, because what we focus on increases.

If we want to create solutions, or more of what we do want, we must switch our focus to exactly that - what we want. We must stop looking for what might be wrong. This is not the frequency for finding ideas!

PROFIT FROM UNLIMITED THINKING

Once we have disciplined our minds and have a clear head, then ideas are much more likely to pop in. Ideas, like much else in metaphysics, try to match a predominant vibration and may not always appear to be an exact match. However, it is important to follow up every lead, as it will eventually provide the best fit to the problem.

If you are riddled with debt, it is unlikely that you will come up with winning lottery numbers. Well, you might. However, the vibration that caused your debts would eventually create the loss of your sudden abundance too. A better vacuum-filler would be an idea to consolidate your debts. You contact your lenders and work out a payment plan. You take control, and not some automaton in a call centre whose daily harassing calls can reduce even the strongest nerves to jelly.

Business likes to brainstorm. In my experience, the best ideas come to the still and silent solo mind. However, the same principles apply: clear the mind, expect solutions - and be open to them.

MANAGING YOUR EXPECTATIONS

> *"I have learnt through bitter experience the one supreme lesson: to conserve my anger, and as heat conserved is transmuted into energy, even so our anger controlled can be transmuted into a power which can move the world."* Mohandas K Gandhi
>
> *
>
> *"...impatient as the wind..."* William Wordsworth
>
> *
>
> *"And so each new venture*
> *Is a new beginning, a raid on the inarticulate*
> *With shabby equipment always deteriorating*
> *In the general mess of imprecision of feeling,*
> *Undisciplined squads of emotion."* T S Eliot

How expectations can be buffeted by emotions! My own are reflected in my choice of the wise words above. Anger, impatience, undisciplined squads of

PART 4: MANAGING CHANGE

emotion... Yet anger, for example, properly controlled, can be a powerful force for good. Righteous anger is a form of passion and provides an enormous charge to whatever we do. Impatience is an alternative perspective to energetic drive. Intolerance of circumstances and situations can make us fight for a greater cause.

Since our emotions underpin our expectations, we need to understand them better. We expect to hear from this headhunter, that lover or customer. We anxiously wait for a cheque or contract. When the call, contract or cheque does not arrive to expectation, we feel anger, fear, uncertainty.

But there are ways to keep emotions from overload from life's little annoyances. These are, after all, just annoyances. If the need appears to be so immense that it assumes a greater importance than an annoyance, more work would have to be done on self-conversing (see Part 5). More work would also have to be done on what we really desire.

To seek a job but to hate working is contradictory self-talk. To be open-minded, but to take at face value the market today, or what the middlemen say is limited thinking. If you really want something sincerely enough, ways will be created. That is unlimited thinking. That is an unlimited truth.

Obviously major debt is more than a mere annoyance. This has not happened overnight and could need as long to put right. People have committed suicide under the burden of financial pressure. Yet taking out multiple credit cards and toggling balances from one to another, for example, is not managing expectations sensibly. Seeking help at any stage, however, is a wise move. The immediate pressure will be lifted in a fate now shared with someone authoritative.

The most important element of managing expectations is to remember that we are not alone. It can be a challenge when events appear to be moving in a backward direction. But we live in fortunate times, blessed with many support organisations. The good ones will be able to separate you, and your self-esteem, from your problem. The choices you made then can be re-made or re-adjusted.

It is vital to retain self-esteem in order to unshackle yourself from the issue at hand. Managing expectations invariably means clawing back the power you have given to the debt, the job or the lover.

> *"Out of the kitchen, to stew is to fret, to worry, to agitate. In the kitchen, however, to stew is to have great expectations."* Molly O'Neill

Emotional responses are often inappropriate because they stem from a primitive response pattern.[27] Our memories and experiences colour our reactions which can result in a pre-programmed response. That is why self-knowledge is so vital. If we are aware of our trigger points, we can aim to avoid or neutralise their effect.

Sometimes we feel a lack of control in our lives which can affect more sensitive souls and those prone to depression. Depressives in particular can gain immeasurably by stimulating their creative tendencies.

Negative emotional responses can create unwieldy stress. Stress in itself is generally unavoidable, but it is not always a bad thing. Stress can motivate and stimulate action to change. What is important is to recognise the signs and control the levels so that intensity is contained and redirected.

However, if the need is pressing, stress energy can unfortunately build up negatively. The biggest challenge in counteracting this negative stress is in

---

[27] Gael Lindenfield: Emotional Confidence

PART 4: MANAGING CHANGE

taking that first step across to a different thought or action. When your gut is getting steamed up about something or someone, it is difficult but not impossible to launch into a stress reducer.

Breathe deeply. Count to ten. Chant your favourite mantra. Read a funny book. Listen to a calming piece of music. Whatever your choice, it still involves the discipline of doing it. Managing expectations means being disciplined.

Never forget that stress is actually cumulative energy, and should be used as a positive force. In the workplace, for example, it can be used as a launch pad for finding a job with a better fit. The stress attached to being overweight can lead to joining a slimming club. Support organisations and clubs are excellent for maintaining momentum or handling downturns.

Downturns happen to all of us. Positive thinking cannot stop a recession or a divorce or ill health. What it can do is change mindsets, and, in effect, make a silk-like purse out of a sow's ear. Mastery of the world starts with mastering ourselves. You are the silk purse. The sow's ear is merely the circumstance which currently challenges us.

Change can sometimes make us become forgetful, losing concentration, becoming irritable or depressed. It is vital to stop and take stock.

If your health is playing up or your sleep patterns are regularly disturbed, once again, stop and take stock. It may not be the most pleasant of prompts from your inner voice, but it is a sign nonetheless to take time out and re-focus on what you really need and want.

We best manage expectations when we can fool our subconscious: the fake-it-till-you-make it syndrome. This does not mean going out and buying an Aston Martin on tick. It means absorbing the essence of Aston Martin-ownership. How would we feel, dress, walk, talk and act if we owned an Aston Martin? We are raising our game, and our personal vibration, and thus the opportunities which we attract.

> *"Of all days, the day on which one has not laughed is surely the most wasted." Chamfort*

I disagree with Twain that there is no humour in heaven. I am utterly convinced the Big E has a splendid sense of humour, and that when we realise the power of illusion over ourselves, we too might permit ourselves a wry grin.

Make sure your sense of humour remains at a high level, especially in times of challenge and change. Read humorous books, watch funny programmes.

Try to see the ridiculous in any negative situations. It will transfer its power back to you.

> *"Time is but the shadow of the world upon the background of Eternity." Jerome K Jerome*

I once read that time is God's way of making sure everything we thought, felt or desired did not happen simultaneously. Put like that, it is easier to accept the natural ebb and flow of managing change.

The changes in our lives should be viewed over a period of time in order to make more sense of them. To view our life changes from a historical perspective will also provide the necessary objectivity to meet any fresh changes that we might be facing.

PART 4: MANAGING CHANGE

> *"Comparison, more than reality makes men happy or wretched."* Thomas Fuller
>
> *
>
> *"I murmured because I had no shoes, until I met a man who had no feet."* Persian Proverb
>
> *
>
> *"If you compare yourself with others you may become vain and bitter for always there will be greater and lesser persons than yourself."* Max Erhmann

Comparisons may well be odorous, but, applied judiciously, they can also be quite useful sometimes. When fears insidiously start to take root, it can be levelling to know that even the highest achievers have experienced fears and uncertainties.

Despite almost continuous success, many powerful businessmen feel uncertain about their education or class. Many more fear their past mistakes coming to light. But what is the worst that can happen?

Most of us have experienced fairly abysmal events at some time in our lives. Little skeletons hide in most closets but we move on. Taking a healthy look at the mistakes of another - that is without criticism or gibing - can help us to handle our own human failings.

Likewise, sensible comparison could help us to set a value on ourselves and our services. As with everything, the Principle of Balance needs to be applied. We might indeed be better in some ways, and but rather less in others.

Comparison should never be used to find fault as that will inevitably boomerang back on us. However, if we find that someone in our field of activity has achieved significantly more, without necessarily being better qualified, or more able, it could and should act as a spur to greater effort. If you like, they can be interim role models.

Never allow comparisons to bury your dreams though. Often we place a high standard on what we

PROFIT FROM UNLIMITED THINKING

should achieve, based on our perceptions of role models. Yet, the step-by-step, brick-by-brick approach is fundamental to continuous and consistent success.

Sometimes, when we test out the waters of unlimited potential, we can find ourselves taking a massive step backwards. The accoutrements of success evaporate and we can find ourselves paralysed by the "what-will-others-think" syndrome. Will they think I am a failure? How will I be able to prove myself now? What messages about myself am I projecting?

I was once reduced to driving a £250 banger, and an ex-work colleague remarked "How the mighty have fallen!" Luckily for me, I have never really measured my self-value by the car I drive, although that definitely was a bit of a heap, and it took a little longer for my sense of humour to return.

In Status Anxiety, Alain de Botton, talks of failure and success measured by the reactions of others. De Botton compartmentalises collective thought generationally. While acknowledging the mass mind, the purpose of unlimited thinking is to be individual within the collective, in order to raise the ultimate value of the collective.

As we set about managing the changes in our lives, we will be marching to the beat of a different drum for a short while. We cannot afford to lengthen that period by allowing the comments of others to throw us off balance.

> *"The principle of supply is the realisation that we already have, even though appearances may not testify to that." Joel S Goldsmith*[28]

It is vital to understand the importance of the invisible and unsensed, which I will cover in greater detail in Part 5.

---

[28] Invisible Supply: Joel S Goldsmith

PART 4: MANAGING CHANGE

Things happen beyond our current normal sensory patterns. It is this ability to tune into another dimension which forms the basis of true unlimited thinking. That is what we must learn to effect and be in control of.

This act of control-and-merge happens in a total awareness of being in the immediate and eternal present - effectively, the Principle of Now - and will eventually materialise in some form or other in our lives, provided we try to maintain consistency of thought and emotion.

It is an extraordinary act of faith to believe while the evidence is as yet unseen. Try it - now.

> *"God told us to love our enemies not to like them"* Niebuhr
>
> *
>
> *"Who can endure the crassness of the common herd! Are folk not presumptuous, warped and absurd: Putting barriers between self and the thing they should see, Self measuring by self the whole community!"* La Fontaine
>
> *
>
> *"The people, and the people alone, are the motive force in the making of world history."* Mao Tse-Tung
>
> *
>
> *"I believe that more unhappiness comes from this source [the family] than from any other - I mean from the attempt to prolong family connections unduly and to make people hang together artificially who would never naturally do so."* Samuel Butler
>
> *
>
> *"The family is the association established by nature for the supply of man's everyday wants."* Aristotle

In Part 1, I briefly mentioned the structures that form our sense of self: our families, friends and colleagues, our social and religious affiliations, not to mention our various hobbies and special interest groups. When managing the changes in our lives, as well as our expectations, our biggest challenges will undoubtedly come from other people.

We need them, generally as a support mechanism, often like a hole in the head, and, sometimes, to get away from, permanently, if our spiritual growth is seriously impeded.

However, that is not an excuse to duck our obligations. The Principle of Balance encompasses karmic cause and effect. If we have been responsible for bringing children into the world, they are part of our spiritual duty. Postpone or ignore that duty now and it will come back to haunt you at some point in time and space. Opt for quickfix bankruptcy and your financial responsibility will remain on your spiritual balance sheet.

We might need to distance ourselves from over-critical relatives and friends, but not to the extent of causing hardship and pain. So, to manage our expectations fully, we need to understand their needs and desires as well as our own. We need to empathise, even if that means doing so from a distance.

Set boundaries, but do not criticise others, because what you think about them will eventually reflect back on to you - and, generally, when you least expect it.

If you feel that change has been forced on to you, from divorce or ill health, for example, the quickest way to regain personal power is to take responsibility. Very few events, if any, are one-sided. Our actions and thoughts are cumulative, and the responding kick in the teeth may not always come in a recognisable manner.

Controlled calm is easier said than done when inconsideration and inefficiencies load up on the minus side of your internal see-saw. The straw that broke the camel's back is frequently something as petty as a television turned up late at night, or a neighbour regularly encroaching on your space by a few millimetres. The cumulative effect is like a fly that will

PART 4: MANAGING CHANGE

not leave by the open window, preferring to buzz around your immediate space like a kamikaze pilot.

Newspapers regularly recount tales of neighbours' blood feuds over trees and other boundaries being breached. A universal annoyance seems to be an endless series of call centre messages, when the desire is to talk with a human being. When you do eventually reach said human being, they very rarely want to hear your eruption of frustration.

Forgive yourself when the fuse blows as it may well do from time to time.

In Part 5, I will show you how to use light to diffuse adverse conditions, and promote harmony. And just remember that even persistently annoying flies eventually disappear from your horizon or burn themselves out.

TASKS
!Do you allow your expectations to err on the side of cynical?
!How supportive is your family?
!How often do you think about your problems?
!Do you give up if the solution is less than perfect?
!Do you sabotage your own desires?

PART 5 - GURUS AND YOU

> *"It is the close observation of little things which is the secret of success in business, in art, in science, and in every pursuit in life.... little bits of knowledge and experience carefully treasured up... growing at length into a mighty pyramid... are all found to have their eventual uses, and to fit into their proper places." Samuel Smiles*
>
> *
>
> *Guru: an influential teacher; a revered mentor*

Gurus and self-improvement teachers have probably been around since the dawn of the time. The first Western self-help bestseller was called appropriately enough "Self Help". It was written by a Dr Samuel Smiles, and, along with Darwin's Origin of Species, it was picked by Harvard University as the most influential book of the 19th century.

Many of the early personal development writers such as Dr Orison Swett Marden and Elbert Hubbard were also influenced by Smiles. Napoleon Hill of Think and Grow Rich fame was a contributor to Hubbard's magazine. Others who have contributed to today's dynamic market in earthly self-improvement, with a nod to the spiritual, include Emmet Fox, Joseph Murphy, Dan Custer, U S Anderson, Catherine Ponder and many more.

Today, the self-help industry continues to enjoy exponential growth, although now more attention is paid to its mystical antecedents. Eastern wisdom is enjoying parallel success with its rather more materialistic western counterpart.

However, in defence of those early writers, it probably would have been difficult for them to promote the Bhagavad-Gita or Sufism, for example, without incurring the wrath of more fundamentalist thinkers. It may even have been blasphemous to talk of Jesus' teachings and some forms of spiritual metaphysics in the same breath, although Joseph Murphy frequently did so.

In How to Use the Laws of Mind, Murphy writes: "I receive many letters, a few of which say, 'You will be cast into a lake of fire because you are telling people.... that each man is his own saviour, that all he has to do is contact this God-presence and It will lead him, guide him and solve his problems for him...'".

Although religion continues to be a very emotive subject, we now live in a more curious age. Many of our spiritual leaders have feet of clay and in seeking self-confirmation, we look outside our existing borders for answers. The gamut of accepted modern creeds sweeps from the mainstream to the occult like Wicca and even Satanism, with barely a blink.

Unlimited thinkers will take the purest and best of all wisdom in their quest for enhanced living, whatever its source. This does not mean giving up on the religion of your choice. Far from it. Seeking a wider perspective can add immeasurably to a chosen faith.

Ideally, a guru or teacher should provide us with signposts when we reach various crossroads in our life.

While many allow permanent relationships with their followers, like Sai Baba, Mother Meera and Billy Graham, to an unlimited thinker, a guru is an impermanent bond. They are but one source of information.

SELF-HELP GURUS

> *"If you want to do something with your life never listen to anybody, no matter how expert they may appear. Go for it!"* Michael Caine

When we seek answers to fundamental truths of living and dying, we make others aware of our vulnerability. It is more important than ever, at such times, to make sure that whoever we turn to, can aid our growth - and not take advantage.

Is your guru a leader of men? They may not be leading you into battle, or be powerbroking in the political or business arena, but your guru will share many characteristics with those leaders.

The defining traits of a leader are ambitious, aspirational, honest, open-minded, caring, competent, considerate, courageous, reliable, steadfast, fair-minded, forward-looking, imaginative, independent, inspiring, intelligent, loyal, mature, self-controlled, straightforward and supportive.

Of these, the five that usually rank the highest are honest, competent, forward-looking, inspiring and intelligent. The least valued traits in a leader are ambitious, determined, self-controlled, loyal and independent.

According to Professor Adrian Furnham, followers want bright people with vision, who have clarity and directness. It is probably also true of those who you choose to guide you in your life decisions.

We all have had a mentor or coach at some stage in our lives. Even those who have reached significant positions of power have turned to gurus. In fact, they probably use them much more than the common man.

All those many well-known gurus would not be well-known if they had not created positive results.

PART 5: GURUS AND YOU

They still do create positive results. They have a vital role in preparing the mind to stretch itself beyond its boundaries.

Sometimes your guru can be an author. I have had many gurus whose words have helped me at special and needy moments in my life. To see, read and feel a fresh perspective can be just the nugget required. While I rarely read books from cover to cover, information flow is always valid. For me, that is the best way to stimulate my imaginative processes – learning, but staying out of a particular box.

I also have been to see many well-known names but once has generally been sufficient for me. They gave me an excellent insight which I was then able to pursue better on my own, although for many people, this would not be an easy route to take. Our lives are cluttered and busy. An external form of spiritual or self-help can be invaluable in maintaining personal discipline.

Although a guru is technically a (Hindu) spiritual leader or teacher, nowadays it can take many forms.

There have been many times when I seemed to prefer externalising, and so I made regular visits to tarot card readers, and clairvoyants. I was evidently desperate for some kind of affirmation since the cards or visions never came true. It was almost a form of counselling though more likely a signal that my spiritual life needed an overhaul.

However, when you have a fair pile of problems, it is difficult to sense resolution in some distant star. Most humans prefer to gnaw the bones constantly and that gives no space or energy to solving the issues.

Any form of guru can be helpful but should really only be a temporary measure. The best type of guru is one who allows you to discover your own

PROFIT FROM UNLIMITED THINKING

superpowers – and then offers guidance from time to time to help you to keep on track. I have enjoyed that guidance from many mystics and spiritual writers, and still do, but warily. They have crises of faith too, and this can impact your energy should your trust and faith in them be too strong.

Please note that this is not a criticism of them in any way. Teilhard de Chardin wrote that we are spiritual beings having human experiences, and as humans we cannot avoid those crises. In many ways, it is almost as if the Divine Essence is saying "You do not have all the answers, yet. But come through this and you will have opened another window of knowledge. Oh and a bit of humility won't come amiss either!"

> *"Example is the school of mankind, and they will learn at no other."* Edmund Burke
>
> *
>
> *"Example moves the world more than doctrine."* Henry Valentine Miller
>
> *
>
> *"He or she is greatest who contributes the greatest original practical example."* Walt Whitman

Many people have role models and heroes. It is an important and valid part in the accomplishment of our goals to use that paradigm – but only as a focus for one's imagination.

Swap images, with you in pole position, in order to impregnate the subconscious mind. When the image has become part of your vibratory essence, move on to other more pertinent role models or examples for the new you.

PINS (people in the news) often achieve ephemeral success. They are interim role models because their achievements are built on transitory elements. You want your subconscious to provide more solidity and permanence. So, as an unlimited thinker, you can have your pick of role model as well as guru.

PART 5: GURUS AND YOU

With a role model, you can take the more positive aspects of their lives, or skills, and build them in to your visualisations or learning techniques. With a guru, you have the choice of keeping them at a tangible distance by just choosing to read their books, or maybe attend workshops. Or if you prefer a one on one approach, you may wish to hire trainers, coaches, mentors and counsellors.

The differences between these are fairly subtle, but generally range from broadbrush services to specific niche strengths. Typical of the latter are nutritionists, happiness specialists, diet and fitness experts and many more. By and large their strength is their experience. They have ploughed the furrow and want to share. Because very few coaches and gurus lead perfect lives, that can give them an edge in helping others.

Basically, whatever form you choose to learn from, it should help you to explore ways of being, self expression, language and investigating new possibilities for and about yourself.

Your spiritual teacher or role model should help to remove the barriers from the knowledge you already have, and help you to discover the potential of what you are.

CREATING YOUR PERFECT GURU

> *"You cannot teach a man anything; you can only help him find it within himself"* Galileo

Profit From Unlimited Thinking is about discovering ways in which to unfetter our minds. To think in an unlimited fashion means allowing no restrictions to the power of the imagination, since the imagination is the rooting ground of future success, whatever you choose that success to be.

PROFIT FROM UNLIMITED THINKING

In this next section I want to show you how to imagine and create your own inner guru. It may be an easier exercise for those already blessed with a deep faith. But, if you recall from my introduction, my typical reader is an open-minded cynic, possibly agnostic or even an atheist. With both, I am probably skating over thin ice, but I hope you will sense understanding beyond the words.

> *"God is what man finds that is divine in himself. God is the best way man can behave in the ordinary occasions of life, and the farthest point to which man can stretch himself." Max Lerner*
>
> *
>
> *"Closer is He than breathing, and nearer than hands and feet." Alfred, Lord Tennyson*

Despite the wars fought over religious belief, to most people, their God represents a personal, private faith. That faith is felt deeply within. It is a raison d'être on a utterly subliminal level. Although we may remain with the faith of our fathers, the religion itself frequently undergoes several incarnations. All the major faiths have offshoots of varying degrees of significance, yet most people stay true to their original choice. It is a comfortable and known quantity in which to be thankful for this deep inner belief, or to pray through when times challenge.

Yet we have far more power than we realise. We can become a little too comfortable within our spiritual or even secular structures, and not really seek out or use this power within. After all, it demands recognition of self-accountability - and very few of us enjoy accepting the blame for the inequities of our lives.

By learning how to tap into this power, our lives can become truly exciting and fulfilling. Yet, many people do not want exciting lives. They just want to have an easier run: money to pay the bills, a loving

PART 5: GURUS AND YOU

partner, good health, enjoyable job and, perhaps, a win on the lottery!

All this can come from your inner power. That is the beauty of it. It is as much or as little as you want it to be. Whatever you choose to call this inner wisdom - your Higher Self, genie, an aspect of God or just your intuition, it has enormous potential power which can be turned on full, or just a trickle.

I believe that opening the tap by even a trickle will intrigue and fascinate you to explore further. I believe you will discover a rare enthusiasm about the possibilities for your life. When you find yourself exceeding your sales figures, or achieving the body of your dreams with pleasing ease, you will want to find out what else the magic lamp can bring you.

Since this book is all about unlimiting your thinking and therefore your mind, you are going to take an imaginary quantum leap and you are going to create your perfect guru. As this perfect guru is already an aspect or another dimension of your own nature, it should not be too profound a shock to make its re-acquaintance!

> *Aladdin's lamp: the source of wealth and good fortune. After his good luck and marriage Aladdin neglected his lamp and allowed it to rust.*[1]

Aladdin's genie, in the familiar fable, was not a happy entity. Trapped within the magic lamp, he reluctantly served whoever found it, whether for good or evil purposes. The only restriction to his power was the inability to make someone fall in love as one of the three wishes.

Sadly, when Aladdin had abundant wealth and the Princess was his forever, his need for, and attention to, the genie faded. Unlike the Disney film, the genie of fable, whose deepest desire was to be set free, was

---

[1] Brewer's Dictionary of Phrase & Fable

forgotten - presumably till another pressing need arose.

The genie within that we want to create for ourselves is similarly restricted where love is concerned, as love is many-layered. We may ask for a loving partner, but not for Alan or Anna in accounts to be the next notch on our bedpost. However, our inner genie is not limited to just three wishes.

The idea of creating a perfect inner guru is because we need to feel enabled by a power that is considerably greater than our human self. This unlimited genie can be called upon for anything we need or want, whether that is receiving all that our heart most desires, or just for mundane daily guidance.

For non-theists, the concept of a magic lamp should be an excellent visualisation tool. Then again, we should all imagine our genie or perfect guru to be a powerful source of information, across all points of time and space. Imagine it to be an all-knowing creator... a creator whose appearance can be whatever we desire.

The Kahunas, Hawaiian priests of the Huna teachings, believe there are three selves: the low, middle and higher self. They are usually allied to the subconscious, conscious and superconscious minds.

The superconscious self is the 'parental self of spirit', and is called on to see the future, to guide or even to pray to. When in a trance, ranging from alpha to theta brainwaves, the Huna follower projects an image of him or herself as the tangible essence of that superconscious self.

As well as a Superman-sized deity that is a replica of our human self, we can also create an image of a being of omnipotent light, or maybe a Solomon or Delphic Oracle. In Star Trek Voyager, Captain Janeway uses a hologram of Leonardo da Vinci. How we choose

PART 5: GURUS AND YOU

to see and communicate with our perfect guru is as endless as our imaginations.

> *"I sit down and there is some inner voice that takes over. I don't have to think about it. It's an odd thing to explain. It is an access to something that is going on in the subconscious."* Alexander McCall Smith

Now that we all have a mental image of our own personal inner guru, we can talk with it, pray to it, berate it, love it, ask it for advice and guidance. Or, we can let it, as an omnipotent force with only our best interests at heart, 'take over' .... "Thy Will be done". I do, however, use such terms as 'taking over' with great caution.

Mental illness is sadly increasing, exacerbated by drugs misuse. If you have any doubts or fears whatsoever, then please skip this altogether. The most important thing to remember, is that our superconscious self, or the inner guru we create, should be an essence of great love and light which wants the best for us - and for our world. To be 'guided' into anything that causes hurt or harm is categorically not your superconscious self.

> *"The flow experience, like everything else, is not 'good' in an absolute sense. It is good only in that it has the potential to make life more rich, intense, and meaningful; it is good because it increases the strength and complexity of the self."* Mihaly Csikszentmihalyi

Associations however pleasant should be pertinent. 'Flow' now seems to be an accepted term[2] for the effect of connecting and merging with a higher source. For me, the association with the word-sound remains that of an old lady called Flo who I was very fond of.

In this instance, I would rather see an image of infinity and a constant stream of abundance on my

---

[2] Flow – Mihaly Csikszentmihalyi

internal TV screen. So, no disrespect to Csikszentmihalyi, but I prefer the association of river (T S Eliot's "strong brown god" or Pascal's "moving road"), or even resonance. We resonate with whatever we are in sync with. Like attracts like.

The word "flow" is a more modern term to describe what is basically a mystical practice. One experiences flow or connectedness. Nonetheless, scientists do now accept the term as an "optimal experience" to quote Paul McKenna, a sense of exhilaration and bliss. I would go further and say that, for me, it is also stepping outside of human form and becoming one with a much greater universality. It is infinite knowledge and creative potential, without beginning or end.

Experiencing this flow is non-conformist and not affiliated to any religious persuasion. Still, I would never deny the many great mystics and gurus who developed very deep personal relationships with their God in this way.

I myself am happy with my relationship with the Divine, but most people seek a more pragmatic approach to unlimiting their thinking. If a divine meeting of minds does result, then you should count your blessings.

> *"All are but parts of one stupendous whole, Whose body Nature is, and God the soul.." Alexander Pope*

Resonating with a collective oneness of endless latency can result in different types of spiritual adventure.

When Katherine Hepburn's brother died she said: "It was as if when he died, I sort of became two people instead of one. A boy and a girl." She even took his birthday as her own.

I have an unsubstantiated view that every particle and cell in our bodies has transmitter and

PART 5: GURUS AND YOU

receptor facilities. In the same way that a radio can tune into different signals, so too could our personal particles. In deep grief, it could be easy to assume the essence and energy of the departed loved one.

In Into The Silent Land, Paul Broks writes that brain disorders, as a result of accidents or strokes, are creating astonishing changes for the so-called victim. One woman woke up with no memory at all of twenty-three years of her life, including an "acrimonious divorce". In another instance, a man became "convinced his head was full of water and contained a fish rather than a brain".

Broks found himself asking who are we? Or even what are we? Can our identities be so completely changed by random acts? Are we no more than receivers of multiple external sensations? Is personal identity a self-protective illusion?

Minnie Driver once played the part of a young woman who received a heart transplant - and then found herself irresistibly drawn to the dead woman's husband, and he to her. In The Heart's Code[3], Pearsall writes that the heart stores information which it can then communicate to every cell in the body. Organ transplant recipients underwent "mysterious changes in personality and taste" after such operations.

According to some sources, cells are believed to have unique properties, allowing them to interact and respond within a particular magnetic field. In Lynne McTaggart's acclaimed book[4], she calls it the Zero Point Field, connecting everything in the universe, as part of a 'dynamic cobweb of energy exchange'.

Francis Crick, one of the discoverers of DNA's double helix, more prosaically believes he and his

---

[3] The Heart's Code: Paul Pearsall
[4] The Field: Lynne McTaggart

group of researchers have found the cells responsible for generating consciousness, and the individual's "sense of self". He posits that our minds can be entirely explained by the interaction of nerve cells.

To me this does not undermine either religious belief nor unlimited thinking at all. It allows our inner self to communicate with us in ways that appeal to the more logical, perhaps even the atheist mind.

With unlimited thinking, the adventure of personal understanding is open to any inter-dimensional experience - as indeed it should.

> *"These damned mystics with a private line to God ought to be compelled to disconnect. I cannot see that they have done anything save prevent necessary change."* Harold Laski
>
> *
>
> *"All the wonders you seek are within yourself."* Sir Thomas Brown
>
> *
>
> *"What lies behind us and what lies before us are tiny matters compared to what lies within us."* Ralph Waldo Emerson

Unsurprisingly, I disagree with Laski. The Divine Guru, in my experience, adores change. With change comes evolution and growth, even if the pain threshold is sometimes set a tad high.

Equally, what is not so appetising about connecting and merging with the 'strong brown god', or divine river, is agreeing time and place. The DG fires warning shots from time to time, but we are so preoccupied with the business of living that we simply do not notice. Then kapow! When least expected, change hits. However if we are honest, rumblings of change have been felt in some way for some time.

We are constantly thinking, sending out signals - and receiving answers, although we may not be aware of them. We have feelings and views about all sorts of things which eventually filter back into our experience. If we took a little time to be aware of its

PART 5: GURUS AND YOU

two-way process, then maybe we would be more in control.

I went through a phase of wanting to be guided by actually hearing the voice of my Higher Self. Unfortunately, it was doomed to failure, as it smacked of an altered mental state I did not desire, so I chose to disconnect. Thomas Szasz put it rather more pungently: "If you talk to God, you are praying; if God talks to you, you have schizophrenia[5]."

Mark you, if hearing voices is schizoid then we must all "suffer" in some way at most times. Who has not heard that plodding voice of caution? The couch potato choosing to chill out with a beer and a pizza rather than putting out the rubbish or mowing the lawn? The critic, the fussbag, the over-sensitive, the lusty, the lover and of course the voice of conscience.

But all too often, the most frequent 'voice' is that of GFUDA: guilt, fear, uncertainty, doubt and anger. These are all inter-related inner voices since they can usually escalate to produce anger and other negative emotions such as hatred.

All these joyless 'voices' come from the past-programmed subconscious, or even inter-cellular resonance, and not the superconscious. It is all too easy to forget that, and be lead onto darker paths. If what you hear makes you feel lighter and brighter, full of optimism and hope, and, even compassionate love, then that alone is the guide to recognising your perfect inner guru.

Remember, your genie, god or perfect guru, like you and I, responds to being loved. Richard Dawkins believes that the only god is within us, and that the only spark of immortality is our genetic code, which should make it easier to love than some Unknown Being.

---

[5] The Second Sin: Thomas Szasz

> *"Responsibility, n. A detachable burden easily shifted to the shoulders of God, Fate, Fortune, Luck or one's neighbour. In the days of astrology, it was customary to unload it upon a star." Ambrose Bierce[6]*

Most humans generally prefer to live by a set of structured boundaries. To suddenly take on the responsibility of scripting his or her own life, can be fairly disorientating.

Then, when we do decide to write a screenplay for our perfect life, we labour over details. We become over-attentive to the unfolding of the drama and clog its natural evolution. This is turn creates mistrust and doubt. What are we becoming responsible for? How come these things keep happening which I did NOT ask for?

In one school of metaphysical thought, the various unwelcome events, or less than perfect manifestations, are the 'strong brown god' flowing through, shifting debris as it works its way into perfect realisation of true desire.

Stuart Wilde in Infinite Self believes that obstacles and challenges should be seen as stepping stones to deepen this connection. If we can see past the adversity, we will catch a glimpse of our true potential - our divine spark.

As I quoted earlier from Teilhard de Chardin, we are spiritual beings having human experiences, thus, in acknowledging the experience, we are acknowledging our innate divine power.

---

[6] The Devil's Dictionary: Ambrose Bierce

PART 5: GURUS AND YOU

> *"I believe we are free, within limits, and yet there is an unseen hand, a guiding angel, that somehow, like a submerged propellor, drives us on."*
> *Rabindranath Tagore*
>
> *
>
> *"Angels cannot be seen by man with his bodily eyes, but only with the eyes of the spirit which is within him. Emanuel Swedenborg*
>
> *
>
> *All the Utopias of the world will come to pass only when we grow wings and all people are converted into angels." Fyodor Dostoevsky*
>
> *
>
> *"Angels fly because they take themselves lightly." G K Chesterton*

Although angels are generally accepted as divine intermediaries with all the main faiths, their help is not only available to those who have a religious frame of reference.

Anyone can ask for help from an angel, at any time. They will be heard, and answered. It is not necessary to be in a meditative trance, or to be praying. Despite owning several books[7] identifying them by the busload, it is not even vital to call them by name. In fact, from my own experience, there are no special techniques. It is as simple as asking. The only rule, is one of good manners. Remember to say 'thank you' for the help that you will assuredly receive.

For reasons of association, I have chosen to call these beings lumiels. The word is an invented Latin/Greek composite: lumen, meaning light, and el, meaning of God. It roughly equates with my personal experiences of them. Strangely enough, I did not even ask for their help. They simply turned up when the need seemed pressing.

I do now, frequently, have conversations with my lumiels. I do the talking, and then find myself hearing a song, reading a book or speaking with a stranger, and sensing their reply. When I am feeling

---

[7] Moolenburgh; Virtue; Randolph Price; Graham; Webster; Guiley; Roland etc

particularly transcendent, I can feel the gossamer-light touch of a lumiel's love and it brings tears to my eyes.

With lumiels, there truly is nothing to fear. You will not lose your marbles. And any conversations you may conduct will be very much in Tevye-style. [8]

Lumiels have a refined manner of responding as well as an excellent dry sense of humour. It makes unlimited thinking great fun and takes the sting out of challenging circumstances.

I mentioned at the end of Part 4 that light can be used to diffuse problems and promote harmony. A lumiel can either take the form or image of a perfect guru, or it can become the essence of a solution. By connecting and merging with this light, you will find the circumstances surrounding your particular problem or disharmony greatly improving.

> *"We offer up prayers to God only because we have made Him after our own image."* Voltaire
>
> *
>
> *"More things are wrought by prayer Than this world dreams of."* Tennyson
>
> *
>
> *"If God had granted all the silly prayers I've made in my life, where should I be now?"* C S Lewis

The principle of praying defies logic. What or who exactly are we praying to? If it is just an aspect of ourselves, then why not just ask and be done with it? Why does prayer involve some humility? How does prayer work through the power of the mind? What has prayer to do with unlimited thinking?

Finer minds than mine have acceptable answers to each of these questions, so I shall just attempt to answer the last question. But, another question first: what is prayer?

---

[8] cf Fiddler on the Roof

PART 5: GURUS AND YOU

According to Larousse[9], prayer may have been intended to function as incantations and spells. It can be voluntary, spontaneous, formal or stylised. It can be individual or communal, vocal or silent. Prayer is a heartfelt response encompassing worship, adoration, thanksgiving, confession and supplication. I think we can also fit some unlimited thinking in there somewhere!

The general consensus seems to be that prayer does work. In fact, the power of prayer has been known to positively effect other people, even over great distances, although Larry Dossey[10] has written powerfully about the negative side of prayer.

It should come as no surprise to read that many people pray for harm to come to others. Dossey calls them sorcerers as "what is the difference between a prayer to harm others and the curse of a sorcerer?" He also posits the Legion Principle where the problem is displaced. In the biblical story, the demons were transferred to a herd of swine: the poor wretches, carelessly enjoying their swill, only to find themselves committing mass suicide.

Obviously there is something to be learned. Pray from a lighter, brighter source. Make sure that your unlimited desires create good and not evil so that the energy you send out comes back to you, and yours, in harmonious and positive ways. But, equally, we can see from this parable, the interconnectedness of life - and of each of our actions.

Most people view prayers as a form of communicating with an Almighty Being whose wisdom and power reach beyond our current understanding. That may well explain where the humility comes in!

---

[9] Dictionary of Beliefs and Religions: Larousse
[10] Be Careful What You Pray For..: Larry Dossey MD

Science has confirmed, many times, that prayer or directed intention can improve the health of even those who do not know they are being prayed for. That is another clue to the link with unlimited thinking. Within some greater totality, we create links with everyone and everything, at some point in time and space. You will have to work with me on this as the theory of everything has not yet been revealed.

The concept of unlimited thinking, therefore, subscribes to the view that within this intelligent totality is whatever we need, want and desire. The principle of prayer enables us to vibrate with it and attract it into our primary senses. However, as a form of displacement theory may be in operation, whatever we desire in our unlimited world should also work for the good of the whole.

Finally, the shortest, most powerful prayer, is "Thank You."

> "Thy Will be done on Earth as it is in Heaven" Jesus Christ
>
> *
>
> "Do we move ourselves, or are moved by an unseen hand at a game
> That pushes us off the board, and others ever succeed?"
> Alfred, Lord Tennyson

There is at least one school of metaphysical thought that believes a twin soul is our own soul, rent in two. In 'heaven' is our lighter, brighter, omnipotent self. On 'earth', separated, is the wandering part, forever experiencing, evolving, till it is pure and refined, and able to merge in eternal oneness with its other half.

The plus side to this intrinsic aloneness of the soul is in having a personal almighty creator, ready and willing to make the earthly sojourn a happy adventure for us. After all, our greater glory will be its greater glory too. But are we really able to let go? Can our egos resist the urge to claim total credit?

PART 5: GURUS AND YOU

"Sparky's Magic Piano[11]" was made more than thirty years ago, yet I believe it remains an excellent, modern, parable for humility, and the need to acknowledge the spirit within.

It is the story of a young boy, wanting in discipline, who finds it difficult to practice.

One day, as he is mooching at the piano, he hears it talking to him (a rather spooky voice, but Sparky seems to take it in his stride). The piano tells him that he would not hate practising so much if he knew what a pleasure it could be. It coaxes Sparky to run his fingers across the keys, telling him it will bring forth a virtuoso sound, no matter what he chooses to play, and, that his fingers will even look like they are playing the right keys.

In effect, all Sparky has to do is be willing to go along with it.

Sparky obediently plays something from his brief repertoire, not only amazing himself, but also his mother and his teacher. Apart from his protective father and a music critic, he is taken for a genius, and embarks on a whirlwind concert tour. Naturally, he insists on taking his magic piano everywhere with him because it is, of course, doing all the work.

Then one day, the fame and adulation goes to his head. Sparky really believes it is himself who is the genius. He is rude and unpleasant and starts to take his magic piano for granted, as well as taking total credit for this wonderful gift. He even ignores the advice of his magic piano who warns Sparky to change his attitude "or else".

Meanwhile Max the critic is cooking up his own scheme to bring down Sparky from Pride Mountain. He scours the country, looking for an exact replica to fool the little boy. Dad reluctantly agrees as

---

[11] Available from www.amazon.co.uk

he too believes that Sparky is tricking everyone, and does not want him to get too hurt when he is found out.

Sparky's pet dog, however, notices the swap and warns him. Sparky manages to re-swap the pianos and becomes even more boastful. His comeuppance is as grand and public as the success he has achieved.

In front of a huge audience of the great and the good, Sparky takes his place at the piano. The magic piano, however, refuses to play. Instead of the sublime sounds of a youthful maestro, poor Sparky's dreadful clattering echoes through Carnegie Hall. Cue laughter and jeers. The next scene shows the little boy sitting beside his piano, resolving to practise daily. The voiceover says "I guess it wasn't the magic piano after all - or was it?"

Is it really just a children's tale? Or could it be symbolic of our true selves? Alone, we are not much more than children, learning and practising the game of life. We discover a talent, one in which we lose our sense of self and allow a higher Self to take over. - the *en theos* of enthusiasm. We simply run our fingers over the keyboard.

Like many of us with emergent talents, we initially acknowledge the magic power flowing through. Then as confidence grows, we forget, taking all the credit, only to see our success evaporate like the early morning dew in a desert.

Sustained success comes from acknowledging this higher power as Beethoven, Mozart, Handel and many other celebrated musicians and artists have done over the years.

PART 5: GURUS AND YOU

> *"I thought I would make a fine wooden puppet – a really fine one, that can dance, fence, and turn somersaults in the air. Then, with this puppet, I could travel round the world, and earn my bit of bread and my glass of wine."* Geppetto/Carlo Collodi

Pinocchio is another story ostensibly for children. In fact, the book is far darker and more thoughtful than the abridged cartoon.

The wood from which Pinocchio is carved immediately sets the tone. It is crafty, wilful and rather ungrateful. Even as it is being carved into a puppet, it interferes and causes havoc. Some mystics would say that is more or less the case with the wandering soul.

After much searching on both sides ("It must surely be two years since that day - two years, my Pinocchio, that have seemed like two centuries."), they find each other in the darkness of a shark's stomach. The balance shifts as the puppet takes more responsibility for freeing the ageing carpenter and himself, with the help of a candle to light their way.

Back on dry land again, Pinocchio has to endure months of hard labour to nourish Geppetto and restore him to good health again. Finally, through an act of unselfishness and kindness he achieves his dream of becoming a real living boy.

> *"I of myself can do nothing. The Spirit of God within me does the work"*

The interestingly-named Dr Sharad Kumar (Dixit) Dicksheet, is a 72-year old plastic surgeon who has had two heart attacks, throat cancer forcing him to speak through a food pipe, and is in a wheelchair following a car accident.

Dixit spends his savings, and six months of each year, running plastic-surgery camps across India. He performs as many as seventy procedures a day, and has helped more than 60,000 Indians since he began in 1968.

He says "Look at me. I cannot walk, I cannot even sit or talk. How can you possibly think this is me doing all this? No, it is God doing it, while I am just a name and a pair of hands."

> *"The greatest fault of the day is the absence of stillness. ... Modern man lacks concentration and carries with him an atmosphere of restlessness... and unintentionally brings discomfort to others. Stillness is therefore the most important lesson that can be taught to the youth of today."* Hazrat Inayat Khan

One of the hardest things we can ever achieve is mental stillness. Our minds are either bothered by fears and uncertainties, or simply just by being busy.

An exercise that works for me but which I do not necessarily recommend for others (especially those with breathing problems), is to briefly hold my breath. In those few moments, my mind extinguishes all extraneous thoughts and images.

I then allow myself to inhale, gradually increasing the length of the in-breath. As I do, I imagine myself connected to a Supreme Source. With each in-breath, all negative images are flushed out and I feel a sense of equilibrium.

This is not just a quick-fix solution, it is also a desire to establish a connection to this Supreme Source which can see what I cannot, which has answers beyond my current understanding. But it does take a real leap of faith for a believer, let alone an atheist! It means shifting beyond the boundaries of limited thinking. It means not asking and telling, but listening and following up.

So who or what is this Source that I am handing control to?

PART 5: GURUS AND YOU

HOW WILL YOU KNOW?

> *"Joan: I hear voices telling me what to do. They come from God.*
> *Robert: They come from your imagination*
> *Joan: Of course. That is how the messages of God come to us."*
> *George Bernard Shaw /St Joan*

The Source is either an almighty power in which you already have a firm belief, or an idea that you have created in order to further your unlimited thinking. Either way, it is a powerful and omnipotent aspect of yourself. It is synonymous with discovering the power of electricity for the first time.

Since the realm of divine potential is ethereal and immaterial, we can best make our calls to it through fantasising and daydreaming. However, in order to know when it is responding, we have to become as immaterial, and even ethereal in turn. In biblical jargon, we do have to take a leap of faith, and literally allow it to take over.

Thankfully, unlike St Joan, the vast majority of us will not hear voices. We will not feel as if some alien being is taking control of our minds. We will not find ourselves doing ghastly deeds or changing our lives drastically.

Why would an aspect of ourselves, especially a finer, more rarified one, be so self-destructive? In short, it would not.

We will, however, find ourselves feeling or doing something that feels utterly natural, even mundane, that is in keeping with a present need.

If we can keep our emotions in balance, we may also understand the lesson. This is especially important if the lesson is either an enforced change, or possibly stagnation when you desire progress. For example, progress may require creating a vacuum, or removing a blockage. For me, this has frequently come in the form of giving things away or, more prosaically, doing some cleaning.

As well as faith, there has to be trust that this moment in time, however banal, is actually leading to something better. One thing is for sure, however invisible the 'something better' might currently be, it will eventually manifest in your life.

> *"Your heritage can be a source of your personal signs even if you are not aware of what those ancestral signs are." Denise Linn*[12]

While mass mind thinking ensures some uniformity, the Source generally communicates through our own individual dictionary of symbols. These personal clues will have a peculiar resonance only for you. The trick will then be to correctly interpret the message.

As well as the techniques outlined in Tools to Expand Consciousness, symbolic coincidences can come from the message in a song's lyric, a newspaper article, a name or a vivid or recurring dream. These are just some of the ways, your Source can communicate with you.

> *"Our notions of law and harmony are commonly confined to those instances which we detect; but the harmony which results from a far greater number of seemingly conflicting, but really concurring, laws, which we have not detected, is still more wonderful." Henry David Thoreau*

Although I regret having little of the mind-boggling to report so far in my life, I am a great believer in the power of coincidence. It is just one sign of a greater harmony within and around us. As for my own small coincidences, this is probably because I tend to be receptive to higher powers and try to follow up every lead.

---

[12] Signposts: Denise Linn

PART 5: GURUS AND YOU

In Beyond Coincidence[13], the authors recount several lively examples that, as they say, "send a pleasurable shiver down our spine". They describe the power of coincidence as both unsettling and delightful.

Coincidences are the result of random events coming together at a significant time. Coincidences can be warning signals as well as opportune and helpful. However, I disagree with the authors about the coincidence of malign objects. Having felt negative energy through objects and newspaper photos, I believe the frequency that operates with them differs from the frequency of coincidence, although some similarities remain.

Coincidences are believed to be manifestations of a cosmic consciousness beyond our comprehension and scale. Paul Kammerer's 'seriality' is Jung's synchronicity - disparate events linked by a meaningful bond. And, ostensibly, contravening any perceived laws of cause and effect.

But unlimited consciousness works beyond time and space limitations. What might seem mind-boggling to our limited human minds, can in fact be mathematically explained if the computer could scale high enough... beyond time and space. So, yes, the law of cause and effect could still apply.

This can actually work in our favour when checking for signals, or indeed if we feel bereft of opportunity. Working on the admittedly esoteric principle that somewhere in time and space, we must have done something good, we can be open to so-called "coincidence" coming to return the favour.

We could not possibly remember all our good, bad and indifferent actions. While praying that the bad ones are transmuted, we can stay open to a return on our previous investment of the good ones. It is why

---

[13] Beyond Coincidence: Martin Plimmer & Brian King

proactive seeding or prospecting frequently brings results from untapped corners.

> *Although unable to store water, camels can replace rapidly the water that is lost from the body, drinking up to 60 litres of water at a time. The Macmillan Encyclopaedia*

I once read that if you step off the path that is most relevant to yourself, you will be given three signs that you had done so. You could recognise the signs and, invoking free will, change course. If not, fate would step in. Fate being fairly heavy-handed, the chances are you would be floored by its intervention.

One way of pre-empting Fate's fist in the face, or to reduce its impact, is to adopt what I call Camel Mode spirituality. While we may not be able to store the 'waters of divine light', we can rapidly replace lost direction and inspiration, by bouts of meditation and allowing our perfect inner guru to take over.

In this process of inner stillness, we can not only sense an infinite calm, but, without any Damascene moments, ('..suddenly a light from the sky flashed round him. He fell to the ground...') we just find ourselves thinking, being and doing the right things. The good thing about Camel Mode is that it is utterly responsive to a bit of attention, even if it is a rather shabby way to treat a loved Source.

Some spiritual writers believe sensations within the solar plexus chakra are another sign of communication with the divine. In fact, Doreen Virtue[14] goes on to say that this is our divine centre, while Omraam Mikhaël Aïvanhov[15] stresses that "it is there that you will find your source".

---

[14] Chakra Clearing: Doreen Virtue
[15] Man's Subtle Bodies and Centres: Omraam Mikhaël Aivanhov

PART 5: GURUS AND YOU

Although I have enjoyed reading Aïvanhov, the interpretation of truths can and do vary from person to person.

In the Book of Divine Magic, he writes that 'Everything passes and is transmitted through the hands'. That rather limits the Almighty passing on powers to only those with hands. Which is demonstrably untrue. Many people who have lost their physical hands have been able to positively engage and serve their world. They may not have had hands to act as 'antennae' but the Big E provided something else in counterbalance.

By the same token, the solar plexus chakra is a receiver and transmitter of both celestial and earthly information, as are all the rest of our energy points. Sometimes, we get messages in our gut which are clearly imprecise. We humans can and do choose to interpret these signals to suit our predominant emotion. If our starting point is from an earthbound issue, the response is more likely to be in kind.

> *"And Lot's wife, because she looked behind her as she went, was turned into a pillar of salt." Genesis 19:26*

The chances of 'knowing' are greatly limited if we are constantly looking back. I call it the Lot's Wife Syndrome - it can induce a state similar to mental petrification. Stagnation and the inability to move forward are close cousins.

A businessman I know once enjoyed considerable success and financial rewards. He easily secured positions of comparative power and influence. However, a long-drawn out, painful divorce changed his landscape, and with it his mental attitude.

He believed his options were limited by market conditions and the inability of headhunters to see his potential. Instead of being open to the possible opportunities within a relatively lesser position, he was

PROFIT FROM UNLIMITED THINKING

constantly looking back - and suffering the Lot's Wife Syndrome.

In the Principle of Now, there is no past. Your potential is based on your ability to attract to you what you need and want for the cumulative person you are today - now.

By constantly living resentfully in the past, and looking behind to earlier glories, he was effectively blocking anything worthwhile from coming his way. When untoward change happens to us, we may have to take a few steps back in order to move further forward. So how will we know?

The Source is not some insatiable and vengeful deity, neither are we lead into mindless anarchy and chaos. We will know through a combination of pragmatism, and spiritual release, that comes from letting go and trusting. It comes from taking small steps. Or as Philip Pullman once said: 'It took me thirty years to be an overnight success.'

Esoteric principles are worth a try, if you really want to unlimit the possibilities in your life. It might even happen rather sooner if you let your light shine.

COACHING YOURSELF

> *"They were the ones that people turned to for help or support. .. And they were the ones who enjoyed helping others think bigger, think smarter and think differently."* Thomas J Leonard[16]

Pragmatic self-help can take many forms. We are now living in an era of therapy. Coaching, mentoring and counselling[17] are all similar yet slightly differing services that can help us to clarify our

---

[16] Becoming a Coach: Thomas J Leonard
[17] The Counselling Handbook: Susan Quilliam & Ian Grove-Stephensen

PART 5: GURUS AND YOU

thinking, make decisions, or even to push us forward when we are faltering or want to give in.

Modern therapy starts young and is now even making inroads into the more traditionally resilient fields of employment. School stress, army stress, public sector stress – in virtually every vertical sector and institution, there is a call for therapy or some form of psychological counselling.

The life coaching business is a continuously expanding, high-growth area. In Britain alone, there are more than 140,000 practitioners in either full-time or part-time business. In turn, this growth is spawning colleges of coaching so that coaching the coaches itself becomes the business. Despite this, there are no governing bodies and, in theory, anyone can set up a coaching practice.

But what is a coach and what is a mentor and which should you choose? How do they differ from therapy and counselling?

> *"A coach is like a best friend. Your coach is there to rejoice in your triumphs, support you through difficult times and help you get the best from yourself." Eileen Mulligan*[18]

A coach is there to help you make the most of your gifts and talents. A good coach should be experienced in a particular niche market. To help you to stay positive and charged up, they should be aware of market conditions pertinent to that niche and show you how to find shortcuts.

A good coach will be a similarly-minded person, providing optimism, advice and maybe even a gentle kick in the butt from time to time, where family and friends may have neither the expertise nor the patience. They are an excellent way to keep you on

---

[18] Life Coaching: Eileen Mulligan

track when the effect of self-help books and tapes fizzles out.

However you can have the best of both worlds – learn to be totally self-sufficient and know yourself well enough to call upon your own inner self-coach. Or use a professional. The choice is not fixed in stone. You can use the sounding board either inside or outside of yourself – or both.

> *"Mentoring is a process in which a more skilled or more experienced person, serving as a role model, teaches, sponsors, encourages, counsels and befriends a less skilled or less experienced person for the purpose of promoting the latter's professional and/or personal development."* [19]

When Odysseus went off to fight the Trojan War, he entrusted his kingdom to Mentor, a trusted friend, who was a guide and teacher to his son Telemachus. Mentor taught the boy both mental and physical skills and how to survive those violent times. When later, Telemachus went in search of his father, the goddess Athena assumed the form of Mentor to guide and counsel him.

Nowadays, a mentor can be anything from a career guide to an executive coach. Generally though it is providing personal guidance to help those become more successful in their jobs or lives. Both the mentor and the coach have ploughed similar furrows and can lead you past any pitfalls.

Mentoring though is a form of specifically passing on skills and experience which may not be easy to find in books or other forms of learning. It involves a collaborative approach to developing the mentee's skills, abilities, knowledge and thinking in a specific area. So would it be possible then to mentor or coach yourself - or even become your own therapist?[20] It can

---

[19] The Mentoring Pocketbook/Management Pocketbooks
[20] Self-Therapy: Janette Rainwater

PART 5: GURUS AND YOU

be difficult in some spheres such as operatic singing or sports.

> *"You must be the change you wish to see in the world." Gandhi*

The best way to coach or even mentor yourself is to understand yourself. This self-understanding may involve knowing when to use the services of a professional mentor or coach to bounce off ideas and action plans, or it may be to take stock of yourself and the missing elements in your life.

Very few people have not read or heard of visualisation, using affirmations, setting goals and so forth. We start with good intentions but motivation dips because we have not properly understood the foundations that can make or break our goals.

A key element to most forms of coaching is to create a structure upon which to base your goals and actions. For example, there is the Wheel of Life.

The wheel looks rather like a pie chart except that this circle is divided into an equal number of sections, each of which is marked from zero to ten. Each section is named after what you feel is a major component of your life. These can differ from person to person but we all share common elements such as health, work, love, home, family, friends, money, purpose, spirituality and fun.

The centre is zero and the outer ring is the highest grade. As you fill in your individual satisfaction - or dissatisfaction – marks, you can see at a glance the areas of your life which need some attention or re-balancing.

The secret to continuous success in coaching, whether through yourself or from another person, is to break down any goals into manageable chunks. It is to visualise success or the ideal outcome. It is to keep a journal of concerns and successes. It is to re-programme your thoughts and habits. Not a whole lot different then from the things you have been reading about in the first five parts of Profit From Unlimited Thinking!

BENEFITING FROM SELF-HYPNOSIS

> *"Hypnotic suggestion is verbal instruction to the inner mind, worded so as to make it as attractive as possible to the subject."* Henry Leo Bolduc

Hypnosis usually attracts sensational press. We have all read of stage tricks turning innocent audience members into clucking hens, or those unethical practitioners with baser motives. Then there is hypnotic regression where strange experiences and unbidden, maybe even false, memories frequently trigger major life changes.

Yet we all hypnotise ourselves on a daily basis. We may not be able to step back into past lifetimes, but our daily thoughts and actions, linked to our mental diet, create almost the same effect. In an earlier reference, I mentioned PalmTherapy and how Zwang believed we can reprogram our minds by physical manipulation of the lines on our hands. Linked with accurate affirmation, we could change our thought patterns and therefore the experiences we attract, sometimes quite radically.

While there is an obvious mind-body connection even before the physical act of re-programming, it is the act itself which forms part of the procedure for subliminal conditioning or hypnotic suggestion. The subconscious will associate the physical link with the internally-verbalised thought and process it accordingly.

Not that we necessarily need to be physical. In experiments, Robert Jahn, a Professor at Princeton University, showed that our minds can influence the

PART 5: GURUS AND YOU

throw of dice. Many of us have had less exciting experiments with our computers reflecting our moods - usually those we would rather not have.

> *"hypnosis is an altered state of human activity... in a highly increased state of awareness. ... Yet ...there is no loss of control but an increased vigilance and awareness by the subject of his ability to control and exploit his own capabilities.[21]" David Waxman*

Hypnosis is an excellent way of re-programming past thought patterns. It works because it temporarily lifts any blocks from our conscious critical mind, which is like a semi-effective guard-dog to the automated, processing, subconscious mind.

In putting our minds into a state of heightened suggestibility, any new suggestions to ourself are more easily accepted by our subconscious minds. Placebos have been shown to work because the subconscious mind cannot differentiate between a sugar pill and one with the latest healing herbs or magic chemicals.

In the same way it cannot differentiate between reality and a vividly-imagined, frequently-repeated scenario. In fact, it can take an imagined scenario and start to attract the elements to create it in your current reality, if you can infuse it with enough belief and desire.

> *"If the subconscious were to receive no new programming, it would continue to operate on past input. This, of course, cannot happen, for you are constantly feeding new programming or data into your subconscious mind - your computer." Dick Sutphen[22]*

However, whatever we would like to change or attract to ourselves has to be accepted by the subconscious first. It has to be reprogrammed inside first, before it can materialise in outer reality. If our conscious minds are constantly criticising or even

---

[21] Hypnosis: David Waxman
[22] Finding Your Answers Within: Dick Sutphen

applying a perceived sense of logic, then the subconscious will receive confused and conflicting messages. It needs to be in a state of heightened suggestibility by switching off the conscious mind.

In order to be able to control the process for yourself or through an approved practitioner, it is useful to understand some currently known brain states.

The beta state is when we are in a conscious frame of awareness. In beta state, we are wide awake. Our subconscious or deeper level mind operates in the alpha state, while theta is light sleep and delta is deep sleep.

The alpha or hypnogogic state is when the structures of the brain can be more easily reorganised. In other words, we have achieved a state of suggestibility.

> *"A possibly detrimental situation may arise from this literalness of the subconscious. We do not have to be in hypnosis to pick up ideas."* Leslie M LeCron[23]

Why self-hypnosis when there are so many capable practitioners? Firstly, let me stress that if the problem is severe, then professional help is advised. However, for changing habits or minor ailments, or even giving up smoking, it is possible to hypnotise one's self quite effectively[24]. To hear your own voice is a far more effective tool than that of another[25].

As well as being a lot less expensive, it is a useful way of making sure you 'programme your inner computer' more effectively, and regularly. You will be more aware of the garbage that is regularly fed into

---

[23] Self-Hypnotism: Leslie M LeCron
[24] Autohypnosis: Ronald Shone
[25] Self-Hypnosis - Creating Your Own Destiny: Henry Leo Bolduc

PART 5: GURUS AND YOU

your subconscious and will pay more attention to what you hear and say.

More esoterically though, hypnosis by another means putting your faith and trust in that other person. They may be an entertainer with divided standards, for example. Paramahansa Yogananda advised against hypnotising others. In allowing someone else to hypnotise you, you are somehow also logging in to their brainwaves and values. For this reason, you should spend time in finding the right practitioner[26] if you opt for that route.

People have used hypnosis to improve their sports abilities, to make career changes, to acquire wealth, to lose weight, to find a soulmate and also to lose their fear of flying. Regression hypnosis has taken minds back to birth experiences and beyond, which can be useful if some current emotional patterns are hard to break.

If you do choose to use self-hypnosis, remember that change is effected in thirty to forty days. You will have to set a regular pattern of listening to your tape every morning and evening for that length of time for successful mind programming. Change can occur in a number of ways. You may get rid of whatever is holding you back. You may find yourself allowing new experiences into your life.

You are allowing your belief system to be expanded therefore the more imaginative you are, the better the results. Desire is reinforced with effort. If you really desire change, you will put in the effort and you will see changes.

The script I have included in this book is for giving up smoking. Bolduc and Sutphen include many other scripts in their books. However if you use the same principles in creating the statements and new

---

[26] www.mindchange.co.uk

thought patterns, then you can use your unlimited thinking to personalise your own. The statements should be positive, current and paint a fresh image of the desired result.

Read this script or your own into a tape recorder, making sure to read in measured tones. In order to aid the relaxation process, there should be an appropriate piece of music playing as you read, although I have not found it to be that vital as long as I was in a calm and undistracted frame of mind.

Obviously there should be no lyrics or past associations. You want your subconscious to hear your words, not someone else's. Equally, if Lakmé reminds you of an airline, then that would not be an appropriate choice either! The benefit to finding the right music or sound, is that it will act as a trigger mechanism. It is definitely worth setting yourself that task.

Self-hypnosis primarily works from a state of 'profound abstraction'. As Dr Bernard Hollander writes 'Indeed, this state resembles that in which men of genius have achieved their highest creations, while completely oblivious of their physical sensations and external surroundings[27]."

SAMPLE HYPNOSIS SCRIPT

THINK ME ... A NON-SMOKER SIDE ONE

Cigarette smoking and other forms of tobacco intake are habits that build up over a period of time causing dependency and need.

By acknowledging this need, you built up a desire to smoke even more. Now, however, you have ceased to place your strength in tobacco in any of its forms. You have begun to realise that you can control

---

[27] Methods & Uses of Hypnosis and Self-Hypnosis: Bernard Hollander MD

PART 5: GURUS AND YOU

and even cease smoking altogether, through the power of your own mind.

By changing your thought patterns, you are changing your habits to fulfilling, controlled, healthy ones. The new thought patterns contained in this tape can help you to permanently eliminate the tobacco habit, reducing any withdrawal symptoms and without any adverse side affects such as weight gain.

You have now made a commitment to cease smoking or partaking of tobacco in any of its forms and you are willingly listening to the new thought patterns contained in this tape, knowing that they are helping you to release the desire you have previously held for tobacco and smoking.

Your belief is now going to be in yourself and your abilities and not in tobacco in any of its forms. You are already starting to believe in yourself and to exercise self-control and self-belief.

Have you had difficulty in stopping smoking previously?

By listening to these new thought patterns now, this time you are making the choice to change your inner perceptions about yourself and in doing so to firmly present to your subconscious mind your determination to quit smoking permanently. Changing your thought patterns is the first step because you determine what you are through your mind and your thoughts.

By listening to this tape you are choosing to help yourself through this voice giving you new thought patterns. By relaxing to the music and concentrating on the sound of this voice as it takes you through your new thought patterns, you will achieve what you desire - to be a healthy, relaxed and successful nonsmoker. So now relax and listen to the music that will be accompanying the new thought patterns for a few moments.

PROFIT FROM UNLIMITED THINKING

play music*

A distinguished writer once remarked: "There are literally thousands of prescriptions the mind can write to meet the body's needs."

The power of suggestion - that is putting forward an idea for another to think about - has time and again created many amazing feats, both good and bad, for the mind to carry out.

Every thought that you think is a suggestion with varying degrees of intensity. You are, quite accurately, a product of your own thoughts - and in some cases, the thoughts of others.

These new thought patterns are your choice for you - your desire to be a healthy, successful non-smoker exercising your own self-control. And in complete control of what you think.

Within your mind there are two levels: the conscious mind and the subconscious mind. The conscious mind is the thinking, rational, analytical mind. The subconscious mind is the ultra-powerful force that can move mountains to fulfil your wishes.

If you have listened to any other new thought pattern tapes in the "Think me .." series you will know that your thoughts are your commands.

Your wishes come from your own ability to provide auto-suggestions to your subconscious. How often do you indulge in auto-suggestion ?

Do you use expressions like I can't/ It's so difficult/ I haven't got the willpower/ I really need a cigarette?

Do any of those sound familiar ?

Your subconscious is going to answer all these "wishes" that you have commanded it. Good or bad.

Auto-suggestion, then, is when you provide the suggestions, good or bad.

PART 5: GURUS AND YOU

Hetero-suggestion is when ideas are planted by another person: your parents, your friends, your spouse, your boss. I don't have to give you any examples; I'm sure you can think of a few of your own. Tragically, all too often these can be very critical and harmful and contribute to deeply hidden feelings of ambivalence and a lack of self-esteem.

This can manifest in various external symptoms such as addiction to food, smoking, lack of money, being unrelaxed and stressed.

You are choosing to listen to the new thought patterns contained in this tape because you know it is a good beginning to learning to consciously control your thought patterns. Once you have learned new positive thought patterns, you can then trust your inner automatic pilot to guide you unerringly towards all you desire most.

THINK ME ... A NON-SMOKER SIDE TWO

On side two of this tape is a relaxation programme with new thought patterns specifically designed for your inner mind to guide you to being a healthy, successful nonsmoker.

If listened to for at least twenty eight days, you will help yourself achieve this goal. This may, of course, be the first time you have listened to a new thought pattern tape, so take time now to listen while I count from one to ten.

You will progressively start to feel more and more relaxed, allowing the music to flow over you, knowing that already your inner mind is enjoying this new self-control you are exercising.

You may listen to your tape in any way that suits yourself. There are no rules. You are in charge. And as you listen you may find yourself drifting off. This is fine. Or if you are listening at your regular bedtime, and you feel like sleeping then you will sleep, a deep, calm, relaxed sleep, knowing that when you wake you will feel better than ever before.

I want you now to picture yourself approaching a door. See this door and know that when you walk through it you will be in the theatre of your mind where you can write the scripts to make all your dearest wishes and dreams reality. You are the writer and the projectionist, projecting onto the theatre of your mind what you dearly want.

You are now opening the door, this door to your inner mind ... and you see yourself standing on a stage. And as I count from 1 to ten, you will see yourself rising higher and higher on this stage.

With every count you are being lifted higher and higher till you are floating in the stars. Now whenever you hear the word "stars" you will feel relaxed and sure, knowing all your deepest good desires are being met.

1 - **feel yourself lifted up**
2 - **higher and higher**
3 - **and higher**
4 - **you are floating higher and higher**
5 - **higher**
6 - **you are almost there**
7 - **higher still**
8 - **and higher**
9 - **nearly there**
10 - **you are now floating free in the stars where all your dreams are perfect reality.**

All tension is now gone from your muscles and mind. You are floating free and you have left all tension and cares way way down below - far far away from you and your desires.

Your entire body is now relaxed all over in every way. All tension is gone from your body and

PART 5: GURUS AND YOU

mind ... all tension is now gone from your body and mind.

    play off to music

    Settle yourself into a comfortable position and clear your mind. Keep your thoughts concentrating on the sound of my voice and feel relaxed and loose. Clench any parts of your body that feel tense. Clench them tightly and then relax them again. Feel relaxed and loose.
    Feel your toes relax, and your legs and thighs. Your stomach, your buttocks, clench - and then release all tension. Your fingers and your hands are relaxed and your arms and your stomach. Relaxed and loose. All tension released. Now your chest and your neck and your facial muscles - all the way up your spine feel the muscles loosening and the tension flowing out ...
    Feel your muscles loosening and all the tension flowing out ...
    Help yourself by cooperating with me and concentrating on the sound of my voice. Listen to my voice and use your imagination to paint the words and pictures in the theatre of your mind.
    Now, use your imagination as you know you can and really feel, your body relaxing, one part at a time, as I ask you do so. Think it, feel it, really feel it., Play the part.
    Use your imagination to feel this relaxing power shining on you like a gentle summer sun. Feel its warmth caressing you all over.
    And the relaxing power is now coming into the toes of your feet. Feel it in each of your toes. It is moving down into the ball, into the arches and heels, on up to the ankles. Completely relaxed, completely relaxed... and the relaxing power is now moving on

up your legs to the knees, relaxing all the muscles as it goes, and on up your legs to the thighs, and now to the hips.

Just completely relaxing, and your full attention is on the sound of my voice as the relaxing power comes into the fingers of both your hands at the same time, relaxing your hands. Feel the relaxing power flowing round each of your fingers at the same time.

And the relaxing power is now moving on up into your forearms, relaxing your forearms, flowing round your elbows, relaxing your elbows, and into your upper arms, relaxing your upper arms. And your fingers and hands and forearms and elbows and upper arms are just completely relaxed as the relaxing power now moves into your spine and neck.

Now feel, the warmth at the base of your spine; feel the relaxing power coming in and moving, moving slowly and warmly up, up .. the spine .. and into the back of the neck and shoulder muscles. And the back of your neck and shoulder muscles are now loose and limp. Loose and limp. And the relaxing power is now moving up the back of the neck and into your scalp, relaxing your scalp.

FEEL, your scalp relaxing, and feel the relaxing power now draining down into your facial muscles, relaxing your facial muscles.

And if your eyes are still open, they are now so relaxed and heavy ... relaxed and heavy ... that you want to close them. So close your eyes now and leave them closed until I ask you to open them. And your facial muscles are now completely relaxed, and your jaw is relaxed. Your ears, under your eyes, your nose and throat are completely relaxed. Allow a little space between your teeth.

Your entire body is now relaxed all over in every way. All tension is gone from your body and

PART 5: GURUS AND YOU

mind ... all tension is now gone from your body and mind.

Continue breathing deeply and smoothly.

Feel the essence within you floating freely as you let the tension drain from your body. Just feel yourself floating freely.

Listen to the sound of my voice and keep your full attention on it. Feel your blood flow. Use your imagination to feel the blood flowing; feel it in your arms and your legs. Feel it in your entire body and mind.

Feel this flow as positive energy washing the tension away from your body and mind. Feel your mind loosening your thoughts and letting them float free. Just concentrate on the sound of my voice. And feel your thoughts separate from your mind and float away.

Brush away any lingering thoughts and return your attention to the sound of my voice, concentrate on the sound of my voice. Continue breathing deeply and relaxing completely.

In the theatre of your mind, see your finger paint the word RELAX. See it glow and sparkle as you become more and more relaxed and calm.

And as I count from 1 to 10, I want you to picture yourself standing on the stage in the theatre of your mind. With every count you are being lifted higher and higher till you are floating in the stars. You are remembering that whenever you hear the word "stars" you feel relaxed and sure, knowing all your deepest good desires are being met.

1 - **feel yourself lifted up**
2 - **higher and higher**
3 - **and higher**
4 - **you are floating higher and higher**
5 - **higher**
6 - **you are almost there**

7 - **higher still**
8 - **and higher**
9 - **nearly there**
10 - **you are now floating free in the stars where all your dreams are perfect reality. Your entire body is now relaxed all over in every way.**

All tension is gone from your body and mind ... all tension is now gone from your body and mind.

NEW THOUGHT PATTERNS

I am in charge of my mind and my life and I have chosen to be a nonsmoker. I dislike the taste of the cigarette in my mouth. It has an unpleasant taste and I choose not to damage my life system with its poisons.

I am so pleased with myself for being a nonsmoker and for having no desires at all for cigarettes or cigars or tobacco in any of its forms.

I am proud of my ability to say I am a nonsmoker and to choose not to smoke.

I enjoy the fact that I have lost all desire to smoke. I am a nonsmoker.

I have no more desire to have tobacco in any of its forms and I feel pleased and proud of myself for my strength of character, my willpower and the healthy, attractive self-image I am now projecting.

Being a nonsmoker makes me feel healthy both mentally and physically. I especially feel proud of my strength and power in having the willpower to refuse tobacco, cigarettes, cigars or any poisonous substances.

My energy level has increased as has my pride in being a nonsmoker. I feel healthier and wealthier and better and better.

I smell good, I look good. I feel good - because I am in control. I have chosen to be a nonsmoker. I have chosen to stop smoking altogether.

PART 5: GURUS AND YOU

I have chosen to control my weight too and being a nonsmoker I can now taste the real goodness in food. I am in charge of all aspects of my life. I feel healthy, more confident and very much happier.

Everyone has noticed how good I look and feel and tell me how much better I am in every respect since I became a nonsmoker.

I am completely relaxed and calm and have used my inner creativity to think of healthy, harmless ways in which to release tension and stress. I enjoy repeating to myself often: I am relaxed and in charge of my mind and my life. I am in complete control.

If someone offers me a cigarette or any other poisonous substance I can hear my inner voice strongly and loudly telling me to STOP.

And I do.

I breathe deeply - and I stop myself.

I have learned to put a mental shield around myself if I am near other smokers. I am proud of the fact that other smokers or the smoke itself does not bother me at all. I hear only the words "I am calm and relaxed and in control". And I am.

I have completely erased cigarettes and tobacco and other poisonous substances from my life. Instead I choose success and health and harmony in my life.

I have totally eliminated all need or desire for cigarettes tobacco and other harmful substances and I have a wonderful inner pride in myself and my achievements as a nonsmoker.

I am a success. I am a successful nonsmoker. I am healthy, happy and prosperous. I am a healthy, happy and prosperous nonsmoker.

Now, in a moment, you are going to open your eyes and loosen up. You are going to awaken feeling as if you have had a nice, refreshing nap. You will feel rested and refreshed, your head will be clear, and you will be thinking with calm self-assurance, acting with calm self-assurance, feeling glad to be alive ... at peace with yourself, the world and everyone in it.

On the count of three, you will open your eyes and be wide awake.

One ... feel the blood returning to your arms and legs, you're beginning to come up a little. ... feel yourself coming up and you feel good all over, glad to be alive.

Two ... you will open your eyes and be wide awake.

Three ... and you... are... wide awake.

You are opening your eyes and feeling better than you have ever felt before. Alive. Alert. Refreshed. Open your eyes and feel good.

PART 5: GURUS AND YOU

SOME LAST WORDS

There are two worlds. There is the outer world which appears to exist, and seems solid and permanent, but in truth is an illusion. And there is the inner world which many people deny, and is invisible to the senses, and yet is real and eternal. - Jalal al-Din al-Rumi

It is a good thing that we have to face difficulties and opposition from time to time, because this brings us back to ourselves. - Thomas à Kempis: The Imitation of Christ

What is the use to people of teaching or light, unless they use it? If they are in darkness or sorrow, they ought to see the light. - Meister Eckhart: Wisdom as Divine

Control the mind. Attain one-pointedness. Then the harmony of heaven will come down and dwell in you. You will be radiant with life. You will rest in Tao. - Chuang Tzu

Self-consciousness, as the term is ordinarily used, implies two things: an awareness of oneself by oneself, and an awareness of oneself as an object of someone else's observation. - R D Laing: The Divided Self

When we are no longer limited by the five physical senses and have attained even a measure of spiritual sense, we find ourselves unlimited in terms of 'here' or 'there', 'now' or 'hereafter'.. In this consciousness, finite sense disappears and the vision is without boundaries. - Joel Goldsmith: The Infinite Way

Beyond my visible nature is my invisible Spirit. This is the fountain of life whereby the universe has its beginning and end. - The Bhagavad Gita

The soul refuses limits, and always affirms an Optimism, never a Pessimism. - Ralph Waldo Emerson: Compensation

Education is not filling a bucket but lighting a fire. - William Butler Yeats

Thy destiny is only that of a man, but thy aspirations may be those of a god. - Ovid: Ars Amatoria

He was a wise man who invented God. - Plato: Sisyphus

SOME LAST WORDS

ABOUT THE AUTHOR

Euphrosene Labon has been interested in metaphysics, mysticism and all aspects of unlimited thinking for over thirty years. Being a pragmatic unlimited thinker, she has spent over twenty-five as a professional salesperson and is a Fellow of the Institute of Sales and Marketing Management and Member of the Society of Authors.

For more information on Profit From Unlimited Thinking workshops or Euphrosene's other books, please contact euphrosene@floreo.org or visit www.floreo.org.

TASK NOTES

TASK NOTES

TASK NOTES

TASK NOTES

TASK NOTES

TASK NOTES

TASK NOTES

www.ingramcontent.com/pod-product-compliance
Lightning Source LLC
Chambersburg PA
CBHW020747160426
43192CB00006B/268